A Life on Film

DELACORTE PRESS / NEW YORK

MARY ASTOR

A Life on Film

With an Introduction by SUMNER LOCKE ELLIOTT

ALSO BY MARY ASTOR

FICTION

The Incredible Charlie Carewe
The Image of Kate
The O'Conners
Goodbye Darling, Be Happy
A Place Called Saturday

NONFICTION

My Story

LIBRARY OF CONGRESS CATALOG CARD NUMBER: 77-164844
MANUFACTURED IN THE UNITED STATES OF AMERICA
FIRST PRINTING

DESIGNED BY *Joel Schick*

*All pictures not otherwise credited are from the
Mary Astor Collection*

FOR

TONO AND PATTI

BECAUSE THEY CARED

INTRODUCTION

THEY SAID THEY HAD GOT ME Mary Astor to play the mother, so would I stop complaining about everything. "They" being the casting people for the then celebrated *Philco Television Playhouse* and this being sometime in the mid-1950s when I was one of the stable of writers under contract to the *Playhouse*. It had fallen to my lot in an unlucky moment to be the one conscripted to provide a play at short notice for the recently crowned Miss America, whose tour was being sponsored by Philco. Miss America was an enormously pretty girl and an enormously inexperienced actress; the director was green, too, and the hodgepodge play I had hastily put together to fit their idea was just a hair short of bathos. Besides, it was dead of winter, and the decaying ballroom where we rehearsed was unheated.

It was under these discouraging circumstances that I met Mary Astor. She was the first to arrive at the rehearsal room—in a heavy fur coat which she kept on. She was offhand, cool, rather like the role she played in *Holiday*, and she made no response to my nervous introductory joke when I said, naming a B picture she had once made, "Well, Miss Astor, *Trapped by Television* I see."

We had the first reading of the play, and it was very much worse than we had imagined, and Miss America was very much worse than we had imagined, and Mary Astor said nothing but stared a lot over the top of her glasses, and I thought this is a woman that no one will get close to. To my surprise she asked everyone to autograph the front page of her script. She was collecting autographs, she said, from every television play she had done. It was the first intimation of what it took me a long while to realize: She nearly always likes the people she works with. What I had taken to be offhandedness was her way of covering her terror of live television. Anyway, in that ill-lit ballroom, there she was, a good bit older than when she had won her Academy Award but not much changed; the darkly red hair in the mannish cut, that profile, the freckles, eyes the color of cracked hazelnuts. And the unique voice, a cello voice, Edith Cortright's voice in *Dodsworth*, a voice that has a trick to it: It can make a banal line seem intelligent; it has had experience doing that.

I was profoundly glad of that voice for the next ten days and sorry that it had to say lines like, "What's wrong, dear, is something troubling you?" I was grateful for that voice as things went from bad to worse, as we chopped and changed and altered scenes that grew more banal, and swapped lines and motivations to disguise the inadequacies of Miss America. At one stage we had four different endings; swamped in indecision and arguments we asked Mary for her opinion. Which ending did she think right? "The one that I have to *learn tonight*," she told us.

On the last day of "dry" rehearsals before this leaking, sinking ship of a play was transferred to the cameras, Miss America sat calmly aside from us and addressed her Christmas cards. Mary said to me, but not with malice, "Isn't it wonderful not to know enough to be scared?"

It was all live in those days, no safety of tape to be cut and repeated if something was direfully wrong. Mary played more than just a "mother" to the girl who quaked with terror when the red light flashed and we were "on" coast to coast. Miss America turned in a remarkably good performance, but we all knew who propped her up through it. "What's wrong, dear, is something troubling you?" asked the deep, assuring, reassuring voice of experience. This is the voice of the actress who has been through it all; this is the calm of the veteran who can get you through even if the set falls down.

Mary is un-actressy, though, herself, one of the least actressy actresses I have ever known. She is no more given to ostentatious behavior than she is to big hats.

In fact, the impression she gives is more that of a successful woman lawyer: that has something to do with her native intelligence. This sense of intelligence has been a stamp on all her roles from the somber Antoinette de Mauban in *The Prisoner of Zenda* to treacherous Brigid in *The Maltese Falcon*. It may be the reason she was less successful in roles in which she had to subdue this quality behind sham; she has never been very good at sham; as a person there is so little sham in her that you wonder at her spending forty years working in artificial light.

It has always been the work she likes and not the limelight. "Let's work," she says at rehearsal and if there is too much chat about it, "Oh, let's get back to *work*."

I have seen her angry only once. She was again in a television play of mine (a better one and this time not as a mother but as a rich grasping woman) and she and George Grizzard were to do a scene from it for promotion on the Steve Allen show. I went with them to the studio where we were received with majestic indifference. ("Where is Miss Astor to dress?" "Oh, the girls dress in Number 8.") Because the negligee that was being made for her was not yet finished, wardrobe had been told to send over a suitable substitute; instead of sending a flattering concoction of chiffon and bows, they had provided a tired old lace thing that had obviously seen duty a dozen times on the *Hit Parade*. I found a grim-faced Mary standing in front of the mirror in Number 8. "I'm supposed to promote in *this?*" The eyes were like black glass. "If they want me to promote they've got to help a little to promote *me*." To the amazement and awe of a girls' harmonica band sharing Number 8 with her, she ripped the lace horror from top to bottom (it was Sandra slapping the masseur in *The Great Lie*) and vented several good Anglo-Saxon opinions on the dress and the general apathy around the whole situation and declared that we would now leave. I knew this to be no idle threat.

People were sent running and a frothy thing not exactly right but better had been found for her, when I came upon her in the makeup room. "Oh, I am *lucky*," she said. "Have I ever found a good makeup girl." The fact was that the makeup girl was no more than competent. It was the Astor way of reparation. "Now let me show you a few little tricks," she said to the glowing girl.

During the time we were working together on *The Women* for NBC, she came over to me one day and put something in my hand as she said, "Read this when you have a minute." It proved to be several handwritten pages about Nancy, the part she was playing; Mary liked the part and had decided to write down her thoughts about "this dame." I wish I had kept those notes because they were incisive and well written, and although neither of us knew it then, her first step toward what was to be a new career. Years later, she wrote down her thoughts about another dame, herself, and with that autobiography, *My Story*, launched her career as an author.

Very early in our friendship, I made a reference to one of her films and she froze me with, "I hope you're not going to turn out to be a fan. One thing I *never* want to talk about is all those old *movies*."

Well, now she has written about all "those old movies," all the years of them from the silents to the early talkies to the golden age —and from leading lady to star to "Tell mother" roles—and has told all the things she craftily and stubbornly avoided telling in *My Story*, about the worlds of Paramount and Warners and Metro which are no more.

She acts no more. I write for television no more. Even that medium has become transmuted. But were it still as it was and were I again back in long dispute over casting some role I'm sure I would say as I often did after listening to all the pros and cons of this or that possible actress: "Let's get Astor."

SUMNER LOCKE ELLIOTT

1

IT WAS ALWAYS "TOMORROW." Tomorrow contained total fulfillment. "The future" expanded in all directions, blinding glory without limit. Another Duse was emerging. The magnificence of Bernhardt would be forgotten, and a flash in the pan like Mary Pickford had just better watch out.

"Tomorrow we'll hear from Griffith. Lillian Gish said she'd talk to D.W. and set up the test for Friday." "Tomorrow we'll be on the train for Hollywood." "Tomorrow we have the interview with Jesse Lasky." "Tomorrow we meet Mr. Barrymore."

The "we" not being editorial or royal but familial, the unit that first put the product together that was called Mary Astor, Mr. and Mrs. O. L. Langhanke and daughter, Lucile. "Langhanke?"—who could pronounce it? "Lucile?"—out of fashion, Wordsworth and all that. "Astor?"—a famous name, a famous family, a sound of affluence to it. Also, being an *A*, it would figure high in alphabetical lists. The combination would look brief and well in marquee lights. *Mary Astor*—sounds good. That's your name, better get used to it! The name chosen by Jesse Lasky, Louella Parsons and Walter

Wanger. Legalized for contracts, so there would never be the cumbersome "also known as" for documents. Practiced as a signature for autographs, with big capitals, curly *r*'s and a long-tailed *y*.

The product had been given a name, and we mounted the first steps to glory. At least there was food on the table for a change. Sixty dollars a week was more money than a professor of German in a public high school ever dreamed of, and this one hadn't worked lately. So instead of a diet of rice and coffee, and an occasional splurge at the Automat, we had steak. And oranges and grapes. And *Kartoffel* salad. And *Kaffeekuchen* for breakfast.

Also a pair of new shoes with flat heels. There had been whispers, "She's too tall for Douglas MacLean." "Sorry, she's too tall."

"Tall for her age." Tall, leggy, adolescent, a very young, very virginal fourteen-year-old. Enormous brown eyes, wide open, absorbing the sights and sounds of an environment that was as alien as the streets of Singapore. In an almost perpetual state of shock and embarrassment at being paraded before groups of strange people in an office. "Give us a profile, honey." (What's a *profile!*) "*Here!* Turn your face this way!" A heavy hairy-backed hand grasping the chin, turning it toward an awkward shoulder. "That's fine, dear." The hand sliding down over an undeveloped breast. Suddenly tense, frightened, wanting to run. "Can't you smile, cutie? *That's* better."

"*Cutie!*" I was anything but "cute," and besides, something innate told me it was an undignified word. I expected my father to swing on him, for he was a dignified man. "Dignity" was one of his favorite words. But nothing happened. A subservient smile was glued to his face. Mother was fiddling with a long chain of amber beads, also smiling.

I tossed in my sleep at night, sick of the whole business, wishing I had never seen that tempting summons in a movie magazine. "Send your photograph to Brewster Publications and who knows? You too may win. You may be chosen for Fame and Fortune." That was nearly three years before. A lifetime. I had sent the photo secretly, and something like six months elapsed before it appeared in *Motion Picture Magazine* along with photos of seven other young girls. Eight were to be chosen each month and at the end of the year the finalist would be selected and given the opportunity to have a screen test.

My father had believed every word of it. He quit his job at the high school in Quincy, Illinois, and packed us up and we got as far as Chicago, when our money ran out. The main office of Brewster Publications was in New York, but there was a branch office in Chicago and my father thought all he had to do was to present me in person and the contest would be wrapped up. The word was, "Try again next year. She's too young." I was only twelve years old.

We tried again next year. I was on the "Honor Roll" again, but some other girl won. Grimly, my father announced that the following year we'd be on the spot in New York.

In June of 1920 we arrived in New York with three hundred dollars savings and a dream that had gone stale to me. I had had my fourteenth birthday in May of the same year, and all the changes, the uprootings, the dreary flats, the lack of decent food seemed too high a price to pay. I stopped listening, or paying any attention to my father's enthusiastic plans, his excitement over a phone call or an appointment to see this person or that, and I couldn't even work up much excitement that at last we were to meet Mr. Brewster himself, that I was to go out to his estate in Roslyn, New York, for a film test of the finalists in that year's contest.

I preferred to sit on the fire escape outside of our flat on 110th Street and watch children playing down in the depths of a court below us, or dream in the sunshine, brushing my long hair, pretending to be Rapunzel in the tower.

Otto Ludwig Wilhelm Langhanke deserves a book of his own. My feelings about him are still quite ambivalent, and in my mind he still comes on very strong. He is there in the residue of anxiety when I dream; whenever I discuss my work in movies, he is there as prime mover. He is my scapegoat, my apology when I try to rationalize my behavior. I should be free of him now, but such a powerful personality is difficult to shrug into oblivion.

If he were a character in a movie I would cast a blending of Yul Brynner and Erich von Stroheim. Ambitious, intense, a great deal of Prussian pompousness, a longing for luxury, a deep appreciation of beauty, sentimental about music, Christmas trees and sunsets, cold in his family relationship. And totally impractical. I wish he had transmitted his energy and ambition to me genetically, instead of using me as a channel. He was a rebel, who rebelled against anything new, who got stuck in his own century. His idealism was heady stuff. I respected, loved and feared him. I gave him the devotion one might lay at the feet of a guru. I followed his lead blindly.

[3]

But eventually his lead was so confusing that I became somewhat like a neurotic mouse in a maze. A mouse that learned to think and feel and resent.

In Order To Be Somebody You Had To Get an Education. This was my father's credo, his theme, his daily sermon in those early childhood years. He lectured at length to an audience of two. To Mother and me. Vocally he was a button-holer, a finger-jabber, a lapel-grasper. But only vocally. He never touched anyone except in anger.

We understood that we were to stop whatever we were doing and *listen,* dammit! If we were diplomatic enough to seek a chair, eyes upon him, sitting while he stood, he glowed with pleasure and paced the floor as though he were in his classroom at Quincy High. His pince-nez riding on a thumb looked like another pair of eyes perched on a nose, nodding like an active puppet. In his other hand would be the newspaper or pamphlet or book from which he'd obtained his inspiration of the moment. Then he would take off into realms beyond our understanding with a quantity of words exceeding our powers of assimilation.

What "Being Somebody" meant to him was vague. It was important, obviously. His vocal and facial signals indicated that; serious, frowning, his eyes glittering with exalted tears. Even at seven or eight years I longed to be whatever it might be he was talking about. Finally, later, I could understand the beautiful words themselves: Achievement, High Ideals, Perseverance, and I could nod happily at the idea of sacrifice to brain-staggering work, a clenched-fist determination to Win over Difficulties. High school, colleges, and beyond into the higher studies of literature, music, mathematics, the humanities. He said that after my mind was trained, he would be able to perceive my special talent and would guide me carefully.

I was "guided" into the movies. Movies were Entertainment, and as such, very much beneath Education. I was puzzled, but asked no questions. One didn't. I had become "pigeon-liver'd and lacked gall" but I didn't know that. Besides I did not enjoy hearing how stupid I was. I was a constant failure; he indicated his disappointment with windy sighs and shakes of the head. Knowing his temper and his ability to rage, I felt it was kind of him whenever he restrained himself. I actually felt that he had given up on me, that I would never be very bright or intelligent or Educated, and getting me into the movies was the best he could do for me. So I was very grateful.

[4]

There had been no siblings or playmates—no peer group to test myself on, only one or two brief friendships. I was a failure in my relationships in school, because I was unprepared to accept games and "foolishness." I didn't know how to play—not the way the other children played—and I didn't want to. Jumping rope? Throwing snowballs? Just giggling and romping and competing in running around? Very confusing. My playground was in my mind, phantasizing the material I read or observed during the lovely summer days in which I wandered through the woods on our property, lying beside a brook, dozing under a pine tree. . . .

We had been living on a farm in the outskirts of Quincy before we moved back into town for the brief year in which I became an avid movie fan. My mother and father and I went regularly to the movies on Friday nights. (Mary Pickford, Nazimova, Pauline Frederick, Norma Talmadge, and the D.W. Griffith people, Lillian and Dorothy Gish, Richard Barthelmess, Mae Marsh, Carol Dempster. I had access to all the fan magazines I wanted (*Motion Picture Magazine, Shadowplay, Photoplay, Picture Play*) and I cut out pictures of the famous ones and pasted them on the wall of my room. I was being propagandized and didn't know it. They never told me they knew I was beautiful, and I was unaware of it. In fact, nobody told me anything about that until I faced photographers, painters, sculptors. It was pleasant to hear, but I was skeptical in front of a mirror. Red hair! Curly hair! Not beautiful when you've been called "Red" and "Curly" and gagged on Mother's sentimental pun, "Rusty-locks." Dark brown eyes, with circles under them—an inherited pigmentation and not enough food or exercise. A buttonhole mouth. A short nose, with freckles. Beautiful! Absurd. Now if I looked like Olga Petrova! or Geraldine Farrar!

The "Fame and Fortune" contest was a complete washout for me; for anybody. It was a promotional stunt for the magazine, of course, and Brewster followed through to the extent of having about fifty young girls, including me, parade in front of a camera in the garden of his huge estate, and then announcing the winner in the magazine. I doubt if he went to the trouble of having film in the camera. And my father bitterly complained that the girl who won was Brewster's girl friend. He was probably right. I got my picture in the magazine as runner-up. But no producers came knocking on our door.

However, if it hadn't been for that meaningless afternoon in Roslyn we wouldn't have met Charles Albin. He was a photogra-

pher, mostly of theatrical and film people and a very fine artist. He became a friend: someone in the big lonely city to talk with and share our troubles. He had singled me out from that mob of pretty girls and told my father he wanted to photograph me. I had a facial structure that he liked and a look he called that of a "Madonna-child." There was no question of paying or being paid. He just wanted me as a model, and if he could do anything to help me in getting work, fine. No strings.

Whenever there were no appointments at casting offices, no people to see, no lead to follow through to its fruitless end, I posed for "Allie." His studio was on 66th Street and Columbus Avenue, a huge loft with skylights and a few neutral-colored flats for backgrounds. He used no artificial light, and did no retouching. His art was in his printing. He projected his negatives and controlled the light with bits of cardboard, emphasizing, shading, lightening. He was a painter with light. Some of his work remains. In some of the collections of Lillian Gish and the Barrymores, the small stencil *Albin* is down in the corner. And the photos he made of me eventually got me into the movies.

I could work for Allie—he was quiet and soft-spoken when he talked, which wasn't often—and he never touched me, which was important to me. He sensed my shyness, my frightened-animal reaction to contact. As a family, my parents and I were not physically demonstrative. There were no big hugs and kisses, no exuberant greetings or good-byes, no tears shed on a comforting shoulder, no patting of hands. The easy familiarity of the theatrical business came hard for me. And later even the impersonal hands of painters and sculptors and photographers would make me shudder. It's quite possible that I lost a few jobs because I wouldn't snuggle up to a director or a producer.

It was at Allie's studio that I met other artists and learned about people who were in love with their work, doing without food and luxuries to achieve ideals. There was Gleb Djerjinsky, a fine sculptor, in the loft across the hall, Dwight Franklin who modeled in beeswax miniature painted figures from literature in tiny wall settings—Stevenson's pirates, the poet Villon in prison. A few years later Franklin designed the costumes and sets for the Douglas Fairbanks picture *The Black Pirate*.

Mary Astor, age 14 (1920) *Albin*.

Now it was hungry time for all of us. But there was music playing on a phonograph and somebody dropping by with a hunk of sausage, a cheese, a loaf of pumpernickel and a cup of *maté*.

All this, somehow, I could understand. It was easier than listening to the computer mind of my father figuring out just how rich we were going to be someday. Someday.

We had now been in New York about four months, and even in those days three hundred dollars didn't last forever. We'd begun on the rice and raisins and coffee routine and to suffer from it. We were all getting thin and Mother and Daddy were fighting a lot, with Mother complaining that this was just one more of Daddy's "big ideas" that wasn't going to work out. He'd had others through the years: raising prize White Orpington poultry, and calling the breed "Edelweiss"; growing mushrooms in the cellar, and shipping them to big city markets; an investment in a walnut grove in some southern state; an invention of a cutout easel for photographs, trying to get a patent. He thought big and failed hard.

He'd also tried his hand at writing scenarios for movies. All of which were returned.

He couldn't teach in New York, because that meant going through a state examination, which he "didn't have time for."

But we had to have some money. Among his manuscripts was a translation from the German of Suderman's *Elga*. He made an appointment to see a Mr. Harry Durant of the scenario department of Famous Players-Lasky Corporation, thinking he might be able to get work translating material from the German for movies. Mr. Durant was interested. The same day my father was going to drop off some Albin photographs of me at an office on 42nd Street, just around the corner from the Lasky office. Durant listened to my father's idea for a while and then asked about the envelope of photographs he was carrying. "Oh, those are of my daughter, I'm putting her in pictures." It never occurred to him that someone from the scenario department would be interested. Mr. Durant was not only interested—he went to work, fast. And within a week I had been given a name and a contract for six months.

So we were in the movies. They didn't have anything for me to do at the moment, however, so Mr. Durant thought it would be a good idea for Mother and me to go out every day or so to the big new studios in Astoria, and watch and get oriented. We were also given tickets to the matinees of shows in the theaters and the big movie houses.

The "Madonna-child" (1920) *Albin*.

The first few times I was stunned at being within touching distance of great stars like Mae Murray, Ethel Clayton, Elsie Ferguson, May McAvoy. They were so beautiful, so elegant, so perfumed and poised. But after a couple of months of standing on the sidelines, out of the way where nobody talked to us or even acknowledged our presence, it began to be pretty boring. And as the beautiful ones passed me, I could smell the sweat from the hot lights. And Mother, standing close beside me, would gasp at the "dirty language" that seemed to be the vernacular. Already the glamour was tarnished.

There was a hurry call one day to come out to the studio and do a bit part in *Sentimental Tommy*, an adaptation of the J. M. Barrie book. It was being directed by John Robertson and starred Gareth Hughes and May McAvoy. Allie had taught me screen makeup—he used it lightly for his photographs—so I made myself up at home, and put on quite an act on the subway that took us to Astoria. I held my makeup box on my lap and looked haughty and indifferent to the stares of people sitting near us. Women in

Otto Ludwig Wilhelm
Langhanke (1920)
Albin.

those days used no obvious makeup—perhaps a little face powder. I gave these "ordinary" people the same nose-in-the-air gaze that the beautiful ones at the studio bestowed upon me.

The scene was a double-exposure dream sequence. Gareth Hughes as Tommy was seated on a bench in a garden remembering an old love. She faded in and out standing near him, holding her arms out, a sad look on her face. That was all. I wore a dress with hoop skirts and my hair was tied back with a blue ribbon. I'm sure it didn't take more than a half hour to shoot, so I'd hardly met anyone before I was through and could go home.

The still picture of the sequence was used in the billboard advertising of the movie, but when we went to the theater to see it, the sequence had been cut out. Daddy was sure somebody had it in for me. He was one of those.

A month or so later, I did a couple of days' work in something they called a propaganda film, but the idea was shelved before it was completed. That was all I did in that period of being groomed for stardom.

The contract ended sometime in March, and I was hardly better off than before—except that we'd been eating! The rounds began again, the sitting in casting offices or parading in front of strangers. I blew one chance when one day a director with a very heavy accent asked me, "Kin you ect?" and I didn't know what he was saying. "*Ect! Ect!* Kin you ect?" Still not understanding, I said, "I don't think so." "Ah! Git her outta here!"

I made dozens of tests. And the same complaints followed me everywhere. "No experience. Too tall." I believe insurance statistics show that the increase in stature of people from World War I to the present day has been considerable. I was, and am, only five feet five and one-half inches tall, but the majority of male actors in those days averaged around five feet seven or eight. And the girls were all petite; five feet one or two, or *less*. Petite and plump. I felt like a freak. Lillian Gish looks tiny today. And yet she was almost as tall as I.

Speaking of Lillian Gish reminds me of one heartbreaking period. About the only one that really mattered to me during that job-seeking time. I had met Lillian at Albin's and she had arranged a test for me at the Griffith studios in Mamaroneck. This was a place that in my opinion made really fine pictures. It was a kind of stock company working under a great man and doing some things that have proved unforgettable. I wanted to be part of that stock company.

Lillian was enthusiastic, and as their biggest star she had her own way about a lot of things. She made me up herself, loaned me a dress, and directed me in a test that ran for several reels and took us a whole afternoon. We waited weeks for the verdict. Finally Albin called Lillian, and she said she hadn't been able to sell me to D.W. That he liked to make his own decisions and that maybe it was her fault for pushing me too much. Many years later, she told me the truth. D.W. had got a look at my father on the sidelines during the test and had told Lillian, "The man's a walking cash register. I could never mold this child into an actress with him on my neck all the time."

One of the drop-ins at Allie's studio was another photographer by the name of Lejaren à Hiller. Hiller was a commercial photographer, but an innovator. His ad for a fabrics company would be a luxurious fold of satin draped around the shoulders of a beautiful woman rather than the standard photograph of bolts of material on a shelf. He was experimenting with soft focus, using filters of his own making. He ground the lenses himself in his studio. Soft focus was unheard of at that time. Everything was sharp and harsh and literal. He and Albin had long discussions about it, for Albin achieved the same soft effect with long exposures and "stretching" the negative. Many of the photographs Albin did of me were of this experimental nature.

Hiller teamed up with a group of men with an idea: They would be an independent movie company that would produce two-reelers concerning famous paintings. The gimmick for the stories was how, possibly, the artist had been inspired to paint a certain work of art. The first was about the Burne-Jones painting "The Beggar Maid." It was a story about the parallel between the legend of King Cophetua and the love story of an English lord of the manor and a peasant girl.

What month does the iris bloom in the country around New York? Is it April? May? I know it was spring, and I was not yet fifteen, and sometime during that particular spring day of 1921 I was going to be kissed for the first time. By a happily married man who hardly knew I existed and about whom I cared nothing. But I had never felt the pressure of lips, except the perfunctory family pecks, and I was wondering and worrying and dreaming about it.

I was standing in an enormous paneled living room with very high ceilings. The fourth wall was almost all glass; a portion of stained glass extended up both sides of it for about six feet and made a border across the bottom. The stained glass was a realistic design of white and yellow and purple irises; through it, blending in with the design, could be seen a great informal garden of irises in full bloom, and it was impossible at a distance to tell where the glass flowers ended and the real ones began.

We were on location for exteriors of *The Beggar Maid*—I believe it was in Redbank, New Jersey—and we were using the gardens of the home of Louis Comfort Tiffany, the artist who originated the exquisite *favrile* Tiffany glass. I had wandered into the great house, dreaming, worrying, fretting about the imminent love scene, and I thought that window was the most beautiful thing I'd ever seen. I jumped when an old man with very white hair spoke to me from the doorway. "Like my window, eh?" There was no need to apologize for intruding, because he went on, "I suppose you'd like to know what happens when the iris isn't in bloom?" I nodded and he explained, leading me over to some tall cabinets.

"When the weather is just ordinary, and there is nothing particu-

Above: The first kiss. Reginald Denny as an English lord and Mary Astor as a peasant girl in THE BEGGAR MAID (1921). *Below:* Reginald Denny as King Cophetua and Mary Astor as the beggar maid

larly spectacular going on, we remove the iris panels and put in just this abstract design." He showed me some small pieces of amber-colored shapes. "But when there is snow on the ground we have these panels." There were felt-covered sections lying on a shelf but again he took a small one, about the size of a book cover. He held it to the light. It was an exquisite piece of work showing the end of a branch of a long-needled pine with a blob of snow on it. The snow had form and color; it was bluish in the shadows and it twinkled in the highlights. It had the look of crushed diamonds.

I shudder when I see what passes for "Tiffany" glass today.

Incidentally the love scene that was shot that day was accomplished without any rockets going off in me. It was tender and decorous, and I had the feeling, "Is that *all?*" I would eventually find out that love scenes performed in front of a camera and fifty or a hundred people were nothing like the real thing.

Many years later I told Reginald Denny that he was the first man who ever kissed me, and he said, "Good Lord! how *awful* for you!" Very British.

The picture was shown at the Rivoli Theater in New York and received considerable local artistic acclaim. Hiller's photography and the simple statement of the story were new departures in films of that day. My new name was up on the marquee of the theater, MARY ASTOR IN THE BEGGAR MAID. My father and mother couldn't stop talking about it, they were so thrilled. As for me—well, it was the beginning of the feeling I was to have always: "What's this got to do with me?"

But I was working, at last. And work begets work, so from now on there would always be better than rice and raisins on the Lang-hanke table. Much, much better!

We all know about insecurity these days. This era of great knowledge and little wisdom has it all figured out. Lack of parental love causes insecurity. I doubt that I knew I was insecure. If I'd been asked, I probably would have described the word literally—like being about to take a pratfall on a slippery sidewalk.

I know that I felt bored and sullen during long conversations when everyone talked *about* me, and not *to* me. Looking at some photographs, Allie said to my father, "She has an ageless look. See the way her eyes are set, wide apart, that lovely droop at the outer edges?"

I muttered under my breath, "Like a houn' dawg."

"What's that, Lucile? What's that?"

"Nothing."

"Well don't *mumble!*"

Without ever having heard the verb "to compensate," nevertheless I compensated. I got crushes. I fell in love with almost anyone who looked *at* me, who spoke *to* me—who even just smiled at me.

However, nobody dared to make a pass at me for I was heavily chaperoned. I was as zealously guarded as the crown jewels. The security extended even to going to the ladies' room.

I learned that movies were hard work, but I didn't mind that because I had found an escape from, and a substitute for, the home environment. All through my career I was to feel the greatest security within the walls of a studio stage. My need for familial love was satisfied. I "belonged" to the people of my particular studio set. I could fall asleep in my portable dressing room with bedlam going on around me. I was safe. And I loved my "family." The people I worked with. We might have fights and disagreements, and there would be bores, or stupidity or selfishness or meanness or bad behavior—just as in any family. But I was the shy one, the member of the family who got along with the others, the peacemaker, the compromiser. And I was rewarded with love most of the time.

My mother never let me out of her sight at the studio. She did most of my talking for me, and supplanted the directors' directions with some of her own which she would whisper in my ear as she fixed a lock of my hair. Even so, there were people to watch, to listen to, to learn from. I didn't talk much. I would sit in one of the canvas chairs just outside the lights, watching other people do their scenes, wondering at their skill, wishing I could do as well. I would pull at my mascaraed eyelashes in an expression of nervousness until Mother would catch me and shake her head, frowning, so then I'd bite my nails, and if nobody was watching her, she'd slap my hands. Or I'd memorize my subtitles or titles. That needs a bit of explanation, I suppose. It is commonly thought that in silents we didn't talk. But we had to, of course, a kind of improvisation, until we came to the subtitle written into the script. These had to be accurate. The cutter would use the first few feet of the subtitle on the actor. Say, for instance, the lines that would be shown on the screen read, "I saw your brother just an hour ago. He seemed to be upset about something." You would see the actor say, "I saw——" then would come the title, and back to the actor on "——about something."

It was a disciplined life on the sets, of course, but it was a more comfortable discipline than that which I had at home. I was out from under the eyes and voice of my father, and this was a relief and a rest. At home I had Bach and Chopin to practice for hours, but at the studio I could hum "trash" like "Barney Google—with his goo-goo-googley eyes." Or "My sweetie went away, she didn't say *where*. She didn't say *when*—"

Off the set, too, I was never alone. Dates, parties, amusements were unthinkable. If we went to the theater or to a concert it was for "educational purposes" and the three of us went together. The small apartments we lived in afforded no privacy, and I was not even permitted to close my bedroom door. My life shuttled between home and studio, and the time away from the studio was scheduled in work sheets written by my father:

"9:30–10:00 Help Mother with housework.

10:00–11:00 Read marked articles in today's newspaper.

11:00–12:00 Piano practice, concentrate on Czerny today."

I never became a rebel. I was trained never to talk back—never to question or disagree.

It would take a very strong personality with a perceptive mind, someone who would care enough to get angry about the fact that I was growing up as a meaningless pretty little vegetable, to stir me into awareness.

This not-so-young Lochinvar was about to appear out of the West. More accurately, in Hollywood.

"OU ARE SO GODDAMNED BEAUTIFUL you make me
feel faint!" a famous collector of beauty whispered
into my ear during a test for a picture called *Beau
Brummel.*

I was a very young seventeen, a veteran of three
years' work in movies having made six feature-length films and
about a half dozen two-reelers and had become, I thought, very
blasé about the glamour of it all, partially, I suppose, because I
had played nothing but adult roles. I was too tall and too serious-
faced to be cast as a child or an exuberant adolescent. I had
worked with some of the top stars, Richard Barthelmess and
Dorothy Gish (and with a newcomer named William Powell). I
had a bowing acquaintance with other stars who had sets on the
same stage. In silents there were always two or three companies
using the same stages. In New York they were converted lofts or
garages, except for Famous Players-Lasky with whom I was again
under contract. In Hollywood the F.P.-L. studio was a rambling
green-painted barnlike building on Vine Street shaded by pepper
trees.

With Richard Barthel-
mess in THE BRIGHT
SHAWL (Released 1923)

I came out to Hollywood in April of 1923, and worked with Jack
Holt, Agnes Ayres and Thomas Meighan, among others, and almost every day I saw Pola Negri and Gloria Swanson who were in
the midst of a feud about cats: One wanted them fed and taken
care of, the other wanted them Out! Out! Nita Naldi would shock
the tourists by smoking a cigarette in a foot-long holder and wearing
a Japanese kimono which she would adjust elaborately, revealing
that she had nothing on underneath and a very voluptuous body
indeed. There would be little gasps, and the set would soon be
cleared of visitors who would carry home a juicy story of immoral
actresses.

As far as acting was concerned, I simply did what I was told to do.
This I was good at. For too many years I had searched for cues as to
my father's disposition and desires. And this ability called forth
praise of "How beautifully she takes direction!" You bet I did! In
silents the direction went on during the action; after the camera
turned, I'd hear, "Now look at him, Mary—that's it—you can't
believe it! Tears come to your eyes—reach out and touch his arm—

gently, gently." The more experienced actors would refuse anything but the minimum of offstage cueing, like perhaps, "You hear the door slam—" but I wouldn't have been able to carry a whole scene without help. Not because I'd forget what we had done in rehearsal, but because I was afraid I'd do it wrong. You see, I was "stupid"—I really thought I was—and that was the role I played in life. It was very safe.

When Paramount loaned me to Warner Brothers to play in *Beau Brummel* with John Barrymore, I was called for an afternoon of making just a short test, just some film in a costume approximating one I would wear in the picture, mainly for the producers to see how Mr. Barrymore and I would look together on the screen. The Warner Brothers' new studio was an impressive white building on Sunset Boulevard and only a few blocks from the apartment on Hollywood Boulevard where we were living temporarily. Our home base was still New York, and the studios at Astoria on Long Island.

Mother and I walked to the studio that hot afternoon in September, and I was carefully drilled on what I was to say to Mr. Barrymore when I met him. I was half sick with anxiety and nervousness in anticipation of being in the presence of this great man. I had seen him on the New York stage with his brother Lionel in *The Jest*. And of course in the movies in *Dr. Jekyll and Mr. Hyde,* and I had read every word about him I could find in the movie magazines.

Mother said, "Now, Rusty, you say to him, right after you shake hands, you smile and say, 'I can't tell you, Mr. Barrymore, how pleased I am that I'm going to work with you. I feel it is a great honor, and I shall do my very best to please you.' You hear me, Lucile? Are you listening!"

"Mm-hm."

After putting on some makeup and fixing my hair and putting on an Empire-style gown from the Western Costume Company, which didn't fit very well, I went downstairs to the main stage, Mother following at my heels. There were no other sets standing, just a flat and some lights over in a corner and a skeleton crew for the test. I walked the long dark mile over to the little set and met Harry Beaumont, the director, who took me over to a white-wigged gentleman in a red Hussar jacket and modern gray slacks—evidently it was to be only close-ups—and Mr. Beaumont introduced me to Mr. Barrymore. He took my hand and said with a nice grin, "How do you do, Miss Astor, I've been looking forward to this. I saw your picture in one of those horrible movie magazines when I was coming out here on the train and——"

Harry interrupted with, "And this is her mother, Mrs. Langhanke."

"Mrs.—ah—Langhanke?" he asked, pronouncing the name very well, and Mother nodded happily. "May I call you Mrs. Astor? It would be so much easier."

"Of course, Mr. Barrymore. I can't tell you how pleased we are that we're going to work with you. We feel it is a great honor and we'll do our very best to please you."

The well-known eyebrows went up.

"We?" He gave the small word the full force of his sarcasm. He paused long enough to let her fluster and say, "Well, I mean of course," and said, "Yes, of course," and took me by the elbow and walked me into the light.

Metaphorically it was the beginning of a very important light, for in the next three years he would teach me that I was a person, that I was somebody in my own right and not just a "goddam trained seal." Like D. W. Griffith, Barrymore had spotted the similarity of my father to a walking cash register, but unlike D.W., he did something about it. It was the beginning of respect for the business of acting, of learning that it was a craft that was never completely learned. Most important, he taught me that there was a world other than that which was run by Otto Langhanke. There were books, all kinds of books, besides those containing the poetry of Goethe and Heine; there were other kinds of music than Wagner and Beethoven and Bach—a lilting song from a musical comedy was not necessarily trash—and there was laughter and kindness and fun. It wasn't necessary always to approach the world with a clenched fist of determination or a bowed head of submission. It was a major beginning, then, but it was also the beginning of trouble, love, disappointment.

At the moment though I had a festival feeling—as though banners were snapping in the wind and sunlight. The charm of Mr. B. was the real thing, and the first time I had encountered it in anyone. He had magic and magnetism. Such charm is rare; when it is cultivated, it fades in and out with inadequate power like a flickering light bulb. But when it is real, it seems to be steadily nourished in vitality —by an energy of spirit perhaps. It is secure with self-knowledge;

he knows who he is, he has no need to boast or to be modest, no need to seek attention, or to reject it.

Now I was the recipient of this charm, and I felt expanded and at ease. For he made me feel that there was only one person in the world—me.

I said, "Your nose is sunburned———" Mother having used up my speech.

"Well it's a pretty big nose," he laughed. "It's a hell of a disadvantage in a fight or in the sun. I've been fishing off Catalina for tuna. With kites."

"With kites!"

He explained that to me while his valet came in and patted some Stein's greasepaint onto his peeling nose and forehead.

Offstage Mr. Beaumont said, "All right, we'll run some film now. Just stay as you are and keep on talking."

I heard the rustle of the camera, but Mr. B. paid no attention.

"What do you think of the script?" he said.

He really wanted to know what *I* thought of it! "Well," I said, "It's not really very historical. I mean it's not the way it was—about George Brummel."

"Of course it isn't." He took it for granted I'd done my homework. He said, "George Brummel never gave a damn about anyone but himself———"

"And I don't think there ever was a Lady Margery Alvanley!" [The part I was to play.]

"I doubt it. But this is the *moo-vies*. And there *is* a Lady Margery, and I think you'll be divine."

From offstage where the camera was still running, Beaumont said, "Just take her in your arms a minute, Mr. Barrymore. Let's see your faces close—" He drew me to him saying, "Get your face downstage—they want to see you." He touched my cheek with his finger and I leaned my head onto his left shoulder. He tightened his grip, and said, "You're so beautiful—" and Harry Beaumont said, "Now let's see the profiles again." We parted and he was smiling, "It's quite true—you have fantastic beauty," and to forestall any adolescent squirming under compliments, he went on quickly, "Raise your chin a little—remember you are a lady-in-waiting to the queen, and as such," he stepped back and cocked a knee in a courtier's bow, "dear Lady Margery, I give you my homage." Bowing over my hand, he kissed it gently. "Isn't that enough, Harry? It's hot as hell in here. Come on," to me, "let's get out of these lights."

The star system was in full flower at this time and all the nuances were reflected on the set. The star and his leading lady (or a feminine star and her leading man) had all the best of it. Like a king and queen they were above reproach. They were not called from their dressing rooms until everyone else was present. The director would line up the shot with the cameraman, rehearse the "lesser actors" sketchily; if there were extras, they would have been given an earlier call, instructed as to where they should be, or should go or do— whatever.

A director, a star and the lead had canvas chairs with their names on them, and no one dared to sit down in those chairs. The property man would have them ready for us when we came off the set, side by side, and a little apart from the common herd. And no one would be so familiar as to draw up a chair and make conversation. Even poor little "Mrs. Astor," if she wanted to speak to me, would beckon from afar. I'm sure she hated it.

Mr. Barrymore was of the theater rather than the movies and so the etiquette was adhered to most strictly. He was addressed as *Mister* Barrymore and I as *Miss* Astor. The lesser lights, even those who had played leading roles but were taking smaller parts because of the importance of this picture, were first-named: Irene Rich, Carmel Myers, even older distinguished actors such as Alec Francis, Clarissa Selwynne, Willard Louis. There were canvas chairs for them too, of course, but no names on the back and they got them themselves.

The picture was filmed at any easy pace, no production schedule, no pressure from the front office. If we had been working hard on a difficult scene, we'd be given a rest.

The routine of making a silent was similar to that of today as far as the actors and directors were concerned. A scene was blocked out, rehearsed and shot. The difference was in the techniques. Except for a special scene that could not be taken again—a battle scene, a car falling over a cliff—there was only one camera, and that was mounted on a tripod and hand-run with a crank. If you said the words, "a thousand and one," neither fast nor slowly, you had the rhythm of one turn of the crank for normal speed. The camera could be speeded up or slowed, but the projector ran at a constant speed. If the camera was cranked faster than the projector, the action would be slowed down in projection; if the camera was

John Barrymore as Beau Brummel, Willard Louis as the Prince of Wales, and Mary Astor about to break up over their conversation.

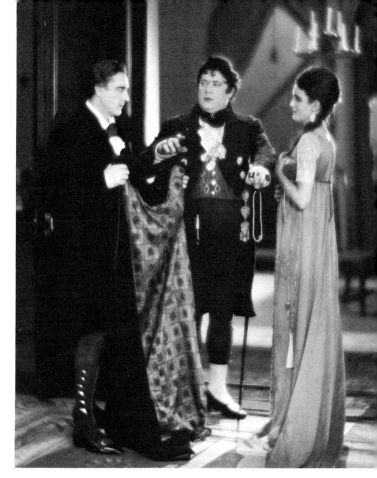

Mary Astor in bridal veil and John Barrymore in hussar costume in BEAU BRUMMEL (Released 1924)

slowed up, the action would be speeded up. This was the only trick the camera could perform.

Another big technical difference was the lighting. Film negative was slow and so the lights had to be powerful. "Luggin' iron," was how the electrician described his job, for all the lights were mounted on iron pedestals and they were heavy and cumbersome. Overhead as general illumination were the banks of Cooper-Hewitts, which gave out a pale, sickening greenish-blue color. They were our original neons. Most of the other lights around the camera on the floor were carbon arcs; the smaller ones with two arcs in a reflecting box were called Klieg lights. A glass slide and a "silk" protected us from the Kliegs to some extent, but all of us at one time or another became afflicted with what was called "Klieg eyes," a very painful damage similar to snow blindness. There were carbon-arc spotlights up high, and to light the backgrounds there were the great brutes of sun arcs which hissed and crackled and whined. "Inkys"—incandescents—were to replace all these; some were already used in close-ups, but they were not strong enough for general lighting.

The heat was unbelievable, sapping our strength. So occasionally they'd cut the master switch, leaving a couple of work lights on, and we'd sit around in the cool gloom and talk or make jokes, or take a walk and have a Coke. This was quite customary. In those days, no one was expected to stand the pressure that became part of the making of movies later on.

The story of *Beau Brummel* lacked historical accuracy, but the era supplied beauty and Mr. Barrymore and I supplied a pair of stunning profiles in many a romantic close-up. We all wore beautiful clothes and behaved with impossibly beautiful manners. Willard Louis as the Prince of Wales and Mr. Barrymore made bawdy jokes during their scenes (it was a silent picture, remember), only occasionally using the lines from the Clyde Fitch play from which the picture was adapted. After the picture was released the following year, there was a great deal of mail from the deaf who were able to read lips: They were very shocked.

The world was a lovely place that seventeenth summer of my life. It never again would be so romantic, so storybook beautiful, or quite so romantically tragic. One could even put it into the idiom of the narrative subtitle of that period: "The parting from her lover

John Barrymore in his Hamlet outfit, Mary Astor in
rental costume for special Albin portrait (1923)
From VANITY FAIR. *Copyright © 1925, 1953 by
The Condé Nast Publications, Inc.*

made her heart ache and caused secret tears to flow upon her pillow.
Her only consolation was that someday, somewhere, they would
meet again, and perhaps, just perhaps, they could proclaim their
love to the world."

Well, things don't come out that way, except in the movie scripts.
The lovers were to meet again, but many things intervened. Time,
for one, geography for another. New York, England, Hollywood
were not hops in a jet plane. Parental influence was strong. My
parents were impressed and flattered by the great man, but they
were not about to lose their little investment to the questionable
clutches of a man of forty-two. So there was a lot of dreaming and
waiting in the next few years, and work, and work, and work.

THE CHRISTMAS OF my seventeenth year, I spent—we spent, Mother and I—in Natchez, Mississippi. Someone has been quoted as saying, "A tree is a tree and a rock is a rock, so shoot it in Griffith Park." This wasn't my particular experience. I saw the United States as part of a movie company. We worked on locations in Maine, Connecticut, Louisiana, Mississippi, all around New York State, New Jersey, and later Canada, east and west, in those few short years alone.

The picture in Mississippi was *The Fighting Coward,* adapted from Booth Tarkington's story "Magnolia." It was an unimportant film with no stars, simply a vehicle for director James Cruze who had become famous for his picture *The Covered Wagon.* A cash-in-on-the-name-quick type of picture. And they're never any good. It was all non-Faulkner southern—with white pillars and moss-hung trees and duels fought for the lady's honor, and colder than the devil. Cullen Landis was the young hero, and our love scenes were played on great sweeping lawns in front of a magnificent southern mansion, and we had to chew on ice between scenes so our breath wouldn't show.

We were handsomely entertained by the owner of the mansion. There was an elaborate buffet supper, to which the company was invited. The crew got drunk downtown, and had a better time I'm sure. "The company" always means director, producer or unit manager, head cameraman, publicity man and the actors. The crew consists of carpenters, electricians, property men, their helpers. Soon that would include makeup people, wardrobe and hairdressers, but at that point we all handled our own makeup, clothes and hairdos. Until they realized it cost them money. For example, I forgot a parasol when I went to Texas on *The Rough Riders.* It had to match the interiors, and it was sent special delivery down to us, but it cost the company in time lost.

The mansion was decorated with hothouse flowers and lighted only by candles, millions of them it seemed to me: crystal chandeliers, wall sconces along the walls of the great staircase, tables and side tables in the dining room all blazing.

I remember feeling gauche and ill at ease in all this grandeur. If it had been a set and I were wearing hoop skirts and curls and had a part to play I would have been quite comfortable. But I had to be myself, with no character to hide behind and that was not—safe? Perhaps. Jimmy Cruze was sweating with the duty-socializing, wanting to get back to the hotel and work on the script. Phyllis Haver, once a Mack Sennett beauty, was giggling, "Gawd, darling, did you *ever!* I'd love to see if they've got real feather beds up there. I bet they do!" Mother was trying to out-lady the lady of the mansion. We all consumed a great deal of food—hotels on location being notoriously lacking in decent meals.

Another evening our gentle hostess escorted us to a Holy Roller meeting. The lady made sure we got in and had chairs in the crowded, hot room. In a voice tinged with something that made me shiver, she said, "Move ovah theah, niggah, let these white folks in and git some good chairs, heah?"

In the company there was a very well-known and good actress playing a stereotyped southern Mammy. It suddenly occurred to me that I hadn't seen her around the hotel—at the company tables for breakfast and dinner or at the buffet supper—only on the set. She was a jolly sort of woman with a great whooping laugh. I hadn't heard that laughter since we arrived. I understood now, a little.

The making of movies didn't stop for holidays. So Christmas that year was celebrated in the hotel with a dime-store foot-high green paper Christmas tree on the bureau. People made long-distance phone calls, and we ate a stringy turkey dinner in the hotel dining room after working all day.

There was no Screen Actors Guild then, so when we started a picture we worked until it was finished: nights, Saturdays, Sundays, holidays. An easy pace, granted, but a constant one. When it was all over everyone rushed around to get another job. If you were lucky, you were under contract and a new assignment awaited you—either with the home company or on loan to another company. The studios often loaned actors they had under contract because they made money on the deal. They could up the weekly salary and collect the difference. We were a piece of property—sold, borrowed, lent, used.

I went back to New York to do some dreary easily forgotten pieces of movie magic: *Unguarded Women* and *The Price of a Party* for Paramount; back to Hollywood for *The Fighting American* with Universal.

Listen to those titles! Thousands of feet of film to feed the hungry box office. And they were the money-makers. They only took six or eight weeks of shooting, and paid for the gamble on the bigger films. They also built stars by familiarity. People cared a lot about actors, and seemed indifferent to the vehicle they watched them in. Everybody was handsome and beautiful or mean and ugly; there was some excitement about whether the boy would get the girl, and then of course he did; and nobody in the audience had to think as they got away from their business or marital troubles. There was never any reality, any kitchen-sink drama, or ordinary troubles, just real big ones that never happened to anyone—avalanches, suffering at the hands of the Huns, or being shot at or starving to death. And everything always came out right in the end.

"It all comes out right in the end." "Everything happens for the best." We were the representatives, the proof of these clichés of consolation. We were the hope peddlers; we pushed it in all sorts of brightly colored capsules: Love Conquers All, Crime Doesn't Pay, Honesty Is the Best Policy, Hard Work Reaps Rewards, The Rich Are Unhappy—the Poor Are Happy, Good Triumphs Over Evil. These silver linings to all clouds were the stuff of dreams and human beings like to dream. Movie theaters were quiet, dark, hypnotic. Organ music throbbed gently and a huge brightly lighted silver square held one's total attention. You could forget, you could identify—or you could sleep. People didn't kick the habit for years.

Why this was a peculiarity of the movies of that time I don't know. Whether it was the taste of the producers who selected the material or their knowledge of what the public wanted I have no idea. The producers weren't all the stereotyped ignorant, illiterate, cigar-smoking money grabbers. Men like Jesse Lasky and Walter Wanger, who were my bosses at that time, were intelligent and cultured. Films were adapted from stories by good writers: Joseph Hergesheimer, Adela Rogers St. John, Percy Mackaye, George Ade, Booth Tarkington. And yet, somehow, before they reached the screen these good stories would be poured into the mold, stamped with another come-on title, and even I knew they were just silly.

I was reminded that nothing could be silly that paid me a thousand a week. Possibly. But I had seen plays and read books, and I had a longing to do something *good*. I'd seen Eleonora Duse on her last tour, breaking box-office records. I'd watched Winifred Lenihan in Shaw's *Saint Joan;* there were plays I've never forgotten, like *The Green Hat* with Katharine Cornell, *The Miracle* with Rosamond Pinchot, *Craig's Wife, The Guardsman, Desire Under the Elms.* The theater was good but movies were just puerile.

John Barrymore had stimulated my interest by his own great respect for the theater and the acting profession. It fascinated me to learn that there was something called a relationship with an audience. That there were techniques that "made 'em listen." An audience was not just a bunch of people out there but an entity with which one communicated. He told me that I could learn a great deal by movie work, but that I would never reap the rewards of audience-actor relationship unless I went into the theater. But in the meantime, "learn everything you can." For him, acting was never self-expression. It was the duty, the purpose, of the actor to be the expresser of the writer. The medium between writer and audience. He wanted me to play Ophelia with him in the London Company of *Hamlet* and later Lady Anne in *Richard III.* My father said no: It was "impractical." Of course it was. No money in it.

I felt the stirrings of ambition, of an intuition that real goals could be very rewarding. That hard work could be more than just long hours, hot lights, fighting boredom, traveling on trains, freezing or boiling on location.

But I wasn't the boss of my life. I was conditioned from birth *not* to make decisions. "I make the decision for you, until you are older," and I never got old enough.

So back to Hollywood to make *Enticement* and *Playing with Souls.* That gives you an idea.

There was a new dance called the "Charleston" which I learned so I could do a few steps if the script called for it. My hair was long and Daddy was against cutting it, so I wore bobbed wigs.

Coolidge was reelected, radio was becoming a threat, just a grain of sand in the comfortable shell of the movie business. There was the Leopold-Loeb trial. J. Edgar Hoover became head of the FBI. There was something called the Teapot Dome scandal.

There was also a new fad called crossword puzzles. *That* I was interested in. It occupied the long sitting-around hours on the set. In *Enticement* I was playing a bobbed-haired, Charleston-dancing young bride who shocks her new husband's (Clive Brook) staid English family. I had a book of crossword puzzles and I had learned a word from John Barrymore that I'd never heard before. I filled in all the four-letter word spaces of the puzzle, both up and down: "Crap, Crap, Crap, Crap." An avalanche in the mountains around Lake Louise, in which I was saved by Ian Keith, showed me the error of my ways and I was reconciled to Clive Brook. Crap, Crap, Crap.

In *Playing with Souls* I stood by my sweetheart, William Collier, Jr., who believed himself illegitimate, but it all came out right in the end: There had been a fire where the records were kept or something. Crap, Crap, Crap. A thousand dollars a week. Or was it more now? I didn't know. My father never told me.

Aside from these soporific little epics I was condemned to, there was much going on that had great entertainment value. And one of the people who contributed so much to this art in itself was Douglas Fairbanks, Sr.

Doug was a great acrobat, and he played a Robin Hood type in every picture. Grinning, he gaily leaped over every difficulty and helped whoever it was who was in trouble. His productions were lavish and beautiful and he surrounded himself with attractive people. The stories were all in the fairy-tale category, so the impossible was never ludicrous. He did almost all of his own stunts himself, except when the risk might mean an injury that would delay the picture.

Once during the filming of *Don Q, Son of Zorro,* while he was watching his double do a jump from a wall onto a running horse, he said, "It's not good, he's too soon, he ought to swing out more." He stopped the camera and told his double, "Let me show you, Jim. Go on back to where the camera is. I'll show you, you've got to *lean* away from the wall, like this." And with everybody watching and no

With Douglas
Fairbanks, Sr.,
in DON Q, SON OF
ZORRO (1925)

camera running, he did the whole stunt, and the crew and everybody laughed, and the double said, "Why don't I just go home?"

Working with Fairbanks was a kind of pleasant social event. He
and Mary Pickford entertained lavishly at "Pickfair" and there was
always someone visiting the sets, and work was interrupted to show
people around and make them feel like an audience while we did
a scene for them. I was introduced to Sir This and Lady That and
important people of all kinds. Everybody visited Doug's set. And
they were always photographed with Doug, given tea or lunch. It
was very pleasant. It was nice to get paid for—and had little to do
with acting.

Before we had started shooting *Don Q*, Elinor Glyn (the writer
who dubbed Clara Bow the "It" Girl) was a guest at luncheon at
the Fairbanks private dining room. There were a dozen people
present. Donald Crisp, who both acted in and directed the picture,
writers, my mother and myself. I was under discussion—or rather

my appearance as Dolores De Muroz. The trouble was I didn't look very Spanish. My hair was stubbornly curly and Doug didn't want me to wear a wig. A hairdresser was called in to make suggestions. But it was the imperious Miss Glyn who solved the problem. She called for a comb and some butter. Sitting at the table with my lunch still before me, I endured her combing out my long hair, brushing it briskly—a few hairs going into the food—and then dipping her hands into a bowl of soft butter and applying them to my head. Talking all the time, she parted my hair in the center, smoothed it and patted it down sleekly and into a bun in the back, and then called for a high jeweled comb which appeared miraculously. She stuck it into the bun at an angle and said, "*That's* the way she should look!" Coiffure by Elinor Glyn. And that's the way I looked in the film, although I think they managed to get something less unpleasant than butter to hold my hair sleekly to my head. They had not begun to make hair sprays or hair lotions as yet, of course.

Perc and Ern Westmore were handling makeup and hairdressing on *Don Q:* As I remember, it was the first time these departments had been created. Greasepaint came in a stick—somewhat like a big lipstick. Stein's Pink #2, I remember, was what I used. And it was pink, whitish pink. It was applied in streaks all over the face, and then smoothed until it filled every pore. With a towel wrapped turbanlike around the head, you leaned over and using a powder puff loaded with a pinkish powder slapped it all over until the grease had absorbed it. Really very similar to the method clowns use. Eyebrows disappeared, eyelashes were coated, lips covered. Then it was brushed off nice and smooth.

Lipstick was a dark red. Reds went black on film, but if the tone was too light one's mouth would look white. The men used a lighter lipstick and less base makeup. There was eyebrow shadow, brown, and mascara, black, and then something that was called "cosmetique," a black cake of guck that was melted over a spirit lamp and then applied to the ends of the eyelashes with a match or a toothpick. This was "beading": It accomplished what false eyelashes do today.

As technical improvements made the film faster, the makeup began to look even more masklike and white on the screen. It was no good using darker tones of pink because they tended to "go black" if you moved into a shadow.

With mother, Helen Langhanke, in Temple Hill house.
Note the "Oriental" stained-glass windows (1925)

One day in the makeup room Perc Westmore and I played around with mixing the Stein's Pink with just a touch of the brown eye-shadow. We melted it together and stirred it up and put it on, and there was an ivory cast to the color that had never been used. On the screen it was miraculous. Bones began to show, skin looked natural and the tiny muscles of facial expression that had been blanked out before now were more evident. It was the beginning of panchromatic makeup. I wish I had held a patent on it!

1925. A nineteen-year-old girl was a young girl then and that was the way I was treated. Not listened to very much, and therefore not talking much. Also, older people talked over my head. They made jokes that I didn't understand, or wasn't supposed to, and if I did, I smiled gently to indicate that I *didn't* understand.

It always flustered me when someone asked me a direct question. I had the dreadful habit of quickly turning to Mother so that she would take the ball and run with it.

I was standing with one of Doug's visitors one afternoon, watch-ing Doug curl the whip: the gimmick that was used in *Don Q* as the weapon with which he bested his enemies. He was seated at a table and with a small flick of his wrist the whip snaked over to the fire-place. The end was to catch fire on a coal and he was to draw it swiftly back and light a cigarette with it. One of those little scenes that takes a lot of time and patience and sometimes fifty takes to get right. The thing won't light, or it's too far to the right or to the left. The visitor, a lady, I think she *was* a Lady Somebody, very British, was watching in a cool detached manner. She turned suddenly to me, and I remember her eyes were very bright, twinkling and intelligent. She said, "D'you *really* like working in films?"

I flashed a look for Mother, but she wasn't close enough, so I answered in the phrases I had learned to use with interviewers, visitors, etc. I said, "Of course, I love it! It's so exciting! And working with Mr. Fairbanks is just wonderful. I'm *very* lucky."

"Really!" she said, with a smile. But I could hear her saying, "You did very nicely with your little speech but I don't believe a word of it."

I had to move away with a polite excuse, farther back where I could sit down, because my heart had started to beat too fast. Insincerity always did that to me. It made me clench my nails into my palms and grit my teeth. I longed to say what I really felt. "It's fun sometimes, but I'd rather watch other people than do it myself, because I really don't know what I'm doing half the time. I dress in beautiful clothes and I pose and make faces. And I do this *all the time*. Nothing else. But I'm stuck with it. And I don't know how to get unstuck! I would like to go to school. I would like to go to parties and flirt with boys of my own age." Instead I was all messed up in an affair with a man twenty-five years older than I and I was terrified if I ever so much as whispered a thought of my own.

I was never totally involved in movies. I was making someone else's dream come true. Not mine. I hadn't even had time to discover what my dream might be. But anyone would think me crazy for not wanting to be a movie star.

Think of all that money and everything! We had bought a big house—not a beautiful house, but a big, sham-Oriental, complete with lotus towers. We had a maid and an English chauffeur named Parker and a Pierce-Arrow limousine (with the lights on the fenders).

That day the Lady asked me if I liked being in movies, we finished work around five. It took me a half hour in the dressing room to remove my makeup (with Nujol and turkish toweling) and then we waited for the limousine and chauffeur to take us home.

Parker and the Pierce Arrow (1925)

It became six o'clock, and I was hungry and tired, and Mother was fussing because she was afraid there'd been an accident. We went out to the front gate and stood and waited some more. Finally the car drew up in all its heavy grandeur and Parker leaped out and held the door open and Mother squawked to Daddy who was in the back seat. "Where've you been? We've been waiting and waiting. Did you phone Tillie? I bet the dinner is ruined." Daddy sat quietly with his hands on his malacca cane until she ran down and then said patronizingly, "One cannot simply walk out in the middle of a game of three-cushion billiards."

Well, of course not. Especially when you are a member of the exclusive Hollywood Athletic Club and you play with the best men —no Jews, of course.

Mother wouldn't leave it alone. She said, "Well, I'm just about dead. I've been running up and down stairs. We were doing some scenes in the tower and every time Lucile needed her makeup fixed or her mantilla would get blown by the wind or something, it was just trot, trot, trot all day."

"What is the matter with the brothers Westmore?" asked Mr. L. "Aren't they paid to do that?"

Mother squirmed a little and said, "Yes, but it's my job, and I don't want them to get the idea they can paw over her any time they want to———"

I ventured a protest, "They don't *paw* over me, Mother!"

Mother made one of her "Hm!" sounds. "Oh, they're nice boys, but I have eyes in my head."

On this shattering truth I gave up, leaned my head against the window and tuned out. And stayed tuned out, for the argument went far afield and continued on and on, through dinner, through an hour's practice at the piano. I climbed the stairs to my bedroom and finally fell asleep to the sound of loud talk and slamming doors.

It *was* nice to be a movie actress, in some ways; I could be in a studio, protected. Listening to nice, modulated voices like Donald Crisp's and Warner Oland's and being gently teased by them. Maybe Miss Pickford would come over for a while; she had been so nice the day she'd said, "Douglas, that child has been in the sun for an hour, why don't you get her a lemonade or something?" People were *nice* to me in the movies. Yes, it was wonderful being a movie actress.

Toward the end of the picture Doug and Mary gave a dinner party for one of the male members of the Royal Family, here from London more or less incognito. I can't remember who was there. But just look over a list of the stars of that time—they were *all* there. It was literally a command performance, for several of the talented ones did a little act or a dance or something. Charles Chaplin did a balloon dance, without balloons, with the magic of that later great mime, Marcel Marceau.

Afterward there was general dancing, and I became a wallflower. I sat on a couch with another young actress, who said, "I don't like to dance," in one of the loveliest voices I'd ever heard. It was strongly accented, very low and whispery as though it just took too much energy to talk. It would be years before the public would be privileged to hear that voice: "Gimme a visky, ginger ale on the side and don't be stingy, baby." Garbo, of course. I had heard of her: She'd come from Sweden, had made one American picture and there were great possibilities for her future. Indeed there were! We talked about the party, about clothes, about movies; we discovered we were born the same year, 1906, that we both had trouble sleeping; I took hot milk before going to bed, she liked chocolate, "something sveet." That's all. I never saw her again, except in films.

WE COMMUTED TO NEW YORK. With studios about equally divided between L.A. and New York at that time, we would travel back and forth two or three times a year by train. I don't think I have missed a single type of public conveyance for travel across our continent—except the stagecoach. Buses, trains, the trimotor Fords that left one deaf and dizzy, then the DC's and finally the jets.

Of course today we don't want to lose time. We want to get there and be on the job, we don't want to spend time in traveling. Lose. Spend. These are tension words. There aren't enough of them for our usage today. We've forgotten the pleasures of "have," "take." We're really not very good to ourselves. The *size* of our country, the beauty of it, the variety of its topography—the *feel* of it. That's what one can "have" if you "take" time. You can't get it in books or on TV. That's what we had on the Santa Fe Chief.

To me, the word "distance" has a pleasing resonance. Horizons of the sea and the land—way out there. It's like stretching; it makes you feel better.

We left L.A. on a Friday, for instance. Saturday we were in Albuquerque, Sunday in Kansas City. Monday in Chicago for a stopover and then the Twentieth Century Ltd. got us into New York on Tuesday.

Of course it doesn't sound very pleasant if you thought of it as being "cooped up in a train for five days." But nobody felt that way. Everyone had a relaxed air. We got to know a few of our fellow passengers. We took walks through the train in informal clothes, got off at the big stations where there would be a half-hour stop and had a little exercise. Inevitably there was a little old lady with a Pekinese, saying, "Him gets so restless!"

And then the gathering for meals at our regular table. And what food! We would have brook trout for breakfast, caught that morning in some sparkling stream and trucked to meet the Chief. Kansas City stocked us up on steaks and roast beef. Fresh vegetables, eggs, morning-baked bread all along the way. The best cooks and waiters, the whitest tablecloths and napkins, sunlight pouring in on the glittering tableware and glasses, the smiling face of "our" waiter who wanted to know how we'd slept, and hoped we'd take the flapjacks this morning, with the little sausages, perhaps? And a couple of fresh eggs? Brought aboard this morning. Or perhaps some winter evening, on the plains of Kansas, snow swirling outside the black windows, and inside all was warm and comfortable and secure, with occasionally a bit of excitement at being delayed for an hour because of the storm.

The transcontinental trains seemed to be one of the unchanging elements of our lives. We always took a drawing room, although two compartments would have been better. Daddy would say, "No sense to it. Three beds. What more do you want?" Well, privacy. But privacy to him was in itself suspect. "Privacy? To do what?"

Even so, we got along fairly companionably during those trips. Our only pet, a canary named Tweetums, accompanied us in a small wooden traveling cage hung on a clothes hook. He loved the noise of the train and the music from the portable phonograph with its endless Mozart records. Whenever it got a bit claustrophobic for me I could always say I wanted to go out onto the observation car for a while. I was permitted out of their sight on a train—I suppose because there was nowhere I could go. And I'm sure they knew my manner was too chilly and shy for me to be picked up by some stranger with ulterior motives. Even so, inevitably there would be some parting admonition, "Don't be gone too long! They're going to call lunch in a little while." (The small, hand-carried chimes—*ding-dong-dong*.) And I would close the door on a remark from my father, "What's the matter with her, anyway? Why can't she sit still for a while?" "Well, Daddy, she's just a kid, you know."

All I wanted was to *look*. To do my scenery viewing without the salting of comments: "My that mountain looks close!" "Pine trees up there." "Look at that cute little stream!" "There's a nice farmhouse—barn's just been painted." I wanted to sit in a corner of the observation platform and watch the rails disappearing into a single pewter line, feel the wind, listen to the scratchy drift of cinders on the roof, and let the mountains and the trees and the flying telephone poles and the fields and the farms all just happen—without thinking about them, or *saying* anything about them.

Sometimes when I had been assigned the lower berth at night (we exchanged and rotated upper, lower and wall berth, which had varying degrees of comfort) I would lie awake in the dark for hours, while my parents snored, and watch the stars, so close in the desert, and wait for that wonderful mourning wail of the engine whistle, coming from what seemed to be a mile up ahead of us. A scarf of smoke whipping by, a shower of sparks. And the stars doing their slow dance to the rhythmic conversation between the wheels and the rails.

At the stations we had an audience, because the fans knew that movie stars traveled on the Chief, and there would always be a dozen or so waiting for a glimpse, for a gracious smile and wave, or even an autograph. Good publicity. It was part of the job to be seen and smile "graciously." Really, the patronizing sound of that word! But that was what was expected. We were only a little less than gods—living an unbelievable existence. Wearing mink and sable and dining on pheasants' tongues and champagne, and smiling graciously.

The crowds increased in direct ratio to the distance from Hollywood. There might be a couple of kids in Albuquerque, no one in Needles or Dodge City, but Wichita would have a couple of dozen, and by Kansas City they'd start to get a bit more frantic and squeally and in Chicago it would be a mob. Of course in New York they were everywhere. A few would pool a taxi and follow us around on a shopping trip, for example, getting a new set of autographs wherever you stopped. I once asked a girl, "What do you do with all these?" She shrugged elaborately. "Sell 'em. What else?"

I was living right in the middle of that era called the Roaring
Twenties and described as "gin-soaked," "flaming," "decadent." In
victory and triumph our boys had returned from Over There but
peace did not bring love. Youth rebelled against the establishment.
Parents? What did those old fogies know about life? Teachers? Out
of date. Freud was the teacher—about sex, the ego and the id, you
musn't be repressed. Nietzsche had the real philosophy. The common complaint was that the older generation had ruined the world
before passing it on to us. They professed "to find all gods dead, all
wars fought, all faiths in man shaken."

Sloppiness in morals brought sloppiness in dress. The girls parked
their girdles and wore skirts above their knees, open galoshes and
cloche hats. The boys smoked pipes, wore puffy pants, porkpie hats
and floor-length racoon coats. *Ziegfeld Follies* and *Artists and
Models* showed women in the nude on the stage. F. Scott Fitzgerald
hit the bitter, cynical emotional note in his books. Edna St. Vincent
Millay declared,

> *Life in itself*
> *Is nothing,—*
> *An empty cup, a flight of uncarpeted stairs.*

The Twenties were roaring up to one of the biggest letdowns in
the history of our country. We were really swingin'—like a pendu-
lum.

Men worked for a peaceful world. The United States ratified the
two Nine-Power Treaties of the Limitations of Armaments Con-
ference and the signing nations agreed to respect . . .

I don't see the Twenties as a carefree, kick-over-the-traces, happy
time. The emotional climate was one of disillusionment, a painful
reassessing of values.

As for me, I was kept securely in my ivory tower, for I'm sure
that my father felt the threat to his source of income, and because of his fear of change. I could read and observe and listen—
but I could not participate because I was locked in and I was
kept busy.

I made two pictures that summer of 1925, and when I wasn't
working at the studio I had vocal lessons at Carnegie Hall and press
interviews (Louella Parsons, Harriet Underhill). I modeled for
clothes for publicity purposes: I was photographed in Bonwit
Teller fashions, and for Georgette hats; I modeled Jaeckel furs
for Maurice Goldberg; Lucas Kanarien photographed me for a

cover of *Motion Picture* magazine. And I took dancing lessons with Ruth St. Denis.

The films were *The Pace That Thrills* and *The Scarlet Saint*. If you can believe it.

In *The Pace That Thrills* there was this boy, Ben Lyon, out for all kinds of big thrills like race cars and stunting airplanes and amateur prize fights, and his steady girl (me) who was just as rich as he was but who took it in stride, very sensibly; then she endangered her own life with him in one of his big paces that thrilled, and it shook him up and everything came out all right in the end.

In *The Scarlet Saint* there was this boy, Lloyd Hughes, and I played a girl called—I'm not kidding—Fidele Tridon. This girl was stupid enough to sacrifice her honor, at least she made it *appear* as though she were a pushover, much to the humiliation and grief of her handsome but weak young man. Who then straightened out and had to stand up for her and everything came out all right in the end.

The Scarlet Saint was the first of seven pictures Lloyd and I made together. They thought we'd make a great team and teams were "in" at that time. We didn't. We were the most unsexy pair ever to appear on the silver screen.

Our locations were at a ball park or a racetrack or somewhere close by, and it was a hot New York summer. I can feel the heat and smell the smells we encountered as we drove over the Queensboro Bridge to our apartment in Flushing at night after a working day. I was on an at-home schedule also. A quarter hour of vocalizing, then dinner; then an hour and a half of piano practice.

I woke one night to a curious sound. Mother's voice, tense, furious, not loud, but with a through-the-teeth anger, "You're killing her, Otto! You're just killing her. For what!" She was peeling off my stockings, slipping a nightgown over my head. I had muttered something about lying down for a minute when we got home, and apparently they just couldn't wake me up.

The thing that sustained me through that long hot New York summer—besides the imperative of authority—was that I was hooked on the very stuff I was peddling: the hope stuff, the belief that everything would come out all right in the end. There was some justification for my expectation.

As my family put it, we had "renewed our friendship" with Jack Barrymore in May of that year, still 1925. We had not seen him since his great triumph in London with his Hamlet, and he was to go to the Coast for two pictures with Warner Brothers. And he wanted me to be with him. The first was to be *Moby Dick* and the second either *The Tavern Knight* or an adaptation of Byron's *Don Juan,* directed by Lubitsch. Doug Fairbanks wanted me for another picture, there was a Richard Barthelmess film that was also open. But my contractual obligations to First National cut out everything except *Don Juan* in September. Still, that was enough to dream on.

I had additional dream material. For two weeks in May I spent every afternoon with Jack at the Ambassador.

It was a complete mystery to me why I was permitted these afternoons alone with a man like Jack. My chaperonage was complete, a form of nineteenth-century European—or Latin—care of the young lady. I wasn't allowed to go to the corner to mail a letter. I might be kidnapped or something.

It had been a less complicated matter when we were working on *Beau Brummel* two years before. Jack came up to our apartment a few times to work with me. He wanted to teach me, to give me what he knew about acting. He had started with some rather noisy and self-conscious-making breathing exercises and control. The ponderous presence of my parents irritated him, and in exasperation he said, "We *must* work alone." So during the months of *Beau Brummel* he would send a car for me and my mother on Sundays to bring us to the Beverly Hills Hotel, and we were "alone at last" in his suite while Mother sat out on the veranda of the hotel with her sewing.

Later that same year when we returned home to New York, Jack was playing in a return engagement of *Hamlet* before taking it to Boston and Philadelphia. And he proposed that I study the part of Ophelia with him. This was a very wonderful thing, of course, and I got "up" in Ophelia as though I were going on as understudy. This meant a series of afternoon sessions with him, except on matinee days when I frequently went to the theater (*with* Mother) and saw the performance backstage.

But now, two years later, it seemed to me that the fiction was worn pretty thin. We were working, true—reading plays, doing scenes together—but . . .

I remember the gist of a conversation we had one afternoon during this time. It was rainy, blowy weather and the wind moaned and sang around the tower apartment. We were still sitting at a room-service table with the remains of a favorite luncheon: cold vichysoisse, cracked crab, cheese, fruit. I was wearing Burgundy satin lounging pajamas which he'd had made for me with the initials M.A.B. on the pocket of the coat. I would hang them in his closet at six o'clock when the lobby phoned that my father was there for me.

I asked Jack what he had said to my family to get us these times together. I said, "Daddy always sits over in a corner while I'm working on my singing lessons with Mr. Stuart."

"Maybe he doesn't trust Mr. Stuart."

"Stuart's an old *man*—" and then I saw he was laughing. "They're not *stupid*," I said, huffily.

"I didn't say they were."

"Well, I can't believe that they think that every day for six hours we act out bits of Shakespeare together, that all you do is teach me how to speak and move and think in terms of characters in a play."

"Do you find it dull? Aren't you learning *anything?*"

"No, of course not. And of course I am. But they seem satisfied with what I report to them at night."

"And I think they're satisfied with what you *don't* report to them at night."

This shook me, good.

"I don't believe *that!* Why if they had an inkling they'd—why they'd——"

"They'd what? Now let me tell you something," and he got up and started to pace around the room, nervous as always when he talked about my parents, for whom he had little regard.

"They have no intention," he went on, "no intention whatever of losing you, of allowing you to get married and get away from them."

"How do you know that?"

"I felt out your old man one night, and I got nothing but a fishy stare. I put it to him in his own cold-blooded idiom. I told him that I thought so much of your potential as a great actress—oh, I said I thought he'd done a hell of a job so far, but now I thought it was time for you to emerge from your little cocoon. That I would like to take over—I would even marry you, keep you in my protection, train and develop you as a person and as an actress."

"What did he say?" I was popeyed.

"He said he wasn't quite ready to relinquish his job. It was out of the question. Absurd."

Jack came around to the back of my chair and put his hands on my shoulders, saying, "I asked him, 'Doesn't she have anything to say about that?' and he answered, 'Nothing. Nothing whatsoever.' "

"Of course not," I murmured, automatically.

There was a long, raw pause, and the silence built up, and he went and stared out the window. Finally he said, "You don't have the guts, the vitality, to be an individual, do you? It would be an impossible thing for you to say, 'I want to be with my beloved—I want to go with him, and the hell with you.' "

I shook my head, miserably, and said, "Not just now."

"They are damn foxy, you know? They are shutting their eyes to what is really between us—it's their way of letting you out on a rope but keeping you feeling guilty, so they've got you."

"I just don't believe that. They're very straitlaced, truly."

"My ass!"

That evening I babbled on about the scene we'd worked on all afternoon. A chunk of the fourth act of *Hedda Gabler*, between Hedda and Brack. We had, as a matter of fact. But I saw them nod their heads, interestedly, and then exchange looks, Mother pursing her lips a bit. And then I remembered Daddy telling me one time that many European fathers took their sons to an older woman, a whore, for their sexual education.

It is difficult for me to find this girl in my memory. I've used all kinds of mnemonics: a perfume I wore, Rigaud's "Un Aire Embaumé," music we played on the piano in Jack's apartment, making duets out of Debussy's "Après Midi d'un Faune," "Rhapsody in Blue," "Wildflower," "Fascinating Rhythm," "Limehouse Blues." There was a hat I loved because Jack had designed it: a cloche of deep purple velvet, crushed in to fold at one side and held there by a bird's wing of gray feathers that curved down around my cheek. What else? Very little. Small emotional associations. But she still remains someone I think of in the third person, with small approval. I find her hard to accept, a growing person, and not growing: with no aggressiveness, no pride, no assertiveness. Painfully aware of her prison and yet not making the slightest effort to find a file in the cake with which to saw at the bars.

That mumbled, shamed, sad phrase, "Not just now." Jack had said repeatedly, and it wasn't an on-the-make line, for it had been a couple of years now, "I could make it happen, baby—I really could! I could teach you things that make an audience want to wrap you in their arms. I could make you a truly great actress—there aren't many in a century, you know—you could be one of them. You could move among the greats forever."

Being "great" seemed like an enormous responsibility. A burden. It seemed to contain too much hard bravery. And I was not to learn the simple ingredients of courage for some time. The mediocrity of material, which I sweated over for so long was, in part, my own fault. The breaks happened to me; I didn't make them happen. I never in my life went into the front office to do battle for a script. I never risked suspension for refusing to do a picture. Authority buffaloed me, and my only weapon was indifference. "Not just now."

Not ever, really. I didn't want to fight, and it would have taken a battle, I thought, to overcome my present condition. Inertia won. It's easy and comfortable now to say that it would have been a dreadful, heartbreaking life with this unstable man, great though he was. It's easy because we can never know what might have been.

Right up to the last moment with our tickets bought and reservations made, I worked on added scenes for *The Scarlet Saint*. The contract for *Don Juan* was signed, the picture was scheduled to start the first week in October, but I had at least two weeks of costume and wig fittings, tests and publicity assignments. My impatience was monumental, and I was worried. There had been a good deal of publicity during the summer about the making of *Moby Dick,* and that new girl, Dolores Costello. Jack had phoned us from the Coast several times, and once I was able to say, guardedly (the family was always listening), "I hear that Miss Costello is really lovely."

"She is. She's divine. Can they hear me?"

"No."

"Don't worry, my goopher, she's just a chicken."

So, finally we entrained on the Twentieth Century Ltd. I wore a new soft gray Patou coat, and my hat with the dove wing. And I smiled graciously and waved to the fans at the stations all along the way home.

And Jack met us in Pasadena with an armload of roses, and everything was just the same. Nothing had changed: And I was lying to myself and I knew it. For everything was changed, and couldn't be changed back.

DON JUAN with
John Barrymore (1925)

Don Juan had nothing to do with the poem by Lord Byron, and Lubitsch had declined to direct it. Alan Crosland was at the helm with a heavy hand. It was a turgid, rambling, sumptuously staged melodrama that had something to do with the Borgias. They were played by Estelle Taylor, Warner Oland and Montagu Love. In small parts there was an exotic, almond-eyed young girl by the name of Myrna Loy, and a slim, aristocratic bit of decoration whose name was Hedda Hopper. The story was forced into an impossible mold. The Borgias were mad at Don Juan because he was in love with a girl from the wrong family. They tried in several ways to eliminate the girl and finally succeeded in driving her off to a convent. That was the preview version. After the preview the audience opinion cards were so against the unhappy ending that we had to re-shoot several sequences so that Jack and I could ride off on a white horse into the Renaissance sunset.

Every picture in the making very quickly establishes its own atmosphere. It's like a big party, in a way. It's good, it comes off, or it doesn't. The director's the boss, and he usually sets the tone. John Ford's sets, for example, always felt "good." Everybody worked hard, but there were laughs and conversation about something besides the picture. Some directors took their power very seriously and held the company with a rigid hand. Mervyn LeRoy ran a nervous company, because he was fidgety and liable to blow his top over some minor detail.

Don Juan never jelled. Jack was tired from the physically rough job of *Moby Dick,* and he didn't like the story. He was drinking a lot and had horrible hangovers, and Alan Crosland didn't have the strength of personality to hold the company together. He was a nice man. He'd walk around, well dressed, brushing a waxed mustache with a finger and saying, "All right now, please, people—" but his crowds of extras were noisy and unruly. The sets were huge, dark, gloomy, smoking with torches; the costumes were elaborate and heavy. Velvet, brocades, metal lace.

By this time, Jack was deeply involved with Dolores and was feeling considerable guilt about me, so he picked on me for trifles of mistakes in scenes, or walked away from me after a scene in apparent annoyance. Mostly he simply ignored me. The simple psychology of guilt behavior: *You* are the one who is in the wrong.

Alan Crosland took me and my mother aside one day and said to Mother, "Mrs. Astor" (the name had stuck!), "what can we do about our lovely Mary? I mean she's not photographing very well.

Is she getting enough rest? Or what? She has these circles," tracing them with a finger, "very dark under her eyes, and the cameraman is having difficulty—"

Mother delicately hinted that it was a certain time of the month, I shook my head, but she ignored it, and Alan said, "But my God, she doesn't menstruate for three weeks, does she? I saw all of last month's rough cut last night. There are some really bad close-ups which we'll have to retake; but see that she gets her rest, O.K.?"

There was turmoil at home. I had, too late, started a campaign for freedom. It was only a scratching on the wall with my finger-nails, but it called forth loud discussions, much pacing of the floor, much slamming of doors. I had dared to say I didn't want Mother with me on the set every minute. That I wanted to be like the other actresses and have a maid to dress me, and not have Mother running up to tug at my dress or pat my nose with a powder puff. Mother was tearful at my "pushing her out of her job" but I was softly stubborn and suggested she come to the studio as a guest, that it would be more dignified for her. And my father, furious, yelled (he just couldn't *talk*!), "You want to reduce your mother to the level of a visitor, a nobody—a tourist—after all she's done for you!" and on and on.

I got a maid, and Mother would show up at lunch time and stay until we finished for the day—or night. It wasn't much. But it was the opening wedge.

After Alan Crosland's firm order, I was firmly ordered to bed at an earlier hour, and Mother would give me a teaspoonful of her "pink medicine" which she used occasionally, which knocked me out cold.

After all there was nothing more important than how you look in the rushes. Everyone inhabits two worlds, has two faces. The private world of heart and mind. We feel lousy some days but it mustn't show! Not to the people we meet in our public life. This was most particularly true in movies, because any great changes in one's physical or emotional health was penetrated by the camera. In the theater you can have a bad night, give a miserable perform-ance, look like hell—but it's only one night. On the screen to photo-graph a happening of a few minutes might take a week of work. Say you felt great on Monday, you walked into a room and played a part of a scene. You did another piece on Tuesday. Then Tuesday night you had a fight with your wife and got drunk and Wednesday when they took the close-ups of Monday's work, you wouldn't look the same at all. And so, the actor's protest, "I gotta work in the morning," was quite reasonable. It meant, I mustn't have an emotional blowup, I mustn't stay out too late at a party, I mustn't (well, shouldn't) drink too much, eat too much. You've got to look good in front of that lens. If you were not supposed to look good in the scene, you accomplished it with makeup and lighting. We didn't have time for the Stanislavsky method. Blood was ketchup and tears were glycerine—or fumes from a menthol inhaler blown into your eyes (if you'd been crying for a couple of hours and just ran dry).

It's a very odd feeling the first time you see yourself on the screen. I'm sure everyone says as I did, "That can't be me." Of course it can't. It isn't the way you experience yourself. And it is totally different from the mirror image. You don't walk like *that,* and what an odd shape your head is from the rear! If you are an actor or a public figure of today, you will constantly correct that image, until it is closer to what you want people to see. The shock of hearing one's voice is even greater, because we don't hear our own voices. The sound is too mixed up with all the resonators in the head and throat and mouth which impinge on the hearing apparatus. Both the image and the voice can be trained, until they become like an instrument you play without effort or self-consciousness. True, you can put untrained actors in front of a camera and get an effect of great reality. But have them do it again next week and the week after that, and next year. That spontaneous reality will have disappeared. It takes training to make a sentence sound as if you'd just thought of it—to look at another actor as though you'd never seen him before. Emotion is easy. Everyone is emotional. But to bring it up on cue, to the right pitch, controlled or out of control, takes training and experience. I have heard young people on the set saying, "I don't feel it." "This isn't my reality." Of course it isn't. It isn't supposed to be. You don't even have the same name. You are expressing someone else's reality.

As well as I know the actress, Mary Astor—every movement, every shade of voice, and I learned to manipulate her into many different kinds of women—she is still not "me." A year or so ago I flipped on the TV set and then went into another room for a moment. I heard some familiar words and said, "Hey, that's Mary Astor!" *not* "Hey, that's me." It was a rerun of an old movie. And if you're curious, yes, I watched it for a while and then switched to another channel, where they had a better show.

This "not me" feeling has developed a quirky thing in my relationships with people. I am quite jealous of "Mary Astor." I am more comfortable when an acquaintance has passed beyond the stage of being "thrilled" to meet her. Of talking about her and how much they remember about her, in this picture and that, of how beautiful she was. I squirm around in my skin and hope to be noticed a little, like Cinderella at the chimney.

I am proud of the product I developed and sold for so many years, the product called Mary Astor, but I'm glad when after awhile that look goes from people's eyes. The look they would direct at something in a museum. Or a zoo.

This schizoid feeling is shared by many actors. For example, if I meet a famous actor for the first time, we are immediately on the footing of fellow workers, and neither of us goes on about the other's accomplishments, or how thrilled we feel about meeting each other. But let a "civilian" join the group and we put the record on, and we say, "Thank you! Well, isn't that nice of you to say so! Really! You remember that!"

Of course I—the I that isn't M.A.—have my idols too. I was in Rome not long ago, and I would have loved to have met Sophia Loren, for the same reasons anyone would—I think she's fabulous. It could have been arranged, I'm sure. But there was no *professional* reason for meeting her, and so I didn't do anything about it. I felt I would have been intruding—like a "civilian"! On the other hand, for years I have had a great regard for Eva Le Gallienne, one of the truly greats of the theater. I was signed by my agent to appear in a play with her, rehearsals were called for Monday—the usual thing. The night before, the doorbell rang in my apartment and a woman in a camel's hair coat stood there saying unnecessarily, "I'm Eva Le Gallienne. Sorry, I should have phoned first, but I was in the neighborhood——" And I didn't gasp or faint or anything, nor did I feel like saying, *"You're Eva Le Gallienne!!!"* I said, "I'm glad you came, you must be frozen, what would you like to drink?" We were two women who had a job to do together, and we both knew we had to cut through the guff of social amenities and establish solid communication quickly in order to get on with that big job.

So what do you do when you meet a celeb? Well, you don't need to deny that it's exciting. It probably is, so say so! But don't go into a long thing about what you remember, or what you and dear

Henry used to say whenever the person had a film at the local theater. And *do* skip the line, "You've always been my favorite." It may be true but we're awfully suspicious of it, because there isn't an actor who hasn't heard it before, and we can't *all* be your favorite. How would you feel if one of my contemporaries walked in right after you'd said that to me? Then you'd have to say, "Oh, you *too*, Miss Crawford, you've always been my favorite too." However I *do* understand. The first time I met Lillian Gish—July 1920—I babbled, my knees felt weak. It was at Albin's studio in New York, and I said it: "Oh, Miss Gish! You're my favorite actress! I've seen all of your pictures and I think you're wonderful!"

I seem to have dropped *Don Juan* with a thud, but *Don Juan* is easily dropped. It was a very unhappy time, and the picture's only claim to fame was that it was the first silent film to have recorded Vitaphone music as a background.

Philip Gibbs wrote a novel called *Heirs Apparent*. Undoubtedly he worked very hard on it. Everyone was writing in that post-World War I time about how the youth of the day was going to hell. I didn't read Gibbs's book and I wouldn't have recognized it in a script called *The Twentieth Century, Unlimited*, which was changed to *Running Wild* and then changed to *High Steppers*.

It introduced a lovely young Mexican actress called Dolores Del Rio. A typical case of Hollywood logic: It was about England's postwar generation. Dolores Del Rio's great Latin beauty was disguised very well. They curled her hair, thinned out her brows and made her lips smaller. Of course her accent didn't matter: silent picture.

I was teamed with Lloyd Hughes and we started work early in January of 1926. Lloyd was a nice guy, who should never have been an actor and who knew it. The whole thing embarrassed him. He was very good-looking. Black hair and blue eyes, a good smile, and a hated cleft in his chin. He could never take being made up as part of the job. The makeup man would come at him to pat down a greasy spot with powder and he'd immediately clown and camp and lisp—and you sort of wished he wouldn't. His masculinity was hardly in question. In those days everybody had to have makeup or look very dirty on the screen. But he just felt foolish. When we had to rehearse love scenes he'd say, "Now lemme see—I put my arms around you—and uh, which way's your face going to be—I have to kiss ya, honey, oh boy, oh boy!" Once I said, "Lloyd, please, just pretend for a few minutes that you're in love with me, can't you?"

Lloyd Hughes, Mary Astor's co-star in seven movies

"Why shore, honey, that'd be easy. But I'd never kiss you in front of all of these people if I was." Even the accent was a sort of hick-for-the-hell-of-it. Supposed to be funny. Well, as I said, we were not a very sexy pair on the screen.

Eddie Carewe, a very good director, could see my difficulty and took me aside one day and said, "Don't let it bother you, don't let it make *you* awkward." But I did. I didn't yet have any control or mastery of techniques which enable you to make love to a telephone pole or a blank wall. As yet, someone chewing gum in my line of vision offstage could throw me. And we didn't have the added discipline of sound and words and lines to be learned and ways of saying things. It was considered humorous to "break up" a fellow actor with a wink of the upstage eye or even by saying something that had nothing to do with the scene.

Gradually it was simpler to dismiss things I had been taught. I didn't hear Jack's voice anymore saying, "*Think!* The camera's a mind reader. Don't let your thoughts wander to what kind of shoes you're going to buy, or to plan on what you'll say to so-and-so when you see him. *Sustain*—even though you've made the shot fifty times."

I remember we were sitting at lunch and I said, "May I have some more butter, please." He used it. He said, "Before *any* scene—go over how long you've known him—or her. You even say 'Pass the butter' differently, according to how you feel. Right now you're bored—I can hear it. There's always something *under* what you're saying—caused by a million things. How does it make you feel? Suppose, for instance, the guy says—maybe he's your husband— 'I've quit my job.' And your line is, 'Pass the butter, please.' O.K., now don't giggle like an ass. Listen, there'd be a world of difference if you think, 'Well screw him, I'll get somebody else to buy me a sable coat.' Or if you feel happy that the guy's finally got up enough nerve to do something that was your idea all along. Now let's try it. Let's improvise. I'll go out and come in and tell you I've quit my job. I'm ah—let's see—a shoe salesman, and I'll tell you I've quit my job and you invent something and let me *see* you thinking."

A few years ago I was working with some Actors' Studio people in a TV show, trying to make sense of the nomenclature they used. I asked one of them, "What do you mean by 'subtext?'" He explained. My thoughts whisked back thirty years to "Pass the butter."

But then, with the material so simple, so uncomplicated, no sound ("That's no excuse," Jack would say, but I'd stopped listening), it was just plain *easier* to do just what one was told, to simplify it into shallow emotion: Are you angry? insulted? happy? lonesome? There were angry expressions, insulted expressions, and you just used those expressions, got off the set and made jokes and had some fun.

And I began to have lots of fun. My blighted romance had blasted away some of my sensitivity and I got tougher with my family. I was filled with bitterness, and I didn't like the taste of it. I didn't understand why I no longer was so affected by my father's anger or my mother's tears. I think I rather enjoyed it. I wanted to hurt, although I didn't *know* I wanted to hurt.

I said to my father, "I'm not going to practice singing anymore, I don't want to learn to sing, I have nothing to sing about, I hate singing." And I didn't mind very much when he shook me by the shoulders and yelled at me about insubordination. I just said, "Don't ever put your hands on me again." I had decided to stop being shy and nervous, and I began to have a good time.

I had a very good time indeed on a bit of fluff called *Forever After*. It was adapted from a play that had been fairly successful, I believe, mainly because of its stars, Alice Brady and Conrad Nagel. It had charm and nostalgia, small-town, prewar, young love. Like Booth Tarkington's *Seventeen*. Lloyd Hughes (yes, Lloyd Hughes) and Hallam Cooley vied for my affections with a ukelele. I wore Mary Janes, flat patent-leather pumps, and my hair down.

It was a big day when a sixteen-year-old first put her hair up. It was a signal of maturity—or at least it said, "Now I'm to be thought of as being on the marriage market." There was many a scene of that transition, when the girl-next-door-type was seen coming down the staircase to meet her date, and you cut to the boy starry-eyed that she's wearing a long skirt, high heels and has her hair piled up on her head, and a subtitle unnecessarily read, "Gosh!" And then there'd be the comic bit when she'd trip on her high heels getting into the boy's beat-up Model-T.

This picture was full of that kind of schmaltz. I thought I had quite an acting problem, now that I was a poised mature woman of twenty, having to be convincing as a sixteen-year-old. For at sixteen you had a whole bunch of mannerisms, like pouting and simpering and never being quite still, and tee-heeing a great deal.

I was a rich girl and my parents didn't want me to marry Lloyd Hughes because he was only a poor boy even though he was a football hero. But Lloyd went to war and became a hero Over There and got wounded and went to a base hospital and guess who was there? In a starchy white uniform with a red cross on her veil, leaning down to put a cigarette into his mouth. He breathed her name, "Jennie," and passed out again and tears coursed down Jennie's cheeks. And then, back in the States, he was decorated for bravery and there was no more opposition from the now proud parents.

But I had a good time. For now, after some real battles at home, I'd been turned loose. I started to smoke, right in front of everybody, and once in a while I had a *cocktail!* That popular drink called an orange blossom: orange juice and gin.

I also got engaged, because that seemed like fun. I didn't know it was really another kind of getting even with my father. The boy was an assistant director—that made him a "nobody." His name was Irving Asher—and Daddy was a Jew-hater. I fixed him!

My father had a legal document drawn up, putting the house on Temple Hill, which at the time was very valuable property, jointly in our three names, with the proviso that no one of us could sell the place without the consent of the other two. For which read: "If the

With Edward
Everett Horton in
FOREVER AFTER
(1926)

young lady gets any more ideas, like wanting some money, she can't kick us out." His thinking didn't go so far as to realize he might not always be the recipient of those handsome weekly checks. Nor did mine.

My "having fun" was simply conforming to what everyone thought I should do in order to have fun. I had had a very embittering experience, much rougher than I was equipped to handle. Nothing came out all right the way I'd been living. I had to get on with the business of the pursuit of happiness. So happiness was a young man calling in an open roadster, having dinner at Montmartre, dancing or going to the theater, driving to the beach for a swim and a cocktail at someone's house in the Malibu Colony, learning to make wisecracks, laughing a lot. Shaking off the yoke of shyness, of thoughtfulness, of observation. Doing instead of watching. Conforming.

I also conformed to what others thought I shouldn't do or like. Things that were "boring, darling." Things that were pompous and dull like Dostoevski and Walt Whitman and Henry James and Proust and yes, by now, Freud. Hemingway was exciting with *The*

Sun Also Rises. Carl van Vechten's *Nigger Heaven* was unbelievable, and if you were a swot you read Carl Sandburg's *Lincoln: The
Prairie Years.* I was a swot. I still read. No virtue, I was a compul-
sive reader, the kind that reads every word on a ketchup bottle.

We danced to "I Know That You Know," "Do-Do-Do," "The
Girl Friend," and learned a new dance, "The Black Bottom."

Hollywood was called "the jungle of moronia" by our eastern
friends and they were right. But movies spread a lot of money
around. Movies were making a lot of money because the public
liked recognizing the familiar. And they stayed away in droves from
anything "artistic." The word in itself was suspect.

And yet there was some real art being sneaked to the public.
Via the "lowest" forms, the slapstick comedy. It was well mixed
with pies in the face and chases, a hot foot, a mustachioed police-
man getting a kick in the pants. But people like Chaplin, Buster
Keaton, Laurel and Hardy were great mimes. They stayed free.
They bought no successful novels and plays to guarantee circulation
value. To them art was not vague or dull or esoteric. It was something that reached out to people more truly than ephemeral concoc-
tions called drama.

I especially liked Chaplin, but I thought there must be something
wrong with me because he didn't make me laugh. I didn't think it
funny when he would sidle up to a group of people and do all sorts
of idiotic things to make them notice him, to make him part of the
group. I kept wanting to say, "Don't try so hard!" but I was really
talking to myself. And I should have listened.

To have talent was not enough. To have a driving ambition was not
enough. To know the right people was not enough—that just
opened a door. The very fact that a person chooses the occupation
of acting might be interpreted as a sign that he's not capable of
adapting himself to reality. Of course I didn't choose my occupation, but I stayed in it and I was a nonrealist. And yet *non* isn't the
apt prefix. Let us say that we held reality at arm's length and
watched it. And we watched ourselves. Not the way a vain person
admires himself in a mirror, primping and posing, but inside and
out. I remember once I burst into tears over something and rushed
to the bathroom mirror to see how I looked when I was *really* crying. We never merely experienced something happening. We experienced it and watched ourselves experiencing it.

[57]

This objective adroitness I'm sure had a lot to do with actors being thought of as not quite worthy of one's trust. We were liars. Not because we lacked integrity, but because of this dexterity with attitudes, emotions and words. It was a pretend business, and the closer we came to pretending it was real, the better we were. The trouble was, it wouldn't stay fastened down to working hours. It could not be confined totally.

Even today's actors who work hard at digging out the reality are self-enchanted, look-at-me beings.

In a recent interview, a very popular young actress said, "Uh, don't pay too much attention to the way I look . . . and I'm not talking like myself either . . . I mean, the girl in the picture I'm doing is uneducated, bitter, cynical, and right now I'm talking like her. Talking bad, using a lotta bad English . . . I let it happen . . . it's the way I prepare for a role."

She's right. It works. What I'm not sure of is, Does she ever know when she is "talking like herself?" I know, she uses a lotta better English.

It was, and is, a pretend business. Not a mimic business. Many young people have disappointed their ambitious relatives and friends when they tried to break into the acting profession merely because they could imitate someone: "You should see him take off Jimmy Cagney!"

It is also not a phony business. I mean it. Because if it's phony, an actor has failed, and you say, "I don't believe him." And good actors are not phony in real life, either. They still may be lying! "I met Alice Apfelschmalz the other day, and why, she's just like the girl next door!" The hell she is!

Of course, in the Twenties, to be like the girl next door was not the thing. Many actresses went the whole way on the strange and other-world performance in real life. Appearing in public, but untouchable, oh, smiling graciously, of course! They surrounded themselves with a court, and they spread their peacock feathers and everybody went "ah—a-a!" They made entrances; they appeared here and there, unpredictable as summer lightning. Heads turned, crowds gathered, busloads of tourists paid to be driven by their houses. We were all Elizabeth Taylors and Richard Burtons. There weren't so many of us then.

I was neither a peacock nor the girl next door and heads turning in my direction always gave me sweaty palms.

THE HIGH SPOT of "having fun making movies" was the location trip to Texas for the filming of the exteriors of *The Rough Riders*. They found a man who was a real double for Theodore Roosevelt. His name was Frank Hopper, he wasn't an actor—I think he was a teacher. But that didn't matter because there were only a few shots of Roosevelt in the picture. You see it wasn't so much about the Rough Riders as it was about two young men (Charles Farrell and Charles Emmett Mack) in love with the same girl, me, and I stayed at home while the boys went off to fight in Cuba. Still, there were a lot of production shots of trainees, marching and forming up and leaving on the train where I tearfully waved good-bye to them.

Victor Fleming's great talents as a director were not completely lost as he was a good "big production" man. And he did get the feel of the period, the zeal for a cause, the heat and dust of Texas.

Our special train arrived one hot afternoon in August at San Antonio. The mayor of the city greeted us with a military band, a welcoming speech and a sheaf of slightly wilted roses for me. I have a picture of the great event. I was wearing (God knows why—Texas in August!) a black satin dress with black chiffon balloon sleeves, a black lace droopy hat festooned with some kind of petals. The mayor is about to kiss me on the cheek and is leering at the camera, and I am smiling graciously.

We were driven with police escort to the St. Anthony Hotel where we had a late sumptuous lunch, and where General Elting made me an honorary member of the First Cavalry Brigade—more pictures of me smiling graciously.

I had Mother *and* a maid with me. I couldn't get away with traveling unchaperoned, but Mother said I wasn't to pay any attention to her because she intended to have a good time. (Daddy had stayed home.) And bless her, she did. She just ate up that Texas hospitality, and annexed a couple of Army officers who thought she was pretty cute.

I've often wondered how long it took San Antonio to recover from that onslaught of Hollywood. For there was not only our company of about 150 people, but a still bigger one, the *Wings* company, with Clara Bow, Richard Arlen, Buddy Rogers, etc. They were the stars—but there was one small bit to be made memorable by an unknown, Gary Cooper.

I had very little to do except wear the corseted, bustled, ruffled—hot—clothes of the period, stand and wave at the boys as they drilled out on the field, or stand and wave good-bye to them at the railroad station when they went off to fight in Cuba. (You know the shot: Camera is mounted on the observation platform and the girl is standing in the middle of the tracks waving and weeping as the train moves away slowly. Her figure becomes tiny and pathetic in the distance and ever so lonely. Why everyone else stays on the station platform where they belong is never explained.)

I was in San Antonio until the end of October, and because I had so little to do I spent the time visiting the *Wings* company which was shooting at the other side of town. Partly because it was greener fields, and partly because the author of the film, John Monk Saunders, was a very attractive young man. Bill Wellman, the director, Saunders and Dick Grace, a great stunt flyer, made several World War I films emphasizing the war in the air, but they never topped their production of *Wings*.

Visitors—nonprofessional—were not allowed within a half mile of the area because of the danger of low-flying ships and the falling debris from explosives. They had a whole area mined and marked with red lines (photographs black, remember?) and men could go over the top and be "killed" by a diving plane as the technicians fired off the lines of buried "squibs"—small explosives like fire-crackers—to simulate machine-gun bullets.

Cameras were all over the place, on parallels, on the ground camouflaged with shrubbery. They would have only one crack at it —maybe a two- or three-minute scene that had been meticulously rehearsed on paper and in dry runs. But once the explosives were set off, it was another day or so before it could all be set up again.

Between technical delays and bad weather, the two companies had time for a great deal of fraternizing. Romances broke out like heat rashes, there were a couple of weddings, at least one divorce, and I'm sure a few local irate husbands and outraged parents. If there were roughhousing and drunken brawls and somebody got hauled off to jail, they were sprung the next day. You just can't hold up production, you know!

With understandable business acumen on the part of local theater managers, two of my pictures opened with great ceremony and red carpet stuff—just like Hollywood! *Don Juan* and *Forever After*. And I made personal appearances and received flowers and signed autographs and smiled graciously and got sweaty palms. . . .

I broke off my engagement to Irving Asher. Being engaged was a drag for both of us at that distance and I'm sure that both families were much relieved.

Anyway, I had a fine romantic Texas summer going for me, complete with harvest moon, dancing at the country club, swimming, learning to play tennis, learning how to drink tequila—the real way, with a bit of salt in the arch of the thumb and a bite of lemon. And hold onto your hat!

Groups of us would go to El Poblano for Mexican food, to Wolfe's Inn for platters of fried chicken. I just hated having to go back home!

But the Texas romp was over. The whole big romp of the Twenties was almost over. Technical progress was always greater in films than the product displayed, and soon it was going to take over. Photography, lighting, in many pictures was incredibly beautiful. Sets were realistic; clothes and costumes cost a fortune in the production budget. But with a very few exceptions the stories remained banal, and again with exceptions, acting was definitely still two-dimensional. Actors emoted—everything had to be understood visually. Rarely did you see anyone's back to the camera. You even had to register a thought head-on, right to the camera, with the eyes barely missing the lens. Even so, these actors were the beautiful people, the fantastic people, and this great technical progress was going to put many of them out of a job. Vilma Banky and Rod La Rocque, Mae Murray, John Gilbert, Norma Talmadge, Marion Davies, Pola Negri, Renee Adoree, Leatrice Joy, Gloria Swanson, Bebe Daniels, Barbara La Marr. Those wonderful "faces"!

There was much talk about sound, about "talking pictures," and most people thought that it would be a loss to an art form. It was felt that instead of being more realistic it would be a sort of two-and-a-half dimension. Theater had sound, *and* color *and* three dimensions, and true reality. Actors from the theater had difficulty in movies—it was a real translation—and a movie-trained actor rarely made it in the theater. There was a little something called sustaining a scene which a film actor was never called upon to do. His acting was done in bits and pieces—anyone can sustain an emotion for thirty seconds or a minute—and then it was all spliced together in the cutting room.

I remember the first legitimate plays I appeared in, and my difficulty in sustaining a scene. I would speak a line and then drift into nonattention until a cue came along when I spoke another line. Elliott Nugent who had been an actor in the theater and an actor in the movies (besides directing and writing) fixed it for me. "Don't leave us, Mary! Just think of it as being on camera *all* the time." And yes, I really said it: "But Elliott, what do I *do?* The conversation is clear over there on the other side of the stage!" And he said, "Listen. Just *listen*, baby!"

There is a similar story of one of the dumb-blonde type. The new young thing who had just won a contest or something. I think Mervyn LeRoy told it: "Now, honey, all you have to do is take the spoon in your right hand—that's it—now stir the coffee—that's fine." "But," said the D.B., "but, Mr. LeRoy, what do I do with the other hand?"

We had all found little tricks, little skills to enrich the voiceless expression of ideas or emotions. Lillian Gish's hands were poetic understatements, Gloria Swanson had expressive shoulders, and of course fans of today have watched Garbo's single, eloquently raised eyebrow.

And all of us knew the trick of "cheat your look" which, if it wasn't done right looked terrible. In the big, single-head close-ups with the other person's shoulder and part of his head in the foreground, if you looked directly at him, your eyes crossed because he was too close. To avoid it you drew an imaginary line at the level of his eyes until you could see beyond his head and could focus on something distant.

There were those who used the trick all the time even when it wasn't necessary in longer shots; then it was a *dirty* trick. It forced another actor to keep moving into his range of vision, *downstage* to look at him, and finally, unless the director corrected the matter you'd be playing a scene with your back to the camera. If you were a bit tricky yourself, you'd permit it and keep turning your shoulders deliberately and then you'd get a close-up of your own because the cameraman would report, "We couldn't see her face!"

You had to see the face, you know. You *had* to see the face, the trademark, with *its* trademark: Mary Pickford's dimples, Doug's grin, Erich von Stroheim's monocle, Mae Murray's pout. A cameraman had taught me the value of a small "eyelight" for close-ups which would put stars in your eyes. The face, the gimmicks, the appearance took the place of genuine emotion.

> *Stand on the highest pavement of the stair . . .*
> *Lean on a garden urn . . .*
> *Weave, weave the sunlight in your hair . . .*

(And don't forget your keylight and your backlight!)

> *Clasp your flowers to you with a pained surprise . . .*
> *Fling them to the ground and turn*
> *With a fugitive resentment in your eyes:*
> *But weave, weave the sunlight in your hair.*
>
> (T. S. ELIOT.)

But soon we were to be supplied with that most expressive organ of emotion: the larynx. Weeded out would be Brooklynese, southern accents, European accents, nasal voices, voices too high, voices too low, voices too "common," voices that squeaked, voices rough from liquor (later to be called "husky" and "lovely!"), stutterers, *uh*-ers, *and-a*-ers. Those who had had theatrical experience were pretty smug.

Not just yet. Maybe when they had stopped experimenting it would all come to nothing—we hoped. But they couldn't stop experimenting. The public *wanted* to hear us. Background music and sound effects would not be enough, even though it would kill off a lot of us.

The work on *The Rough Riders* trickled on through November. We were back in Hollywood and we had a few interiors and local exteriors: a band concert at Sunland, a house exterior at Flintridge. But it was like the end of a long cruise. The "lifetime friendships" petered out, the things that were funny, the party feeling, was gone. We were back home and there were problems and responsibilities to attack.

My father had been busy spending money. And there were "gifts" we had to be pleased and grateful for. (Bought with whose money? *Our* money, never "mine.") Mother had a new blue Chrysler roadster, which Parker would teach her to drive. She'd become infected with the exhilaration of freedom in Texas—from me, from her husband, from the house—and *her* eyes were brighter too. Daddy was going along with it, being generous, very generous. For me, he had bought a great new Duo-Art grand piano. The reproducing kind, not just a mechanical player. It was supposed to "stimulate my flagging interest" but also to supply him with the piano music he liked. I just wasn't giving the usual evening "concerts." I had other things to do than play Chopin and be told I was lousy.

We were taken on a tour of the improvements to the house that he had begun in our absence. Wrought-iron fences, gates, new driveways, full-grown olive and palm trees. He said he was "making the property more valuable." That's what he said. He was also buying a lot of stocks on margin. He was going to be a rich man if it killed me. His set smile told me he couldn't trust me any more. He was going to be secure even though I might go out and get myself engaged to people "after my money" or God knows what. I was a real disappointment, that I could see. So he made plans to put in an enormous swimming pool with a sandy beach and a waterfall.

I had another movie to make. Back at the home company, First National. Costume fittings, publicity pictures, interviews. This one was to be a comedy called *The Runaway Enchantress* which was changed to *The Sea Tiger*. The locale was a Spanish fishing village. Milton Sills, Alice White, Larry Kent. At the studio by eight to put on my makeup, on the set at nine, quit about six or seven—or eight.

In THE SEA TIGER
(1927)

To break in the new Chrysler, Parker drove me in the roadster instead of the Pierce-Arrow limousine. But as soon as we came to Cahuenga Pass (now a freeway) to go over to the Valley where the traffic was thin, I would slide into the driver's seat and get a driving lesson. Parker could have been fired for "endangering my life"—I *am* quoting accurately—but I think he had his own unspoken ideas of the restrictions imposed upon me by my father.

I didn't care much for the script. But then I never did. I saw it in terms of what I would look like, what I would wear, and who the people were I'd be working with. Milton Sills was pretty dull. Alice White was fun, it was a big break for her, and we had a hair-pulling scene in the picture, which promised to be interesting.

I was glad to have a change from the months of corsets and bustles and button boots and big hats. And of being sweet and tearful. This time I was a movie concept of a Canary Island peasant girl. (Still sweet but not tearful.) Barefooted, my hair in braids (by Westmore), wearing a carefully torn skirt of heavy linen and a blouse that would slip down over one shoulder for someone to leer at and for me to toss my head when I caught them leering.

I just didn't dare stop and think: What's become of being an actress? I concentrated on my social life, my clothes, my driving lessons, golf lessons and a new beau. The new beau would be my husband in about two years.

There was a social experiment being tried out among the people in the business. Somebody decided it would be a great thing if we had a club of just film people, meeting once a month for a dinner dance at the Biltmore or the Ambassador. With the dining and dancing closed to all outsiders. Anytime we went out we always had people looking at us or wanting autographs, and we could never be ourselves. Imagine! It was to be called the Mayfair Club, and it had a big membership.

Of course the press was represented, and there were wandering photographers to catch the elite being themselves. And hundreds of fans at the auto entrance.

Kenneth Hawks (Howard Hawks's brother) and I went to these parties because it was fun. The food was good, the music was the best. But as for movie people being themselves, it was absurd. The men wore top hat, white tie and tails. Everybody got a good look at everybody else, and who was with who, and who got drunk and who looked terrible, and the columns duly reported the long lists of important names the following day; and if your name wasn't there you called the paper and raised hell. The final commentary on the experiment was made by the madam of the local, very fancy and expensive brothel.

There were, one night, a great many lovely girls dressed in beautiful gowns, identical in style and color—red. Now, there'd been slipups by local dressmakers once in a while. Miss X wore mauve satin with fringed bugle beads and Miss Y also had a mauve satin with bead fringe. But fifteen all-red dresses? The women couldn't figure it out, or pretended they couldn't and the men didn't dare. The dancing was country-club style; you table-hopped and danced with anyone you wanted or should. The girls had no complaint about being wallflowers—for what man there would say he knew them? When it finally—very quickly, really—got buzzed around as to the identity of the girls, a wife or girl friend could say, "Did you know who you were dancing with?" "Why no, I thought she was one of the new starlets at Paramount. Some kind of publicity gag—*you* know!"

They disappeared after a few dances, but Madam F. had made her point.

I've often had the question put to me, "If you had to live your life over again what would you change?" It's a silly question, of course, because you'd change a lot of things—with the excellent vision of hindsight. I know if I'd had a little more aggressiveness, if at some point I could have had a shot of the essence of ambition, I wouldn't have had a string of films called, *Sunset Derby, No Place To Go, Sailors' Wives, Heart to Heart, Three-Ring Marriage,* etc. I *was* under contract, but I could have gone into the front office, and said, "I'd like something better," for there were better films around.

But I had accepted the attitude of don't make waves, don't do anything that might get the producers mad at you, that might jeopardize that weekly check coming in. My father, as my manager, could go into an office and fight for better financial terms at the beginning of a contract, but he was never interested in the quality of a script or the kind of part I had. And so, neither was I.

George Fitzmaurice shook me a little one day when he said, "Why don't you take more interest in what you are doing?" He was a good director, with great taste, and a sense of the beautiful. I felt as though I were being scolded, but I said, "Well, Mr. Fitz, I know my lines [titles] and I'm careful about matching my action from one scene to the next, and I know what scene we're shooting, what else can I do?"

He said, "Did you ever look through the lens or the finder of the camera? No. You don't know anything about composition. You're a nice cooperative girl and you come onto the set and ask, 'Where do I stand?' And when the scene is shot you run off and find somebody to talk to. I think you'd enjoy yourself more if you were aware of my problems, for instance, the cameraman's problems, that it's more than a social event." It was excellent advice, but should not have been necessary. Acting had become such piffle to me, that I had just dismissed all other aspects of movie-making.

I started asking questions of the men of different departments and of course they were more than willing to tell me anything I wanted to know: "Why are the sidelines wider with this lens than with that one? Why do you have to trim an arc lamp? What's a scrim for? Can I go into a cutting room someday and watch some film put together?"

Of course, once you start asking questions, innocence is gone.

Being aware of other people's problems led me to question my own actions.

"Ed, why are you putting a 'barn door' on that spotlight?"

"Because it's too hot when you turn around."

"Well, I don't know why I *have* to turn around. Wouldn't it be better if I didn't?"

"It sure would."

"Wouldn't it be better?" "Why does this scene seem so ridiculous?" "Why would anybody in their right minds behave this way?"

And then, oh yes, and then—wouldn't it be fun to play something besides just a "sweet girl"? Of course I couldn't, not with this face, dammit. This *sweet* face with its big brown eyes (and the little lamp that puts stars in them) and its wistful smile. How could *I* ever look like a whore or a bitch or a malicious person or an immoral woman of any kind! Of course those parts are always the more meaty ones. Wouldn't it be fun!

It would be fun, but it wouldn't be for a while. In about a year I would be playing golf with my fiancé, Kenneth Hawks, and with Sol Wurtzel, the production head of Fox Studios where Ken was an associate producer. I would miss an easy putt, and to the astonishment of Mr. Wurtzel, that sweet little gal of Ken's would blow her sweet little top and burst out with "Sonofa*bitch!*" I remember Sol taking off his heavy-lensed spectacles and wiping them and his eyes from tears of laughter, and turning to Ken and saying, "Hey, you know we ought to use her for the gun moll in *Dressed To Kill.* Never thought of her as having any fire—and sure as hell never thought she had a temper!"

Nice little actress, mind you. Pretty, dependable. She could always get reviews saying ". . . she was adequate as . . ." ". . . she was lovely as . . ." ". . . wore beautiful clothes, looked charming . . ." But no fire, no temper, no sex, no nothing.

Dressed To Kill got it on the record, at least, that I could point a gun *not* in self-defense alone, that I could smile like a villain smiles. Small irony: Even in this picture I was pretending to be a hard-boiled gal—I had joined a gang of crooks to recover stolen bonds for which my boy friend had gone to jail. But it was a breakthrough which would survive even the hiatus between silent pictures and sound, for the picture was well done, directed by Irving Cummings and well acted by the smooth Edmund Lowe and Ben Bard, especially. It opened at the Capitol Theater in New York in March of

With Montagu Love in ROSE OF THE GOLDEN WEST (1927)

1928, and the reviews all expressed a mild surprise and pleasure at this "new" facet of mine.

In the meantime, during the year 1927 I had the lovely *Rose of the Golden West* to complete, with director George Fitzmaurice. Exquisite photography, beautiful costumes of the period when the United States and Russia were bidding to annex California. Gilbert Roland was a handsome caballero, our locations were at Monterey peninsula and at the San Fernando, Capistrano (with its swallows) and Santa Barbara missions. Gilbert Roland and I learned to dance the "Jota" well enough for a few close-ups, and I could play the castañets enough to get by.

Then a real goodie came along. One of those pictures that would be remembered, for which Lewis Milestone won an Academy Award for comedy direction in the first year of the awards. It was called *Two Arabian Knights* and it was one of the few attempts at movie-making by Howard Hughes. (He came on the set a few times, and couldn't understand where "the fourth wall" was.) But it was a good one. Louis Wolheim and Bill Boyd (later Hopalong Cassidy) as a couple of American soldiers escaping from army imprisonment in the uniforms of Arabian prisoners were very funny.

[69]

With Gilbert
Roland in ROSE OF
THE GOLDEN WEST
(1927)

I was mostly a pair of dark eyes seen above the veil of an Arabian
princess, but I had to be rescued from drowning in order to become
the love interest in the story. The rescue was rough.

We worked nights on a freighter out in San Pedro harbor, and
the water was cold, murky and oily. I was wearing a gold metal
cloth skirt with a kind of bolero jacket also of gold metal cloth,
and a gold lace-trimmed veil over my nose and chin. Long shots
were done by doubles but when they lowered a platform over the
side of the ship for the cameras, Bill and Wolly and I had to go into
the water for medium shots and close-ups. And there were a lot of
them. Comedy routines of spluttering and the two men rescuing
each other—"Where'd she go? Over there? No, over there!" and all
the time I had to be treading water, waving feebly, and about to
drown, literally, for the metal cloth weighed me down and the veil
over my nose clung to my face and cut out most of my air. We had
to do the whole thing in very short bits or I would have sunk, and
after each shot we had to be hauled aboard and warmed up and
given a shot of brandy, for San Pedro's waters in the spring are just
this side of ice. We were all half-drunk, half-frozen and half-nause-

ated by the taste and smell of oil and salt water. But it was a funny
scene. And you'll do anything to get a funny scene in a good movie
with a good director telling you how great and how brave you are,
and saying, "I hate to ask it, but can we do it just *once* more—just
to be sure we've got it." Wolheim and Bill swore and I chattered
my teeth but we all said, "Let's do it and get it over with," and
went in. I was no novice at this dunking business. I'd been pulled
out, dripping wet, from many of the bodies of water in the country;
I'd fallen out of canoes in lakes in Maine, been rescued from the
rapids of Sault Ste. Marie, fished out of a well in Connecticut,
walked with Dutch wooden shoes into the rocky surf at Montauk
Point on Long Island; but this was the worst—so far. Ten years
later it would be *Hurricane,* and I'd stay wet for three months. And
always the blankets and electric heaters and a jigger of brandy. And
never pneumonia or even a cold.

L ORD TENNYSON SAID, "Let the great world spin forever
down the ringing grooves of change."

Well, let it or not, it does. And literally spiraling,
zeroing in on the surface of records, the ringing
grooves of the Vitaphone were changing our world.
By the spring of 1928 the worst sound film would draw a better
box office than the best silent film. Two years previously, the
novelty of *Don Juan* with a specially scored background on records seemed just that, a novelty. And certainly no substitute for
the live orchestras that played in the big theaters in all the key
cities. Even a somewhat maudlin tale with a fine musical star, Al
Jolson, was considered a box-office freak. Talking pictures! They
could never be anything but a fad. We had no prescience of the
end of an era.

I had wound up my contract with Warners in a comedy which
was Mervyn LeRoy's first picture as a director. Previously he had
been a gag man. A strange job in which he had to think up sight
gags. He'd stand around the set and then come up to the director
and say, "Wouldn't it be funny if—" the cat jumped up and

knocked over a vase of flowers; the guy handed him a trick cigar; a swinging door bumped her fanny and she dropped the tray, etc.

Mervyn did a lot of the Colleen Moore comedies, and the first picture on his own was, naturally, a comedy. In it I was a girl who ran away to a desert island on a yacht with my fiancé—(hang on!) —Lloyd Hughes; and I saved both of us from cannibals because I was a hot Charleston dancer, and got the cannibals interested in learning to dance instead of in popping us into a kettle.

With *Dressed To Kill* I had a new contract with Fox. That was enough of a change for me. A new kind of role and, I hoped, the end of the "sweet girls."

My marriage to Ken Hawks had rainbows around it. We had our own small house in the Hollywood Hills. We played golf together, went to football games, to previews and openings; to supper clubs where the band would play our song as we came in: "And Then My Heart Stood Still." And we had a relationship that could only be achieved because Ken was the kind of man he was. He had values that have become extinct. They are just meaningless words now. Without those words I cannot hope to evoke the gentle strength of a man of such subtle qualities. In present-day semantics he would become "old-fashioned," "square," "dull," and I won't permit that, for he was none of those.

Since Ken at that time was in the production end, we often went to special projection room showings of experimental sound films. Fox was developing sound on film, "Movietone," which eventually disposed of the cumbersome and iffy method of synchronized records. After one of these showings, Ken and other producers would stand around and talk with serious, worried faces; but we the actors, the artists, the superior solid conservatives, would exchange satisfied quips about how the noise would simply drive audiences from the theater.

At that point in technical development, talkies were nothing but a poor imitation of theater itself. Silents were an entirely different medium. It was a way of telling a story—images created the emotion—a direct appeal. There were many reasons why talkies were completely impractical. Everything would have to be straight cuts, no fade-ins or fade-outs, no dissolves. All the fluid movement of the camera would be lost. It would be static, dull, tied to a microphone. You couldn't go outdoors. How would you ever get such scenes as Borzage's taxi army in *Seventh Heaven?* Or Renee Adoree running after the column of doughboys in *The Big Parade?* Even in more intimate scenes, you could never speak while moving around. Of course you could hide a microphone in things. It was only slightly smaller than a breadbox, but it could be done.

I wonder who, in what desperation, first hung a mike on the end of a fishing rod. You still hear, "Get the fishpole," in situations that are too cramped for the huge mike booms. Now, of course, miniaturization has solved that and other problems.

So we, most of us, shrugged our shoulders and went on happily about the business of making silent pictures.

They came out silent in the theater, but when I say, "back in the days of silents," I don't mean "silence." For while we did not have to adhere as strictly to the words of a script, the words were there, and had to be learned and spoken. Sometimes when a scene was going well and a pair of actors were in step we would add something or take a different tack. Today it's called improvisation.

And the making of movies then was the same noisy, crowded, cluttered business that it is today. Noisier. Since the discipline of sound was not yet upon us it was difficult to ask for and get complete silence in the studio. It didn't matter if a carpenter dropped a hammer or went on sawing in another part of the stage; the carbon arcs could sing and the unclothed camera could whir and whisper and it wasn't important. During a take, voices of off-scene workers dropped to a polite murmur.

I remember the difficulty of adjusting to the deathly silence after I started making sound pictures; it was disconcerting, a hollow void. That pleasant murmur, the director's voice saying little helpful things, "Fine, now you hear the footsteps—and *freeze!* Over to the window, pick it up, run. Fine." And we had music as an aid to concentration. (Not necessarily to get in the mood.) It was usually a very skillful little combo of portable organ, violin and cello, or sometimes just an accordion. We used it much the way people today use the radio when they study or work. It put the racket into the background.

Then they began to make awful things called "part-talkies." Everything was normal until the final, big scene. And then Bam! Yakity-yak! And in the orchestra pit of the theater the men put away their instruments and descended little stairs under the big screen and played poker.

Option time came up for me, and since it looked as though there'd

Mary Astor in blond wig with Robert Armstrong in
WOMAN FROM HELL (1929)

be some part-talkies in my program the studio said they wanted me
to take a Movietone test. I selected passages from a good play,
Young Woodley, and worked with a coach, Helen Ware, for several
days. I was quite sure of myself, quite comfortable. I felt as though
all the work with Jack Barrymore would finally be of great value—
breath control, pitch, color, vitality.

The test was thorough, comprehensive. We took a whole day for
the filming. I had felt some nervousness because that microphone
seemed to be much larger than a breadbox and it was so madden-
ingly *there.* In the utter silence, nobody talking, the camera under
blankets, no phones ringing at the stage doors, no hammers dropping, nobody even *whispering!*

Dark. Hollow. Bottom of the barrel. Those were the words they
used to describe my voice after they saw the test. And apologetically,
"almost masculine!" They were sorry about that. The microphone
played tricks sometimes that nobody understood. "Of course it isn't
the way you *really* sound," was the only small comfort they could
offer. It was small comfort also to Jack Gilbert whose voice sounded
feminine and caused laughter in the theaters. They were sorry

about that too, because he didn't really sound that way. He did have a light voice, very similar in quality to the late Leslie Howard, but hardly effeminate.

Sol Wurtzel called my father into the front office to discuss the option. They were, ah, having to make some cutbacks, and, ah, if I would take a 50 percent cut, they might consider renewing. My name was valuable, of course, but it would take work, lots of work and time to change my voice. (I don't know how they expected to do that. I don't think they did either!) And, after all, they were able to get people from the theater who would work much cheaper.

My father turned them down. "We'll wait until they come to their senses," said he. I was the one that did the waiting. And it was the last time my father represented me. Ken had heard of the interview, and of the reputation my father had with other producers for being high-handed and pompous. They didn't like doing business with him, not just because he was tough but because he was totally unreasonable, uncompromising. Ken advised me to get an agent, and he had the unpleasant job of informing my father that none of the producers would ever admit him to their offices again.

So I got an agent, and went the rounds. Nothing. My test had been lousy. My price was too high; they were getting theater people for two hundred a week and I was in the thousands. And after all these years I could not drop to that level. So I waited. And the months went by.

Money was not a problem. Ken was getting very rich in the stock market. We bought a new home; there was a fur coat for me, a diamond and sapphire bracelet, a beautiful Pierce-Arrow hardtop coupe. He was directing his own first picture, an all-talkie with Lee Tracy (of Broadway and the successful *Front Page*). It was a nice little semimusical called *Big Time*. Mae Clark was in it and the colored comedian Stepin Fetchit. It was about a vaudeville team and their competition with a trained seal. Lee and Mae did a song-and-dance routine and fought their way up to the big time and it was very good. Ken had me hang around the set, and asked my advice, because his work had been mostly in the front office. We saw the rushes together and he listened to my suggestions. I didn't realize he was doing it so that I wouldn't feel left out. He was that kind of a man.

But work had become like breathing or walking and I wasn't working and I felt restless. I played golf, I took painting lessons, I

With Fredric March in LADIES LOVE BRUTES, Mary Astor's first talking movie

tried writing. I tried to play the role of young housewife and gave charming little dinner parties. I even tried to learn to cook. But I wasn't ready to be a has-been at the age of twenty-three. Still, I had to endure it for ten months. In those days that was a disastrously long time to be out of work.

Among our good friends were Florence and Fredric March. Florence was about to go into rehearsals for a play with Edward Everett Horton at the Majestic Theater in Los Angeles. It was called *Among the Married* by Vincent Lawrence. It was at Florence's suggestion, "Let's show 'em!" that I got a part in it.

We opened to excellent reviews and within the week I had five offers for the damned talking pictures. Same girl. Same voice. Only they called it "low and vibrant" now. I signed for three pictures to be made at the end of the run of the play.

By this time Ken was working on his second picture, getting up early in the morning; with my theater schedule we didn't have much time together, and we didn't like that part of it. But it was accomplishing what we had both wanted, and it would only be for another few weeks. On matinee days he and Freddie March would meet Florence and me for dinner between shows at the Town House on Wilshire Boulevard—halfway between the downtown area and our homes.

Ken and I were both off on New Year's Day, and we went to the football game at the Rose Bowl. He bought me a bunch of violets to pin on my fur coat, making a joke of the fact that it couldn't be orchids because he'd lost his shirt in the stock market crash. So what! He had his job, his contract with Fox.

The following day was a matinee day. Florence and I waited around for our husbands, who were very late. We sat and gossiped on the couch of the stage set under a lone worklight in the dark, empty theater. The stage doorman called Florence to the phone. "Excuses, excuses," she laughed. She was gone a long time and I was drowsing on the couch when she returned. And told me. Ken had been killed that afternoon in a plane accident during the shooting of some scenes for his picture off Point San Vicente. The two camera planes had somehow locked, exploded and fallen into the sea. There were no survivors. It was January 2, 1930.

In about three weeks I started working in my first talking picture, *Ladies Love Brutes*. It was for Paramount with George Bancroft and Fredric March. It was an important milestone, but I have no remembrance of it. The "Golden Years" of the movies had begun.

WILL ROGERS SAID, "We are the first nation in the world to go to the poorhouse in an automobile."

The stark statistics of the stock market crash, the collapse of the banking system of the United States, the unemployment lines, the men selling apples, the desperate, the hungry—all of it touched us only lightly. We heard about it. Ninety million people a week were paying twenty-five cents a ticket, ten cents for kids, to go to the movies, to escape from their troubles. And we provided that escape. And we were paid handsomely for it. We provided funny, heart-warming people like Marie Dressler, Will Rogers, Wallace Beery; we gave them a darling little girl to love, Shirley Temple; we gave them schmaltzy romance with Dick Powell and Ruby Keeler, Jeanette MacDonald and Nelson Eddy; the glamorous faces of Joan Crawford, Norma Shearer, Jean Harlow—and Clark Gable. Ginger Rogers and Fred Astaire danced their heart-lifting poems of joy. We revealed a lot of lovely legs and provided sexy bedroom scenes—until the Legion of Decency moved in—and then we became strictly Andy Hardy. Well . . . You couldn't stop a gal like Mae West from proving that sin can be beautiful, fun and profitable. And Marlene Dietrich in soft-focus glitter made plenty of promises.

The national situation was tragic, but it wasn't *our* tragedy. It was something that was happening "out there" and wasn't it awful, but did you read *Variety* today? People stood in line at the employment agencies but they also stood in line at the theaters.

This insular quality, the little islands of the studios—and within the studios the smaller islands of the individual stages, our company, our picture, ourselves, myself. We were closer than a family, and yet we were mostly strangers in each other's lives.

When people get together, they talk about their kids, their relatives, their friends in great detail: "Got a letter from my sister in Omaha, yesterday, she's the one who has the beauty parlor . . ." "When Jeff came home from school last night he told me . . ." Our off-the-set conversations never had any of these elements. It was a very "now" life. "You got a headache? Get the prop man to give you some aspirin . . ." "You look great this morning . . ." "Feel marvelous. . . ." After appearance and health were disposed of, there was detailed talk of the work, "Does Joe think we'll get into the other set today?" "Is your wardrobe ready for the courtroom scene?" "I gotta do publicity at noon." "Hey, the rushes were great last night . . ." And local gossip, "Louella said . . ." "Did you make the opening?" "How was the preview the other night?" And occasionally sports—baseball, football, races, fights. I never heard anyone talk of family, origin, schooling, childhood, brothers and sisters. (The biog material in movie magazines was mostly invention, so why talk about it; we had no desire to fool each other.) An actor might say, "Betty and I went to the Trocadero last night and we saw so-and-so." And you might not even be clear about just who Betty was. Wife? Girl friend? Visiting relative? If Betty were just a housewife you had little idea of what she looked like—blonde, brunette, redhead, pretty, plain.

Sometimes when there was work at night and a few visitors came after dinner, someone might say, "Who's that Claudette's talking to over by the prop box?" "That's her husband, whatshisname." "What's he do?" "I dunno—doctor isn't he? dentist or something?" Curiosity over.

Perhaps there is as little personal information given out in business offices, factories, shops—except around the water cooler. But we had more idle time for talking, we had sit-around time by the hour. And we did a lot of gabbing. Very opinionated gabbing. About other actors and movies. About the *technical* ability of musicians, dancers, painters. About books if they were picture material. And jokes, lots of jokes, practical, gag-type, dirty-type, and a sparring for saying the witty thing.

It was as though actors' lives began the day they got their first check for acting, and to speak of parents and peers, of schools, of activities in other lines of business would decrease them as actors, lessen them as individuals. Even their beginnings were spoken of as discoveries rather than as strivings on their part. They might have had hard times, small parts, done a little starving; but it was never spoken of as growth, of learning, of becoming. They had always been there, fully developed, just waiting for the spotlight to pick them up and reveal their talent. And if they were lucky, they got the breaks. It was always a "bad break" or some sonofabitch had it in for them if they didn't get certain roles, never a matter of their own ability. I have never heard another actor say, "Well, he's better for the part than I am," or "I'll be ready for that kind of part in a year or so." Oh no! If the studio would give them more publicity, if their agent would just get off his ass, if they hadn't been working at the time and could have tested, if the company would have consented to a loan-out; if so-and-so weren't the star—he "had it in for him." The product had to be jealously protected. It was unique, the best, the most beautiful, the handsomest, the most talented. Well, would Pall Mall ever say Marlboro was a better cigarette?

We were friends (or enemies) of everybody else in the business. We were worse name-droppers than people who dropped our names. Another actor was a "best friend," "know him very well," "died in my arms," "gave him his first break in that picture of mine." That is, *if* the actor had more than three figures in his weekly check, *if* he'd just received an award or a plummy assignment, *if* he'd just had a spectacular wedding (or funeral), *if* he gave huge parties.

Sometimes we did make real friends. Such a one was Ann Harding, whom I met in May of 1930 when we did the picture *Holiday* together.

I had had to make two of the three pictures I had contracted for during the run of *Among the Married*—but work so soon after

With Ann Harding in
HOLIDAY (1930)
Pathé Picture.

Ken's death had been too much for me and I became ill and the third was canceled. Now I was rested and in better condition emotionally; I had stopped behaving on the reaction level of bitterness against movies: the meaninglessness of Ken's dying for one lousy scene in a movie.

I was trying to accustom myself to being a bachelor girl with an apartment. I couldn't go back to the family and be their little girl again. But living alone was difficult. I had to work, Ken had lost everything and had been in deep debt after the stock market crash, and he'd canceled out his insurance payments in order to try to meet the debts. My father had everything else tied up in the Temple Hill Drive house.

I felt very lucky in getting the *Holiday* engagement. It was the Philip Barry play and nicely translated for films by Horace Jackson. It had a lot of interesting, "fun" people to work with. And the part of Julia was anything but a "sweet girl" role.

Ann Harding and I played sisters. I was the materialistic, status-conscious, tradition-bound girl engaged to a young man, played by

Robert Ames, who heretically wants a "holiday" out of life while he's still young enough to enjoy it. And Ann was the sympathetic one who shares his philosophy and takes him away from me when he refuses to toe the establishment mark. Monroe Owsley played a wonderful, fastidious sober-drunk who would like to be a rebel and didn't have the nerve. And the story bounced off experts like Edward Everett Horton and Hedda Hopper.

And to those who remember Hedda only as a caustic-tongued columnist who wore eccentric hats, I must say in those days she was a most attractive actress. Though never a big star, she always lent an air of great chic to a role; she dressed beautifully and she came on with manner, wit and a cool wisdom. Eddie Horton, of course, was a friend who had shared my tragedy during the run of *Among the Married*. The director was Edward H. Griffith, a quiet man, amusing and skillful. It was a congenial company. It jelled.

These were mostly theater people—legitimate, you understand! And because of the then limitations of sound the picture had to be filmed almost like a legitimate play.

The problems of the noisy camera had not yet been solved. It was sheltered in a booth on casters that made it movable to a limited extent; and the booth held both the camera and the sweating operators and it had one side of plate glass. The microphone was not directional; it was very much like an ear trumpet and could hear over only a very narrow area.

In a scene it was impossible to "overlap," which is natural in conversation. In fact one couldn't pick up a cue very quickly; there had to be time for the sound man to switch off one mike and switch on another, and that required a beat more than is natural. And the sound man was king. If he couldn't hear it, we couldn't shoot it. It caused each of us to groan in frustration many times. You couldn't talk and pace up and down. For example, if the action started with you standing beside a table and then included a move to a chair by the fireplace, you could speak into a mike at the table, but you couldn't talk on the way over; you'd have to wait until you sat down—where there was another mike in the fireplace!

Throughout the technical development of movies we would gain a freedom, and find a new limitation. In silents, voice and speech meant nothing but a camera could be set up to photograph almost anything in the world.

With the advent of sound we were suddenly mummified into a

series of static still pictures—but we could speak. We were slowed up for a while until they put soundproof casings on the noisy camera. Once more, it could be mounted on a dolly, so that it could be mobile. Finally the camera itself got wheels.

I don't really know why *Holiday* was as good a picture as it was considering the limitations at that time. I'm sure there was some razor-sharp editing to pull it all together.

Ann was an actress rather than a star—and there *is* a difference. Her name ahead of the title, which technically made her a star of the picture did not affect or enlarge her status on the set. She was one of the first who disregarded the old star-system behavior of special treatment, special chairs, *Miss* Harding, etc. I had seen her in two of her successes on Broadway, *Tarnish* in 1923 and *The Trial of Mary Dugan* in 1928. To both she brought a new, realistic quality. In the picture she went easy on makeup: no beaded eyelashes, no heavily rouged mouth. She had beautiful skin and used practically no greasepaint and she had gorgeous, natural silver-blonde hair. She was thoroughly a member of the company, hard-working, no nonsense. These very qualities made me like her because I felt so uncomfortable with so much of the phony nonsense that seemed to go with being an actress. With me it was a passive irritation; I felt it but didn't scratch. She did. She said, "I don't want to look like an actress, I want to look like a person." And she did and she was—a person.

Later on, when I was married again and moved to a house in the San Fernando Valley not far from her place on a hilltop, we became good friends and our little girls played together. It was a lovely, warm, comfortable house and I had good times there, meeting people who weren't necessarily in the picture business: mostly writers, designers, musicians. And then, many years later, I was invited to a luncheon at the same house. It had been bought by Rudy Vallee and when you pushed the door bell the chimes played "Your Time Is My Time." The library now held great long shelves of volumes of records and radio shows made by Mr. Vallee, and there was a projection room where one went and saw home movies of Mr. Vallee. And when you left you were given an autographed album of one of Mr. Vallee's recordings.

The technical side of sound filming moved very fast, progressing, as it always has, more rapidly than writing and acting. Film quality, camera lenses, sound equipment, editing, lab work, effects, dubbing

—whatever you needed, you got it. But these departments were almost unnoticed by people on stage. They were in buildings we didn't frequent, hardly knew were there, peopled by strangers we passed on the lot. I have often imagined dialogue between a director and one of these mysterious experts:

"Hey, Bill, we got a problem."

"Yeah—like what?"

"Well, in the script there's this scene—a night scene where the girl comes and knocks at the door of this mysterious house. It's London in the last century—low key light—maybe one street lamp —gaslight—and it's foggy, but not too foggy. We want something that'll kind of lay on the ground, and swirl up once in a while, something that won't disappear like smoke pots."

"You got it."

Later on, faster film, lenses that could almost see in the dark; a camera once more free to move around, perhaps still confined to tracks, but movable. The microphone smaller, more sensitive, mobile. And people's voices sounding human. Still not much "variety" in volume. A shout or a scream and a whisper were pretty much at the same level. If you raised your voice in anger in a scene, the mike sprang away from you as though it were frightened, and if you mumbled it came in so close the cameraman would cry, "Gotta mike in the picture." But now it had the appearance of a listener, turning first to one face and then to the other—like an old busybody!

There was no lack of story material, from the topical to the Busby Berkeley choreographic mess of girls, girls, girls. Girls doing everything in tap routine, playing violins, playing a hundred pianos, coming down gorgeous stairways wearing spangles and feathers. There were gangster stories and horror films, there were mother-love stories and teacup plays where everybody sat around being bright. There were confession tales and great love stories. Some were great, some were—well—and some were dreadful. And they were all a lot of work. The bad ones just as difficult and challenging as the good ones.

The good one, the occasional good one, made one feel, "Now, now! things will be different! From now on I'll get nothing but wonderful stories and great directors and I'll be associated in the public's mind with nothing but the best. And I'll learn and I'll grow, and I'll be great." But it wasn't that way. There isn't a star in the business who hasn't had his potboilers, the films he had to do because he was under contract for so many a year. And just squawking at the front office, or having script-selection rights, couldn't prevent the occasional depositing of an egg at the box office, or having something you thought was good turn out badly. Even Bette Davis, the most famous fighter for good vehicles, did some things she hated, some things she thought were good and was wrong about. (Occasionally, Bette! Only occasionally!)

We were working actors, and that meant we had to keep at it, good or bad. We couldn't sit on the sidelines and wait for that great story, that great part. If we did, we just might wait ourselves out of the business. Or until our value at the box office decreased, and our weekly check along with it. People forget very fast.

Whenever we were working there was the constant question, "What are you going to do next?" and we hoped we didn't have to say, "I don't know." (And even if we *didn't* know, we wouldn't say it!) The thing to say was, "Well, there are two or three things. Myron wants me for such-and-such, or I may go on loan-out to Metro; and if they can hurry me through this picture I may be in time for the one at Universal." Keep at it. Keep busy. Keep pushing. What's your next picture, what have you coming out? You were never "out of work," you were "between pictures." If your picture closed and there was nothing to go into the following week, you harassed your agent, "What about it? Got some scripts for me?"

Free-lancing was ideal, seemingly, for you could have a choice; on the other hand, you might need money, you had nothing coming out so you had to take the first thing offered you. A contract let you sit still, the money anxiety was disposed of, but then you had to make your share of the company's program for the year, and sometimes there just wasn't any choice. *Holiday* was a good picture. It was a stimulating picture, because it was the kind where one said, "*Who* am I playing?" rather than, "What do I do?" There were many more "whats" than "whos." I played secretaries, princesses, crooks, the wife of, the girl friend of. I played many more characters who had things happen *to* them—reaction characters—than those who did things, who moved the story around. I was "Sally at the door, waiting for him" or "Pretty gal, that secretary of yours; now about our deal with the mining company." Or (hero to hussy), "Sure, I'm married, but what's that got to do with us?" and there's a dissolve to me, rocking a cradle, or knitting little things. And in

With Richard Barthelmess in THE LASH (1931)

the big fight at the finish, of course, I was off in a corner watching with horrified eyes, wincing at the blows. These are what I mean by "whats." Just *there*.

I had a lot of "whats" before I got another "who." Still, I was busy, thankfully, very busy. I went to Warners for one picture, still free-lancing, for a picture with Richard Barthelmess, a great silent star who had survived because of a warm, soft voice and a personality that matched. *The Lash* was probably one of the weakest pictures he ever did, and he was no longer young enough to play a dashing, Robin Hood bandit. He was a short, stocky man, and had to wear a girdle to pull in a slight paunch, and he used to cuss because it made him "short of breath," when what he was really cussing about was the inevitable encroachment of middle age.

He had achieved his greatness in such pictures as *Way Down East, Broken Blossoms, Tol'able David,* and many, many more. Anything later was just anticlimax.

We talked nostalgically of the "good old days." We had made Hergesheimer's *The Bright Shawl* together in 1922. We made tepid love in front of the camera and we rode a cushioned, flowered gondola in a reproduction on the back lot of the canals of Xochimilco, with mariachis playing from other gondolas and gardenias strewn on the water. No banana peels, no kids begging for pesos ('Allo— trow monee?), no smell, no tourists. But of course, the story was the period of eighteen hundred something and it was the movies, and there are no smells in the movies.

Right now, I had to dispose of money anxieties and accept a contract for which I had little enthusiasm. It was impossible for my father to retrench, and the expenses of Temple Hill Drive were staggering. I made a weak suggestion that he slow down on his improvements but he came back with one of his, to him, irrefutable arguments: "Why should we cut down? It's you who *must* have your own apartment (at so much a month) your own car at (figures), your own utilities and food and expenses (figures, figures), when if you lived here the whole thing could be consolidated and we'd all be comfortable." Well, I was lousy at mathematics, but it didn't seem to me that it made that much difference, and I knew that I would be miserable. It would be going backward.

So I signed for a year's contract at RKO-Radio. It was a year of "whats," all of them pretty bad. "B" pictures they were called— low-budget. I made six for RKO and two loan-outs in the year. That's a lot of film. But I was solvent again—and close to giving up on the idea of being an actress.

In June of 1931, that same year, I married Dr. Franklyn Thorpe, who had attended me during my illness after Ken's death. I had visions of retirement, of living as a doctor's wife, having children— the whole lovely, secure being-loved-and-loving bit.

But it didn't work out that way. It was my husband who pointed out the unfairness of my mother and father living in a big house with a chauffeur, gardener and housekeeper, and two cars, while we had to find a low rental furnished house. He pointed out that undoubtedly my father, a smart man with money, had a private income by now, thanks to all that money I'd earned over the years. He felt I should receive my checks personally, that there'd been enough of having them to go through his hands and of his giving me only an "allowance."

Well, it did make sense, but I still felt nothing but guilt when I told my father that from now on there would be no more money coming in from me. I suggested that with all the improvements on the house, surely they could get a big price for it, buy an annuity and live comfortably for the rest of their lives. "But this is our home!" he cried, and I felt awful. I told him I wanted to quit work anyway, I was tired, I wasn't getting anywhere except from one picture to another, and it all seemed kind of meaningless.

I was married now, and wanted to do a bit of leaning, of being taken care of—but in the meantime I wanted my husband to get started in a new office of his own away from the clinic, and that would take quite an outlay of cash, so I'd finish out my contract and then...

I was really dreaming. For as my husband pointed out to me we couldn't live on his as yet meager income. He was just beginning his practice in a new city, a new area, and it might take years to become established, and wouldn't it be absurd just to chuck it, those lovely four-figure-a-week checks that were now being sent directly to us? Well of course it would. If I needed a rest why we'd have one, a real holiday together. Do something he'd always wanted to do—go to the South Seas. Tahiti, the Tuamoto Archipelago. Fiji, maybe. So we bought a yacht. A lovely sixty-seven-foot two-masted schooner, gaff-rigged, Philippine mahogany. We got as far as Honolulu. And I gave birth to my daughter Marylyn. And when we got back we had to build and furnish a bigger home. Get back to work, Mary. I did. Three weeks after my baby was born. A picture called *Those We Love*. Directed by Robert Florey from the play by S. K. Lauren and George Abbott. The rest of the cast included Kenneth MacKenna, Lilyan Tashman, Earle Foxe, Hale Hamilton. A "nothing" picture.

Then, a picture that would survive. A picture that would be remade, and have both versions shown on TV an eon later.

What gives a picture this quality of timelessness? That makes the old-movie buffs drool? That glues an audience of my age to a TV set for nostalgia kicks? Just Clark Gable? Clark made pictures that nobody ever heard of. The director, Victor Fleming? One of the best, but the same thing is true for him. I was in a piece of cheese called *Other Men's Women*. In it there were some damn good actors—James Cagney, Joan Blondell—in small parts. I doubt if it made back its cost. Performances? In *The Lost Squadron*, another of those 1931 B pictures for RKO, starring Richard Dix, Erich von Stroheim gave a great performance, but that didn't make it immortal.

I believe there is a *timeless* feeling, instinctive, solid, when some-

With Erich von Stroheim in THE LOST SQUADRON
(Released 1932) *Radio Pictures.*

thing is good, a timelessness that makes what was a good picture then, a good picture now. We knew it, somehow. There was a sparkle in the eyes of those who had seen the rushes—the "dailies" —a quick little nod went around, and knock-on-wood. There was a subtle sense of success, or lack of it, even after only a few days of shooting a picture. It felt right. And if it didn't feel right then, it never seemed to develop. No amount of rewriting, reshooting, recasting ever seemed to fix it. It was like reworking biscuit dough, overmanipulation just made it heavier, less palatable.

Of course, we weren't infallible and a good one might not ring the box-office bell as loudly as we would have liked, but we had a hunch people would like it.

I wonder if it could work the other way. If some strange time machine could reverse things and we could show past audiences some of the films made today. Outside of the obvious fact that the world itself has changed. Outside of the fact that there are students

of film-making who go to movies to dig at symbolism, meaningful-
ness, and engage in chin-pulling arguments and analyses.

Let's take nudity and sex and expose our theoretic audiences of
the thirties to both as they are now. I admire nudity and I like sex,
and so did people of the thirties.

But, to me, overexposure blunts the fun. I once lived in a house
with a breathtaking view of the sea. An artist friend of mine said,
"Don't look at it too often; you'll love it more when you do."

Sex as something beautiful may soon disappear. Once it was a
knife so finely honed the edge was invisible until it was touched and
then it cut deep. Now it is so blunt that it merely bruises and leaves
ugly marks.

I have a theory that a great deal of "Victorian" prudery was a
big put-on. All that stuff about how a woman must merely endure
sexual intercourse. I can imagine a group of high-collared, corseted,
prissy-mouthed "ladies" at their weekly sewing circle discussing
what brutes males were. One of them says, "My Ralphie demands,
absolutely *demands* my—uh—body at least once a night." And she
dabs her eyes with a scented lacy handkerchief at Ralphie's cruelty.
The others shake their heads, look heavenward and murmur, "You
poor dear." But I'll *bet* half of them are saying to themselves,
"She's bragging!" or, "Wonder why my Fred hasn't come near me
for a week. . . ." Sure, it's hypocrisy; it's also one of the games
people played—we played games too, you know! Sex is a natural
act and not something just invented by the young people of today.

Long ago, young girls were kept in ignorance—*nice* girls—until
the marriage night, and found it was pretty shocking; but it was a
Wow! kind of shock from which they recovered very quickly. Men
had to do a lot of pursuing in those days. I still think a man likes to
achieve something that's hard to get.

Nudity is fine in the privacy of my own bedroom with the
appropriate partner. Or for a model in a life class at art school. Or
as portrayed in stone and paint. But I don't like it used as a joke or
to titillate. Or to be so bloody *frank* about.

I had dinner at the home of a very hotshot director of radio in
the late thirties. There were just three of us: the director, his beautiful wife and myself. After a pleasant dinner we went into the
library for coffee and liqueurs and my host and hostess proceeded to
divest themselves of their clothing—all of it—quite casually. Explaining, "My wife and I do this after dinner for complete relaxa-

tion—you don't mind, do you? I'm sure you're not body conscious.
Do the same if you like."

My eyelids seemed to be Scotch-taped to my eyebrows, but I
managed to make polite noises that I'd stay as I was. The director
sat at one end of the couch with a cigar and a glass of brandy, which
a stone-faced butler had served, and his wife made herself comfortable with her head in his lap, discreetly veiling what she was doing
with her long black drape of hair.

He went on with his discussion of the technicalities of radio,
stories, personalities, etc., interspersing his monologue with frequent little winces and comments, "Easy, honey—don't bite, for
Christ sake." After a while he said, "My wife will be very happy to
relax you this way if you'd like——"

But I made muttered excuses that it was late and got the hell out
of there.

Now it's all on film, that kind of thing. And the audiences of the
thirties would not have accepted it. Such erotica would have been
stag stuff. Blue movies. Burlesque and heavy winks and guffaws. Sex
was dealt with, not anatomically, not biologically, not flagrantly,
but indirectly, with considerable charm, humor and promise. I
don't think Garbo with her clothes off, panting in a brass bed,
would have been more sexy than she was.

I'm afraid our time machine would blow up. I guess it's a whole
other world.

My beef about films and plays today is that too often they don't
fulfill their purpose, which I insist is to entertain. Entertainment—
and I don't mean the puerility of the anticipated happy ending—
is a necessity of life; we all need to have time out from living, from
the daily minutiae. We need identification that can purge but not
lower one's spirit, laughter that shakes up the gizzard, and the
wonderful refreshment one feels when even for a moment our
attention becomes total, as though we'd been poleaxed into stillness.

This is not accomplished by shotgun stimulation. Multiple
action, strobe lighting, flashing, psychedelic color, split second
subliminal cuts. It's exciting, yes, but very tiring.

Linear action can accomplish much more: It can build interest
and tension, and then resolve that tension by something satisfying
or thought-provoking. Muscles, nerves, the mind relax.

Material that is used on film, in the theater and on TV is called
a play. We need playtime. The media can be used as an information

center, as a school, for news and town hall discussions and that's great. But I think to use our playtime to rub our noses in reality when God knows we get enough of it every day denies us a real necessity. To "tell it like it is" is an impertinence, because it just *isn't*, not everywhere. Therefore, it becomes propagandizing. And propaganda has no place in entertainment. An ancient wheeze, credited of course to Sam Goldwyn, went, "If you've got a message send it Western Union." Or carry a placard.

So, let us play. Let our play be real enough to be believable—or unreal enough to be accepted as pretend.

The trouble with the unreality of so many movies I made was that it was mainly unbelievableness: The action was all too often absurd.

But *Red Dust* was real enough. Clark Gable was real enough. Jean Harlow was sexy, gorgeous and unreal—and took the curse off the unreality by being funny. And Clark's own native wry humor saved him from the unreality of being too good-looking, too manly and strong. I played the character of Barbara without humor or insight, so that her infatuation with Gable was believable.

Maybe this is the touchstone, the yardstick: real enough. The "it could happen" syndrome, or "it could have happened."

Whatever it is, *Red Dust* is one of those pictures that has had many reruns on TV—and is one of the oldest: 1932.

NOT LONG AGO—a couple of years, maybe—I was in my local bank for the usual reasons, depositing a check or cashing one, and a sharp-eyed lady teller gave me a penetrating look and said, "Will you wait a moment, Miss Astor?" And when anyone looks at me that way or addresses me sharply, the old guilt pops right out: "What have I done now?"

But she emerged from behind the grill, and touching my elbow in a confidential manner, walked me to the entrance. "Tell me," she said, her voice warm with the overtones of a cello, "tell me, what was it like to kiss Clark Gable?"

I was startled into blurting the exact truth, "Good Lord, I've forgotten!"

"Oh, you couldn't have!" Her face pinked up and behind the mask of lady bank teller I saw yesterday's bobby-soxer.

"Well, it was a long time ago," I said.

"Yes, I know that, but there was a rerun on TV last night—didn't you *see* it? I should think that would remind you."

I hadn't seen it. I think I read in the TV listing about *Red Dust* being on around one in the morning.

I couldn't just walk away from that disappointed face, so I smiled confidentially. "It's a long story," said I. Let her read into that whatever she wanted.

Happily she fluttered her fingers in farewell as I went past the guard at the door.

In the car, my poodle, Jasper, was as usual pantomiming "What took you so long?" So I told him about it. I told him the lady had stirred up some memories:

Jean Harlow and that great introductory shot of her cleaning the parrot's cage and saying, "Whatcha been eatin', cement?" And during the production, the tragedy of the death of her husband, Paul Bern, a gentle person who had filled her dressing room daily with flowers and little presents like hand-embroidered handkerchiefs. And Vic Fleming saying when she returned to work sometime after the funeral, "How are we going to get a sexy performance with *that* look in her eyes?"

Now I don't claim to have total recall, but bits and pieces of what people said come echoing back, and it's simpler to put it down as a sequence.

Stage 18—or was it 16?—where the interiors were filmed; hot, no air-conditioning then, just big fans; damp from the constant use of rain machines. Vic being tough about our complaints, "So what! Everybody sweats in the tropics. Let it show, that's the way it is."

The mason jar of moths released each scene to flutter and bat their way around kerosene lamps for realism. (Of course they preferred the brighter, hotter lights offstage and Props had to try and shoo them back into the scene.)

"Hi baby!" (Everybody was "baby" to Clark, male or female.) "Rhea wants you to call her tonight—some damn shindig or other on Sunday—wants you and Frank. O.K.?"

"O.K. with me," I said. "Frank may have a baby to deliver—always happens when you plan something."

Vic (butting in): "Don't forget we're working on the tiger blind Saturday night. *All* night. Outside."

Clark: (Unprintable.)

We had completed several days on the back lot on the rubber plantation set. Shots of Clark carrying me through the mud, gasping from the force of the monsoon.

We had just finished the continuation on the stage inside where

With Jean Harlow in RED DUST (1932)

he carries me up the veranda steps into my bedroom, soaking wet, breathless.

Fleming said, "O.K., let's move in on a tight two."

In the script it probably read something like this: "Close shot. He is about to dump her onto the bed, but her arms still cling. There's a look. A faint, cynical smile crosses his face. This is the wife of his partner, but she's been asking for it. He kisses her, gently at first, then fiercely."

Now Clark was a husky guy and a good sport, but it was not practical for him to be a hero and hold me up for the hour or so the shot would take to line up and shoot. So first of all, a stool had to be found which was the correct height to support most of my weight. Out of sight, of course; they were cutting about elbow high.

A prop man and a carpenter shoved a stool under my bottom as Clark hoisted me up, his right arm supporting me under my knees, his left under my shoulders.

From behind the camera: "Too high! Too high! Her head's gotta be lower than his." The carpenter started in with a saw on one of the legs.

"Wait a minute! Check it in the finder, first, Mac. Let's see where you're going to be, kids."

"Make it fifty-fifty to begin with, Clark, then just before you kiss her, swing her an inch or two, so we get you full face."

We tried it.

Vic said, "Too much, too much—back just a little."

Peering through the camera lens.

Clark said, "It's uncomfortable, I'll never hit it right."

"Yes, you will. Just clear the key light on her neck, see it?"

"Why don't you move the camera?" asked Clark.

"I don't want to move the camera. It's a natural move, Clark."

"O.K., O.K.!"

Meantime the carpenter was taking a tape measurement from the bottom of my fanny to the floor, and getting the legs sawed off the stool. Lighting was being blocked in. And in those days there were lots of lights. We were hedged in by them, in fact. It was getting very, very hot.

Harold Rosson, the head cameraman said, "You can step out for a minute, Clark and Mary. Give me the stand-ins."

We cooled off and had a smoke at the big open doorway. I had my usual bad-tempered argument with the makeup man about too much makeup. He pursued me, carrying a powder puff like an extension of his arm.

Soothingly he said, "The freckles are coming through on your forehead, Mary. Let me just touch it up with a *leetle* bit of pancake."

"O.K., but *no* lipstick, Harry—you know what Mr. Fleming said. All that rain, I'd never have any makeup left."

"Looks so naked."

"That's what he wants."

Half an hour or so later, "Ready to try it!" I went back onto the set.

"Clark's on the phone. Step out of the lights a minute, Mary, but don't go 'way."

One of the prop men—in a raincoat—yelled from somewhere, "You wanna wet 'em down?"

"Just a rehearsal—no rain."

"O.K., here's Clark—let's try it now. Everybody settle down. *Quiet!*" Bells rang, doors were closed. It wasn't very quiet. And it wasn't really important until that final moment when the sound man said authoritatively, "We are rolling." Then it was quiet.

I hoisted myself up onto the stool. As Clark took his position he cracked, "Hey, you've lost weight! That's a relief!"

The Kiss à la Gable in RED DUST (1932)

The head gaffer, kneeling under the camera asked Clark, "This gonna be too hot?" Indicating an eyelight.

"Gee-sus it *is* hot," Clark replied. "It'll make me squint, Gus."

"No it won't. We really need it."

"Then it's not too hot. Whadja ask for?"

The gaffer grinned and said, "Got anything in the fifth on Saturday?"

"Yeah, I gotta honey."

"Lemme in on it, huh?"

"Sure, later."

Finally Vic came in from behind the camera so that he could talk to us quietly. And we started to think about the scene. What happened previously, relationships, emotional levels, etc.

"Let's just move through it once," Vic said. "The look needn't be very long, Clark—she's very vulnerable—if she caught it she might start thinking. Mary, keep it simple. Real. Just *want* him."

He turned and disappeared behind the lights.

"Let's make one, O.K.?" he called. "Don't need a rehearsal. Just mean it, kids. Think. Feel." To the camera crew, "Can we go?"

Hal Rosson didn't like that. "No rehearsal? Well, let me check their position when they kiss. We could move in, you know."

Vic said, "I don't *want* to move in, goddam it! I don't want to move the camera. Let the *people* do it, not the camera."

Rosson interrupted to say, "Give us a look, people."

Clark leaned his head close to me and our lips were barely touching. Loudly, he asked, "How's this?" I jumped a little and he said, "Sorry, baby."

"No good. We're just getting the top of your head."

We maneuvered fractional changes, our noses getting in the way.

"Hold it, hold it! That's fine, if you raise her just a little—too much, too much. Right there, that's beautiful, perfect."

Clark whispered to me, "That's where we were in the first place."

The assistant director checked his watch. It was getting close to lunch time. "O.K., can we go? Let's wet 'em down!"

Clark said, "Here we go again, baby," as we unwound and he helped me down from the stool.

We went over and stood just off the set in a shallow bathtub arrangement made of tarpaper and two by fours, and the man in the raincoat turned the hoses on us. After the heat of the lights, the water felt icy and we gasped and yelled as it hit us.

The assistant said, "Let's go, let's go! Let's get 'em while they're wet!" The makeup man popped in to wipe a drop from the end of my nose. "Git outta there, Harry!"

Now it was quiet. Now we were ready to go. To do what they paid us all that money for. To use our acquired ability to concentrate, to focus all our thoughts and emotions on the scene.

It was pin-drop silence. Then somebody chuckled from behind the camera. Clark's head jerked up, shocked, mad. Then the whole crew started laughing.

Vic said, "Cut it! Cut it!" and came in to us. "It's a very hot scene, kids, but not *that* hot! You're steaming!"

And we were, literally. The hot lights had vaporized the water on our clothes and skin, and it was rising in waves.

After the laughter and kidding and the joke was over, the problem remained. Everybody made a suggestion to solve it.

Then there was a question of lunch time. After lunch we were scheduled to move to another set—a "dry" scene. During lunch time I was to have my hair set and a new makeup. If we waited until after lunch to get this sequence shot, the production would be held up for at least an hour for the hairset and makeup renewal. And time was valuable.

The problem was solved. The water had to be heated. Since the source for the hoses couldn't be heated, we simply stayed in position with the lights on until we stopped steaming. To prevent our drying off the prop man kept us wet by pouring teakettles of warm water over our head and shoulders.

And the scene was shot. According to the script: "He kisses her, gently at first and then fiercely." And it was a print. "Lunch everybody. One hour! Crew back in a half hour."

The weird part of it all is that it never occurred to anyone, including Clark and me, that all this might have had a bad effect on the mood, or on our ability to play a love scene convincingly. But that's the way it was. The way it always is. The way it is today, on any movie set.

So, dear Mrs. Bobby-Soxer, in answer to your question, "What was it like to kiss Clark Gable?" I'm sure you can understand that it wasn't much of a thrill. Of course if circumstances had been different and one afternoon he had grabbed me and pulled me behind a door where nobody would see us and said in that wonderful crumbly voice, "Baby, you're for me!" and (sigh) *kissed* me, why

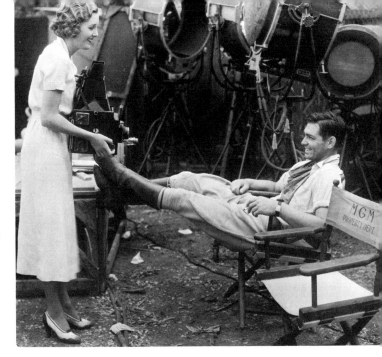

A publicity shot
for RED DUST

then I might have told you what it was like. And I'm positive I
would never have forgotten.

After a picture like *Red Dust* almost anything is a letdown.

A few years ago TV reran a picture I made immediately following
Red Dust. It was a comedy called *The Little Giant,* and as I
watched it unfold on the small screen everything seemed strange
and I had a "Did I do *that!*" feeling. It was really dated.

Eddie Robinson was the star, doing a kind of caricature of his
tough gangster roles. He was a Chicago beer baron, a dese, dem
and dose guy, who was trying to go straight and to buy his way into
California society—Pasadena type. I was the impoverished but elegant society gal who sold him her enormous home.

The thing that was interesting to me was how TV had made so
many things obsolete and absurd. Here was Eddie expressing
comic wonderment at the way "society" lived. Making cracks about
thick rugs and slippery floors, the height of ceilings, silverware and
objets d'art. Seeing a small reproduction of the Venus de Milo on a
table and remarking, "With all her dough, you'd think she'd have
the arms glued back on." I suppose this was hilarious at the time.
But since TV, there are few people who haven't seen beautiful
homes or their reproductions as sets in a film. To make a whole

With Edward G. Robinson in LITTLE GIANT (1933)

picture on the social education of a hood—and a wealthy hood—
who had never seen a game of polo or heard of it, who had never
seen brandy served in a balloon glass ("Whyncha fill it up?") seems
even more hilarious.

Even speech has lost its sharp regionality. I remember a radio
expert in the thirties who could listen to someone speak a few
sentences and then tell within a few miles where the subject had
lived most of his life.

When as a child I went to New York and first heard New Yorkese
with my Middle Western ear, I found it almost incomprehensible.
My "a's" were really flat, with a slide. Glass was gla-uss. And it took
some training for me to hear the difference and select the use of
the so-called English a. I was apt to come up with something like
"Let's get down to brass tocks." And to have "New York" stop being
"Noo Yo-erk" and "world" being "wer-uld" was like trying to learn
another language. Of course these regional differences still exist,
but because of TV we are all like well-traveled people, and extremes
have been smoothed out.

Before the drills Barrymore had given me, my speech was a low-
pitched monotonous mumble, with little lip action.

I found out how hard it was to work with a mumbler when I was with the late Jimmy Dean in a live TV show, before his great success. Live TV was a very precise business, with word cues for camera cuts. Timing had to be accurate in word and action—or you could find yourself off the air or with time left over to be filled with a short subject on the love life of the wildebeest.

We were doing a final dress rehearsal: "From the top—no stops, please." Jimmy was six feet away from me in one scene and I could barely hear what he was saying, and what I could hear seemed to have very little to do with the script. I looked over at the booth, my palms up in a "Help!" gesture.

"What's the trouble, Mary?" asked the director, his voice booming impatiently over the loudspeaker. Paul Lukas, that excellent actor, came to my rescue.

He said, "De trouble *iss* dat ve don't know vat de hell he's saying, ven he's going to say vat, or vere he's going to be ven he says anything." You could understand Paul.

Our answer came over the speaker, "I'm sorry, people. That's the way Jimmy has to work. Do the best you can. It's marvelous in here."

Paul mumbled in excellent imitation of Jimmy, "So for Chrissakes get us some earphones too!"

"What's that, Paul?"

"Oh, notting. I vas just vishing I could be marvelous, too."

We exchanged twinkling, appreciative looks, feeling superior to this newcomer, this young whippersnapper. (Vippersnopper.) We were experienced, we had a sense of responsibility to each other; we knew how to be cooperative, not only with each other but also with technicians, conscious that they too had a job. Experience is apt to make one feel superior; unfortunately it also makes us prejudiced. We become rigid, all-of-a-piece. "This works, this is right, this is the way it's done—the only way."

Jimmy Dean, that vippersnopper, in his thoughtful mumbling way, got the notices. Paul and I were "also in the cast."

But to go back to 1932 and *Little Giant* with that little giant of an actor, Eddie Robinson, the two of us rather sadly doing a bad picture together, knowing it, telling each other, "It might be funny." It was. Sort of. But there was something wrong about Edward G. Robinson taking pratfalls from a polo pony.

For me, it would be four years and eighteen pictures before

Dodsworth. Eighteen pictures, and if you have ever heard of even two of them, you are a well-informed old-movie buff. And if you're my age, you've forgotten all of them, I'm sure. Until *Dodsworth.* I wonder why it is so rarely shown on TV. I'd like very much for this "new audience" to see it. Very dated of course, in the sense that attitudes, values, motives go out of style just like clothes. But the book was good, the play was good, and the picture was wonderful, and I still think Edith Cortright is my favorite character. What she did for me was quite extraordinary. But we'll get back to her later.

I would like to find a common denominator for those eighteen pictures, the reason why they were all bad, most of them just barely successful. It's hard to put a finger on one thing, except with the word "imitation." For there *were* good pictures made in those years: *Back Street, Bill of Divorcement, Scarface.* Highly successful pictures. The trouble seemed to be that producers would try to analyze their success, extract the formula and grind out imitations, more cheaply produced, with "all-star" casts—cheaper because they weren't all stars; they were "all featured players" working under contract.

I was one of those, by choice. My work had become like the spinning of a top, set in motion by my father, whipped by financial necessity. I had been offered starring contracts, more money, fewer pictures, less work—but I was afraid of starring, of being too "successful." It sounds paranoid, but I was practical. Because starring was one hell of a gamble, and I couldn't afford to gamble. I could go on more or less hiding in feature roles, working consistently and not being responsible for the product. "A Joan Crawford picture," "a Norma Shearer picture," "a Ronald Colman picture": If they were bad, it was *their* fault; they were box-office magic or box-office poison. Once you reached their level, you had to stay at the top, for where else could you go except down? I really wanted to stick around, to feel secure. And I did, and I was.

And I also didn't have to go through quite as much of the numbing pretense of being an extraordinary personality; I could preserve a certain amount of privacy which a star could not. They had to be "on"—glamorous—all the time.

Even the amount of publicity I had to do as a featured player was more than I wanted. I used to dread the morning visit of the studio publicity man who would ask, "Any good items today?" Once, to kid him, I said, "I've got a hot one—I sleep only in my

pajama top!" He used it. There were interviews for movie magazines, the Sunday supplements, layouts and fashions for fashion
magazines and movie magazines. It was all a kind of advertising lie,
and the movie magazines especially were insatiable. They had to be
fed constantly, including accounts of my earth-shaking activities
and opinions: "What is your hobby?" "My hobby is my work!"
(Yeah.) "What do you have for breakfast? How do you keep your
figure? What are your complexion secrets?" And if such questions
must be answered, the truth is not good enough: "Bacon and eggs.
. . . Don't eat much. . . . Soap and water and a face cream that smells
nice. . . ." They had to invent something: "Since Miss A. was raised
on a farm she enjoys a hearty meal of hot oatmeal with brown sugar
and cream. . . . She goes on a carrot juice diet one day a week. . . .
An old New Orleans formula of the pulp of cucumber mixed with
a beaten white of egg used as a mask while resting. . . ."

And the photo layouts complete with props. Tennis racket and
an athletic grin. Garden shears and cute heavy gloves and a cartwheel hat. And house pictures. Stirring something at a stove
("Concocting her favorite recipe"), telephoning at a desk, serving
coffee in front of a fireplace. There were no such things as in-depth
interviews then, in spite of the touted "what this lovely lady is
really like off-screen . . ." They hadn't the faintest idea.

Who wanted truth anyway? In the movies, almost everything was
single-track, predictable and happy-happy-happy. If someone were
unlucky enough to have an unpleasant, earthy, normal facet of his
personality revealed in the press, his career might well go down the
drain. For a while in the earlier days, you weren't even supposed
to be married or have children. To my amazement that carried
down through the years as late as 1939, when my son, Tono, was
a few months old and my daughter, Marylyn, was seven. I had engaged a substitute nurse when my regular girl was ill. My housekeeper told me that the nurse had asked her, "How long has Miss
Astor had the children?" After some confusion when she was informed that the children were not adopted but were indeed mine,
the nurse said, "Oh, but they couldn't be! She's somebody in the
movies!"

Well I might not have had the time to take care of children but
I had time to make 'em.

All this is *not* beside the point of the "dreary eighteen." The
facts are that the public did not want the truth. They did not want
to identify too closely with their entertainment. They didn't want

to say, "I understand; I'm like that; I have those sorrows, those joys, those nasty little traits of character."

Jennie Gerhardt, starring Sylvia Sidney, was a three-handkerchief picture. A tearjerker by Theodore Dreiser. Sylvia played a gal who had been seduced by a senator and who had had his child, and it was about scandal in high places. Seduced? You had to feel sorry for the poor senator, because Sylvia's chest measurement was formidable, she had bedroom eyes and a lovely moist mouth, but she suffered and suffered, because she was pure. I was also a pure friend or something. I forget.

The World Changes, starring Paul Muni and directed by Mervyn LeRoy (who had graduated from comedies). Muni played a pioneer in rail refrigeration, and his big scene was when he got the idea and shouted, "Iceboxes on wheels! Iceboxes on wheels!!" I was his wife and I started in by hating the fact that he was a butcher. O.K., he was a meat-packer, and he made a lot of money and we lived in a Manhattan—or maybe it was a Chicago—mansion. But from the beginning I stuck my nose in the air and it stayed there, even though I advanced in years with gray wigs and penciled wrinkles. And through all his contributions to progress the conflict was unchanging: *Me:* "You're a butcher—you smell of blood!" *Muni:* "Why can't you understand?"

Personally I thought Muni was a very attractive man, and as an actor he was very scholarly and as dedicated and hardworking as the character he was playing. But in this thing we were both Johnny-one-note. I remember thinking during the making of the picture that this was a warm, strong, wonderful guy. I didn't approve of his method of working: his total attention to externals, makeup, hair, clothing, manner of walking, gesturing. Every word of the script memorized and actually recorded and rerecorded before he ever went on the set. And the theory that if your eyes twinkled you conveyed humor, if you shook your fist and shouted and allowed spittle to form on your lips, presto! you were an angry man. O.K. So I didn't agree with him. But this wasn't *all* of Muni, and I had a disturbing feeling that the snobbish idiot I was playing could have liked *something* about him, the character. Ah, no, no! that would have been confusing, you see. There would have been people in the audience (who weren't asleep yet) who would have said to themselves, "I thought she hated him?"

These two were rather important high-budget pictures. Technically, sets, photography, costumes, lighting, all excellent. In the beginning I had a bit of enthusiasm—I usually did at the start of a picture—but after awhile I got to the point where I'd come on the set and ask, "Which door do I come in, where do I stand, and what do I say?" And it showed. I was as two-dimensional as the screen itself: cool, indifferent, looking lovely in close-ups. Period. Period. Period. When was I ever going to learn to act! You can't learn if you can't experiment and find what works, and doesn't work. But the hours are long, the schedule rigid, so I did what I was told and saved time and money for the front office. And got a lot of jobs that way.

There were three detective stories, *The Kennel Murder Case, The Murder of Dr. Harrigan, The Case of the Howling Dog,* through which I walked, screaming prettily occasionally. A few suspense stories, *I Am a Thief, Return of the Terror, The Man with Two Faces.* All as good as some paperback whodunit. All enjoyable for me in a sort of social way: congenial people, no problems—set it up and shoot it. Lunch and jokes in the commissary. No sweat. No *nothing.*

Troubles at home loomed with much more importance. There was a squashed frustration that had no place to go. Routine, routine. Getting older, almost thirty, a marriage deteriorating daily. Gotta bust out. Where? How? Quarrels at home discharged some of the energy, but broke the marriage down to the point of no return.

There was an underworld story called *Upper World,* with Warren William and a nice gal named Ginger Rogers who had a lot of sparkle and vitality also dying on the vine: She hadn't danced yet. We'd meet again in 1942 at the Academy Awards dinner where she'd present me with my Oscar.

There were a couple of comedies where I found out something about the technique of farce. It was interesting but I didn't understand it, I didn't know why it *worked.* Later, Mary Boland told me, "Comedy is the *last* thing you learn." Because it's the toughest.

Convention City was directed by Archie Mayo who had comedy technique in his bones, and some experts around him: Adolphe Menjou, Joan Blondell, Guy Kibbee, Frank McHugh and a lot of others. I don't even remember what I was doing there.

The other one was *Page Miss Glory,* which starred Marion Davies well supported by comedians Patsy Kelly, Allen Jenkins, Berton Churchill. Again I stood around watching: "Camera cuts to reaction on Gladys."

But I liked Miss Davies. Most people thought of Marion Davies

With Marion Davies and Pat O'Brien in PAGE MISS GLORY
(1935)   *Harry Wilkinson.*

only as the chorus girl who had it made as William Randolph
Hearst's mistress. She was given every material thing a girl could
want in the world, even stardom. She had a two-story bungalow at
the studio. Bungalow was a term for a dressing room that was off the
set in another part of the lot. A dressing room on the set was portable, and it was called just that, a "portable." Marion's bungalow
was a house that would have looked very well on a street in Beverly
Hills. A few of us were invited there each day to have lunch with
her and W.R. And the dachshunds. Her face seemed to hold that
bright anxiety often seen in women in her position at that time.
But I felt it was not the anxiety of losing that position but of wanting to please a difficult man because she loved him. When he was
not around—he rarely came on the set—she relaxed, but she still
talked about him: "Guess what he said to X last night: It was so
funny—it's not easy for him to be hu-hu-humor—funny."

Whenever we had a chance, Marion and Patsy Kelly and I got
together in Marion's portable on the set for "girl talk." And later in

the day when we were getting tired and cranky, champagne would appear in an ice bucket, and there would be much caution about answering the door and responding to a knock by saying either, "I'm not dressed," or "Oh, it's you—want a snort?" For drinking on the sets was forbidden, and besides Mr. Hearst didn't like Marion to drink at all. Mervyn LeRoy, who was directing, pretended to know nothing about it, but would sometimes say, "Well, guess we're going to have to quit early tonight," when our giggling got a bit high-pitched or when Marion's stutter disappeared completely.

That stutter of hers was the machine-gun type of the first consonants. She was not troubled by it and went through none of the agonies of stammerers, who suffer so much more because the word gets hung up and won't come out. She would keep up her talk and let 'em roll: "I hate f-f-f-fishing. Aha! I know what you th-th-thought I was going to s-s-say!" In front of the camera it disappeared entirely, and not because the lines were memorized, because during rehearsals she stuttered furiously.

She was not sharp and acquisitive, nor was she a dumb blonde. She was bright and funny. Her warmth and kindness could have taught many of us a great deal about the art of loving.

These were the years called by the extravagant name of the Golden Years, maybe because nobody ever had it so good as the moviemakers. In our fortress of films we were safe from dust bowls and grinding poverty, breadlines and alphabet agencies. Oh sure, we made movies about them—things like *Grapes of Wrath*—but making them doesn't have much to do with suffering.

The four walls of a sound stage were impenetrable. Friends were doing the same thing, writing for movies, acting in movies, directing movies. And we went on talking about ourselves, what we were doing, and what we were going to do next. A few broke loose from this safe, tight circle of self, became interested in what was happening in the nation and the world, and got badly burned.

Sometime in 1938, I think it was, Robert Montgomery was driving me home from a luncheon party at the home of a writer friend; the party had been full of wit, anecdote and repartee— about those who were not attending the luncheon, naturally. About who was sleeping with whom, about a new musical, about a great new restaurant in New York where somebody had slugged somebody.

Bob was a lighthearted, intelligent and successful actor, but he'd just returned from abroad, and he had changed deeply. He was sober, quiet, a party pooper. Accused by his hostess of being grim and sourpussed and bad-mannered.

I remember we were skimming along in his convertible with the top down, on Sunset Boulevard near the Riviera Country Club. I tried to find out what was wrong with him, but he just shook his head, "I'm scared." "Of what!" "Of what's happening—in Europe —of what's going to happen. None of us here—we haven't the slightest conception—nobody'd believe it." "Well," I said, "you just probably didn't have a very good time." But the look he gave me shut me up.

There are a few more left of the dreary eighteen—the real ee-uch ones, the bilge, the junk, the unforgivably bad. There are three of them that fail to return to my memory in spite of research: *Red Hot Tires, Man of Iron,* and *Straight from the Heart.* Two at Warner Brothers and one at Universal—that's what it says in the annals of movie-making. They existed and I worked in them, got up early, went to the studio for at least a month on each one of them, played each scene as though it were important, went home bone-tired. And I do not remember a single moment. Oh, I can guess that *Red Hot Tires* was a racing picture, but I can't tell you where we went for the racing scenes. *Straight from the Heart* was, I *think,* something to do with an orphanage and a little four-year-old child who had remarkably hairy legs.

There was *Dinky,* however. It was also pretty ee-uch but I remember it because of Jackie Cooper. Jackie was about twelve or thirteen years old then and I played his Mom. He was a nice kid, very unlike the repulsive child life that infested the sets. He had a pug nose and a belligerent pout. He was intelligent and hardworking and never boring about tedious antics on the set.

We were on location at a military school near La Jolla, which Dinky was attending. I, as his mother, was visiting him. The scene was the playground field where the boys were having football practice. A tackle was supposed to turn into a fight with Jackie at the bottom of the heap coming up with torn clothes and a black eye. They were using real students from the school in the scene, and they had been coached as to how to keep it from being too realistic. The black eye was to come from the makeup man's kit—not from a fist.

But Jackie was an artist—he was having none of that fake stuff.

With Jackie Cooper
in DINKY (1935)
Harry Wilkinson.

Fists flying, he wouldn't stay down and kept coming up to the top of the heap. In the middle of the scene he got furious, exclaiming, "Well, *hit* me, goddam it! Whatsamatter, you got powderpuffs on the ends of your arms?"

The scene was cut, and the boys fell back, quietly and deferentially. Jackie suddenly turned and ran off the set to put his head into his mother's lap (his real mother, next to whom I was sitting). He was crying and blubbering and pounding her knees with his fist, "I *hate* being a movie actor—I *hate* it! I want to be a guy, a man; I don't want fellows like this to treat me like a sissy—I'm no goddam fairy, I got balls, goddam it. Everybody's afraid I'll get hurt because of the goddam picture—" and on and on. I've forgotten how it all was solved, but did I ever identify with that rebellious kid!

Twenty or twenty-five years later I often saw him in the rehearsal halls of NBC and CBS and he would always greet me as "Mom." "Caught your show, Mom. You were great!"

It was sometime in 1933, sometime between *Kennel Murder Case* and *Convention City,* that I found I would have some time on my hands—two, maybe three weeks—before I had to report in to the wardrobe for fittings for the next picture. I needed to touch base, to break the monotony of working all day and quarreling most of the night.

I hadn't been to New York for several years, since 1928 when

Kenneth and I were there on our honeymoon. And New York in the thirties in spite of the Depression was a heady, exciting place to be. An actor's vanity was boosted by the acknowledgment of his importance. He was more than a movie actor followed by fans— although there was that, too. He was treated as a personage, an artist. Not with the swoons and giggles of tourists but with a real deference, a dignified acknowledgment that seemed to say, Of course I know you, of course you shall have the best we can give you: a room, a table at a restaurant, the services at a shop. A cab driver would brush away a doorman and get out to open the door himself. And wouldn't think of "bothering" you for an autograph —not like kids! Somehow it made me feel a little better, just being addressed as "*Miss* Astor," instead of "Hi, Mary."

There were plays and musicals to see, and a nightclub to catch a great talent—shows, nightclubs, people. People on one's own wavelength. Bennett Cerf and Donald Klopfer starting their publishing company to be called Random House. George Gershwin playing bits of his new score of *Porgy and Bess* at a Sunday brunch, George Kaufman to take me to one of the famed Roundtable lunches at the Algonquin to meet other people, Dorothy Parker, Alex Woolcott, Edna Ferber....

It is quite true that working in movies one meets "so many interesting people." Some more interesting than others. That my friendships were with writers for the most part was a matter of unconscious selection. I was an interpreter of the writer, I felt, so I wanted to know more about the intentions of the writer. Also, I'd had this sneaker about wanting to write for a very long time.

It was at the home of Florence and Freddie March that I met a girl by the name of Marian Spitzer, who had been a reporter for the old *New York Globe* and was now writing for Paramount, as well as writing a novel once in a while. We became close friends.

It was at Marian's that I stayed for the first dreadful days after Kenneth was killed. And it was Marian who had suggested this trip to New York. She had written to several people she thought I'd like and had them look me up; among them, Bennett Cerf and George Kaufman.

At that time New York was hectic and exciting, not hectic and ulcer-making. There were fewer people. They weren't tearing down and building up frantically and the voice of Con Ed was not heard o'er the land. Summer in New York was wonderful. The multitudes had escaped for their summer vacations, but many people in theater and publishing and writing didn't have the set two-weeks-a-year vacation, and New York was kind of quiet (it's true!) and pleasant. It was hot, but you could drive in a hansom cab through Central Park and have a cold daiquiri at the Casino and then an icy consommé madrilene and a beautiful salmon mousse or cold lobster or something for lunch.

At night, late at night, you could walk down Fifth Avenue in the middle of the street, just for the hell of it, or sit on a bench near the fountain in front of the Plaza Hotel and philosophize, or pick up a cruising cab and be whisked down to the Village to join a party that was still going. And still talking, talking, talking— theater, theater, theater. What a lovely world it was! And people kept saying, "You should come and do a play!" "Oh, I will, oh, I will!" I'd say. But how could I? I'd opted for another kind of dream—Home, Husband and Children—and Security.

So, having thoroughly sentimentalized the city, the people; feeling "in" about theater and books and personalities, and having my own need to be liked and approved of satisfied for a time, I returned to California in a kind of sulky resentment. Like a child having to go back to school. Back to the glamorous business of movie-making.

9

R ESENT IT OR NOT, what I was doing—and didn't
realize it—was learning a craft. If one is *basically*
an artist, maybe he doesn't need experience and
practice, practice, practice. Maybe it's a little easier
for him. It all comes to him in a glory flash and he
knows exactly what to do to be a great artist. Even the word talent
seems to denote a special gift, an X quality. But I don't think any
talented artist ever created a work of art without the constant
use of the material of his particular medium.

Until the material becomes part of the cells of his body, *sub*conscious, *there* to use without thinking, it is meaningless.

What's a paint brush, a piece of stone, a musical instrument?
They are nothing if you don't have an itch to do something with
them. Then let them be. But if there *is* an itch, then they have to
be handled, explored, *consumed* until they no longer exist as things
in themselves. I think the "itch" is the talent. I think I had the
"itch-talent" to be an actress—but not a movie star. I've often felt,
in hindsight thinking, that I would have achieved more, artistically,
in the theater than I ever did in the movies. But those are useless
and wasteful regrets. And I had my moments! A few of them—

they can be counted on the fingers on one hand—but they were worth it.

So, sullenly, dissatisfied and unhappy, I was learning a craft. The materials began to have a familiar feel. I could, figuratively, walk in the dark and not bump into anything, find articles without thinking or fumbling, know where there were openings to go through, barriers to stop at.

With a few words to a camera operator, "How low you cutting?" answered by a hand signal, I could form my boundaries in the air, my proscenium, the limits wherein I could move—and they were *felt* as though I could reach out and touch them. From then on (until the next setup) I needed to give it no more thought than you give to the edges of a street when you are driving a car normally.

A multitude of varying physical instructions: "Give a little when he comes in." "Move down, rather than up, we need a matching shot from the reverse." "On your move, be sure to clear that inky." "Your look's gotta be camera right." There are literally hundreds of these little sentences between an actor and his cameraman—just little information pieces, little necessities. (What's surgical procedure without the word "scalpel"!)

This kind of thing is my answer to the pseudo-artist who throws a palm to his overheated forehead and exclaims, "I *hate* these limitations!" I got furious at an actor who said that at least once during every setup, and I finally said, "Well, the hell with them, then. Go play your scene down on Times Square."

There are limitations everywhere; be aware of them and work within them. Freedom has its limitations. We're not free to walk on water—not yet.

I learned how to modify my own limitations. To a cameraman: "I need more room, Joey." "You got it," pulling the camera back a foot or switching a lens and saying, "Harry, watch that overhead, spread it a little." From the sound man: "When you gonna move, Mary?" "Why? you need a word cue?" "Please." "Well—uh—lemme see. Gee I'm not sure, Hank." "I don't want to conk your head when you get up, is all." "Okay, move as I put out the cigarette. I'll get it all in before then."

All the time, all around you is a babble of these little instructions, from crew to crew from director to cameraman. When you come onto a sound stage it sounds like bedlam, but it can be sorted out easily—if you know.

It all quits in a minute and then you're on your own. And in the meantime, inside of you, you've been keeping a little pot simmering on the back burner—the character, the relationships: break up the little fat chunks of emotion, and let them mix and spread. You keep up your often wordless communication with the director, you touch and exchange words with other actors. You say, "Can I help?" If he feels crowded, if the pace is wrong; we talk and answer with few words. There is often a very high level of communication between actors, and when there is, something of excellence happens.

And what's the director doing? If you're a pro, you save him time by working with the crew. He shouldn't have the menial task of relaying technical information to his people. He shouldn't have to go through something like the following:

"Now honey, we want you to—ah—see that light there right beside you? No, not that one, the one on your *right, that's* it! Now, when you turn, don't back out of it. You see that funny gizmo in front of it? It's called a cucaloris—I'll tell you why someday, not just now, dear. Well that's throwing some nice shadows on your shoulders and we don't want to lose that—it's a nice effect and—uh —you won't forget, will you dear?"

Or: "Dear, when you're over there against the wall and you're crying—and that's all marvelous, dear, but we can't hear you unless you turn a *leetle* bit toward us. No, I don't *want* you to turn clear around, just kind of drop your head and say the words over your shoulder. We can't put a mike in the wall, you understand."

During rehearsals and between takes you must come to an agreement with the director as to what the scene's about, and what you're going to do to play that scene and project these particular emotions or thoughts or actions. In the studio he is your only audience; he has to look with fresh eyes and be millions of people and decide, "*That's* what they'll think or feel when this moment is shown on the screen." If you know what you're doing, it is up to you to help him preserve this freshness.

It took me years and years to find out that the highest satisfaction I could get out of my work was this achievement of communication between myself and the director, first of all, then with other actors, and then, the crew. And not least of all the crew. The prop man, for instance. I've found him at my side in times of little troubles. Like maybe in a scene where I have to use a cup and saucer, picking it up, putting it back on to a table. Worrying because it's going to clatter during the scene. (Always, the anxiety tremors.)

And I've looked up to see him with a roll of adhesive tape to make a few strips of padding inside the saucer. Thousands of little aids from these most resourceful men.

But at the highest level—the director—I have felt moments of knowing, of feeling, that are like moments when you're in love. You do love, in a way. You don't have to like him, but you have to respect his judgment or you're in trouble. A good director isn't "out there" *telling* you what to do—although I had to learn that too! You may even disagree with him, violently, and you chew it out and try to understand each other. You negotiate and compromise, you talk it out, but finally you *dig!*

I'm not talking about anything old-fashioned now. Just that I learned it. Maybe others learn a little more quickly, nowadays, but you never graduate. I was learning along with the business itself, and I never stopped learning. I like the story, and maybe it's just a story, about Lunt and Fontanne. Lynn said to her husband, "Now, *now* I know what to do with that handkerchief at the beginning of Act Two!" Alfred said, "But darling, we closed tonight, remember?" "Of course, what's that got to do with it?"

There are times, sort of plateaus, when you feel you are not advancing. And if the material is mediocre or banal, there isn't much you can do, except to override it with sheer virtuosity. And never to play a scene as though it were unimportant, or "not worthy of one's talents." Usually I felt that I was the one who wasn't "worthy": I had to overcome the "I am stupid" fixation. Always, all through my career, I wished for someone to teach me how to act. I wished for blueprints, and there were none. There *are* none. That's what I had to learn.

I learned about the "inner image," which goes all the way back to Jack Barrymore's "pass the butter" lesson. It isn't difficult really. But it takes intense concentration to conjure it up when you want it. It's something we all do when we daydream. You can visualize a beautiful mouth-watering chocolate cake or a chilly martini, whichever. Or a mountain pool with the fish jumping. You can see a beloved face or the face of somebody you loathe, and although you don't know it, or aren't conscious of it, your face will reflect these inner images. In the case of somebody you loathe you may even find yourself whispering, "Sonofabitch!"

So it's no trick, really. It just takes energy, lots of it, to concentrate deeply and at the right moment and keep the inner images

With Paul Lukas, Ruth Chatterton, and Walter Huston in
DODSWORTH (1936)   *The Bettmann Archive, Inc.*

going the way *you want them to go*. Then there is the problem of
repetition. In movies it's "over and over" sometimes. And in the
theater it's eight times a week. But the mind is such a wondrous,
flexible instrument that it will present the same image, on command or stimulus, and it will be slightly different each time. That
makes the repetition not only endurable but fascinating.

Of course, fatigue is the enemy, and the mind will balk completely. Then, if you have to do it again, or you've got a night performance after a matinee, you have to resort to the externals
completely—remembering what you did, and doing it mechanic-
ally. And it's never as good. It is bound to be superficial and slick
and the audience knows it. Oh, does it ever!

So I kept going to "school"—the dreary, forgettable, forgotten
eighteen. And finally along came one where it all got put to use,
where what I had learned was used and enlarged by an intelligent
tough director, William Wyler. We got into step very quickly.

He was meticulous and picky and he had a sharp tongue, sometimes sarcastic and impatient. Some would fight him and there were some beautiful battles on the set. But he knew, somehow, that sharp criticism bottled me up completely. Nothing could come out. He could use spurs but not a whip.

Dodsworth. One battle waxed and waned all through the picture. Ruth Chatterton hated Wyler. She disagreed with his direction of every scene, and he was stubborn and smiling and it drove her to furious outbursts. She didn't like the role of the wife of Sam Dodsworth, because the character was that of a woman who is trying to hang onto her youth—which was exactly what Ruth herself was doing. It touched a nerve. But she gave a beautiful performance in spite of herself.

She had been a very famous star in the theater—a delicate "little princess" type of ingenue. I remember her very well in Barrie's charming phantasy, *Mary Rose,* in the early twenties. She had an odd beauty that did not photograph well, so she didn't like movies, and she made it clear that she only worked in them because of the money.

Her home in Beverly Hills was a salon right out of the Victorian age. She always had a swarm of admirers, mostly young men, "sitting at her feet."

She had exquisite skin and pampered it with a daily facial massage administered by one Ada Mae. I remember my good friend Auriol Lee coming in one day during one of these facial sessions at her home. There were others sitting around having drinks and talking while Ada Mae was patting and stroking and pinching away.

"You know, Ruthie, that face of yours is going to come off one of these days; it's going to slip right off into Ada Mae's hands!"

When Ruth and Willie weren't yelling at each other they were exchanging polite poison darts.

It was in the summer, and very hot. Willie had on his usual white linen slacks and white shirt and was sitting immediately under the camera. It was lined up on a big close-up of Ruth, and just before Willie gave the order to roll she said,

"Willie, darling, that *white* suit of yours! It's very distracting with you sitting so close; it's all I can *see!*"

"Would you like me to leave the studio, Miss Chatterton?"

"I would indeed, but unfortunately I'm afraid it can't be arranged."

There was one episode in *Dodsworth*—in the dining salon of the ship that was going to England—where I had a little bit with a nice young Englishman who seemed to be in an agony of nerves. He kept a silly smile fastened to his face and constantly patted his pockets, searching for cigarettes, lighter. Lighting up with shaking hands he'd toss the cigarette away, and pat pockets for a handkerchief with which to wipe sweaty palms, all the time keeping up a running, nervous, disjointed conversation. He said his name was David Niven, and he'd never made a movie before. The rest seemed preposterous, and I'm sure he was inventing. It went like this:

"Bloody hot, isn't it? I *beg* your pardon! . . . I never wanted to be in this silly business . . . wasn't my idea at all . . . they picked me up off a ship."

"What do you mean, a ship?"

"That's right, a ship, a *ship*. It's down in San Pedro Harbor this moment. . . . Whew! Bloody hot. . . . I say, what are we supposed to do? . . . Who's the director? . . . that bloke over there? I jumped ship you know, and look where it got me! 'Twasn't *my* idea."

I never did get it sorted out. It sounded as though he'd been kidnapped and brought directly to the studio! And even though I met him many times in the following years I never did check out the story with him.

Most of my work was with Walter Huston, a warm, easygoing human being. He had played *Dodsworth* on the stage, and it was an enormous personal success. My part, Edith Cortright, had been played by his wife, Ninetta Sunderland. But he had the good taste and the wisdom never to bring it up. There was never any "Nan did it this way" kind of thing, which would only have confused me and made me feel uncomfortable.

The days when just the two of us worked were the peaceful days on the set, and Willie didn't use up nearly as much film. Willie's way of getting an actor into line was simply to take the scene over and over again—I've heard of as many as sixty takes—and then say, "Print take two." Even when he wasn't disciplining someone he used more film than most directors. He was a perfectionist.

I remember one entire afternoon spent shooting a scene of a crumpled letter being blown gently along the length of a terrace.

As Edith Cortright in DODSWORTH   *Kenneth Alexander.*

He wanted it to go slowly for a way, then stop, and then flutter along a little farther, and finally be caught up in a gust and blown over the edge of the balcony. It was the letter in which Mrs. Dodsworth receives the word that she's going to be a grandmother. She crumples it and tosses it away and goes into the house, not wanting to accept it, for she is about to enter into another exciting affair with a young attractive German boy. (I don't remember the name of the young actor, but his mother was played magnificently by Maria Ouspenskaya.)

One day it was getting about that time. Quitting time. Everybody'd had it. And Willie said, "O.K., medium shot. Mary on the balcony. And transparency will work in the background." Everybody groaned and I said, "Oh, Willie!"

He nodded and grinned his evil little grin at me. "You look a little tired, Mary—it's good. Now. What can I tell you? Take your time with it. Long as you want. I'm going to intercut with the stock shots and close-ups of Walter. So? It's got to finish high—but you know that. Just don't rush it. We've got lots of film."

The transparency was a huge rear movie projection of the Bay of Naples, with the city and all the activities of the harbor seen in the distance. It had been the background for this set for a week. The set was the garden of a small villa in the hills. There was a fountain and a wall, and doors leading into the interior of the house, and greenery and rocky paths and flowers.

It was a simple shot and wouldn't take long. All the little flow of questions and answers went back and forth: "Where you going to be, Mary?" "Right here, O.K.?" "Little more to the right—leetle bit more so that vine isn't growing out of your head." "I can't—I'm against the wall now." "Want the wall out?" a carpenter asked. "No, it's O.K. Hey, greens man, cut that piece that's sticking out."

Willie was over talking to someone, but he glanced over to me—a little wordless signal—and I put the little pot on to boil, and the conversation now took about half my attention.

Camera said, "Let's see your look, please."

"About here." I looked—not at the transparency but about three feet to one side of the camera and at a section of the floor beyond the set where there was a big can of sand for cigarette butts. It was marked Put Your Butt in Here. I said, "Can I have a gobo in front of that can?" I knew I'd just read the words Put Your Butt in Here over and over.

With Walter Huston in
DODSWORTH *Culver
Pictures.*

A grip placed the gobo—a strip of black canvas on a wooden frame about ten feet by three—at the place I pointed.

"Do you want a mark?" he asked, a piece of chalk in his hand. Sometimes an X on the black field of the gobo helps one hold a spot to look at. To focus the eyes.

"Don't think so, thanks."

Willie came in. "Yes. Put a mark. I think you will have to differentiate, Mary, a little—only a little—between the steamship and the motorboat. Let's see." And looking at me he took the chalk and marked one spot on the gobo.

"Straight out. Distant, yes?"

And two feet lower. "Look at it, please. Yes. That's good." Another X. He came in closer to talk over the hubbub.

"I think, Mary, you must give up totally—but accepting it—no, ah—no sadness. Just shift your weight a little. I mean, you're getting two feet on the ground, or you'd fall apart. Then—when you want to—see the motorboat, right?"

It didn't take long. I stood there, and I looked and then I raised my arm in greeting and said, "Sam! Sam!" Cut.

Want to hear the pot boiling? I stood there and I looked at those silly X marks on a black gobo, and I thought of the man out there who was sailing on the *Queen Mary* from Naples Harbor, and I wasn't going to see him again, ever. He'd gone back to his wife, even though she'd had affairs in all the capitals of Europe. And because I was who I was, Edith Cortright, I figured that even though it was going to be rough for a while, I'd get over it—maybe. And how beautiful and *final* that damn great ship looked as it was moving away from the wharf. Then, dropping my eyes to the other X mark I saw my gardener in my motor launch and I knew he was returning from having taken the passenger out to the ship, and I hoped he'd done a little shopping while he was in town. And then I saw the other man with him and I saw who it was and—dear God! he *hadn't* sailed—and the tears popped out and I shot up my hand and yelled "Sam! Sam!" And I was never so happy in my life. *Me,* me—and Edith Cortright, for her happiness and mine had fused.

Willie said, "Print it." Willie who took so many takes of everything. I said, "You kidding?" (I was fishing. I knew. One does.)

He shrugged. "It's good, you'll see."

It was good. Everything else was good, just right. All that had previously occurred in the picture was back of this final fade-out of the story. There were cuts of Walter Huston. The audience knew, but they wanted to enjoy the reaction of the woman when *she* saw him. And the background music soared under it. I had a lot going for me. At every theater, at every performance, the audience clapped their hands. It sounded like applause, but it was sheer joy.

Dodsworth was filmed in June, July, August of 1936. There was absolutely no national or world news—except Mary Astor's Diary. (There was lots of news but we were still isolationist-happy.) I had a custody suit for my little girl, and the press made hay. Reporters kept stakeouts at the Goldwyn Studios, and at my house. I was appearing in court at night during the filming and when the picture was finished, day sessions were resumed. It was all pretty hairy, with all the (then) exciting details in fat black headlines. Today I don't think it would rate two sticks on page ten. But at the time, I was under great emotional strain, and I was lucky to be working in a picture that was so absorbing. With guards outside the gate, nobody could get in to disturb us. The reporters could never figure out why they couldn't catch me when I went home—but I was living at the studio, in a very handsome dressing-room apartment, with kitchen facilities.

The diary that caused all the headlines was one I had kept covering the period of about 1929 to 1934. It had been removed from my desk and was to be used by the defense to keep me from suing for the possession of my daughter. It contained entries concerning Kenneth, our friends, his death, the events leading to my marriage with Dr. Thorpe, our trip to Honolulu and the birth of Marylyn. Finally it had a rather overemotional account of a romantic interlude with George Kaufman in New York, and it was this account that was supposed to prove me an unfit mother.

The defense kept referring to the diary in oblique terms, insinuating much, much more. My lawyer, Roland Rich Woolley, told the court that he wanted to stop the innuendos and have the diary produced by the defense and presented as evidence. That night there was a high-level meeting at the Goldwyn Studios. Mr. Goldwyn, Harry Cohn of Columbia Studios, Jack Warner, Irving Thalberg, A. H. Giannini, Louis B. Mayer, Jesse Lasky, all flanked by legal advisers, were out to convince me and Mr. Woolley that it would be better for the motion picture business and, incidentally, for me, not to have the diary brought in as evidence. They had heard of or had seen certain pages in the diary that contained descriptions of sexual acts with almost every well-known actor in the business, with a box score of performance. All I could say was that it just wasn't true and if there were such pages they had to be a forgery. I was not believed, naturally.

The court refused to allow the diary to be admitted as evidence as there were many pages missing, and a "mutilated document" is not admissible. So the diary became a mystery. And as a mystery, rumor begot rumor, with the press using quotes from someone called a "reliable source" who had had access to the diary, and the news magazines and papers quoting each other.

I had achieved the reputation of being the greatest nympho-courtesan since Pompadour. It was funny, it was absurd, and I made jokes along with everybody else—but it was never very funny to me, really, because it just wasn't true.

I know this is going to sound a little strange, but the person I clung to as a friend through all this was the character I was playing, Edith Cortright. She was three-dimensional in my mind, and I knew all about her. She was a lot of things I wasn't, she was a lot of things I would like to have been. She had also been a little foolish and human. But she had complete confidence in herself, and I had very little. She was not talkative, she listened to everyone with a gentle, no-comment smile. She walked tall, she made no unnecessary gestures, or movements. She was *cool*.

So when I went into court and faced the bedlam of sightseers, newsmen and women, photographers, attorneys (in the halls they were hawking ice cream cones and hot dogs for the spectators), when I sat in the witness chair for long hours and answered questions that would have broken me up completely, I kept the little pot boiling that was Edith Cortright. I sat a little straighter, I wore clean white gloves, and kept my hands quiet. I often confused the attorney for the other side by taking a long time before answering his questions, eyebrows slightly raised, "Do you really mean I should answer such an impertinent question?" in my thoughts. I wasn't "smart" or "clever" but I was completely rattleproof, thanks to Edith Cortright. She was my shield. Without her, without the craft I had been so long in learning, I would have been shattered emotionally by the ugliness of that trial.

The outcome of the trial was a draw. As one feature writer, with a purple ribbon in her typewriter, said, "A child is divided. With the wisdom of a Solomon, Superior Court Judge Goodwin Knight made his painful decision—" I was given six months' custody of my little girl and her father was allowed the same. Judge Goodwin Knight was elected lieutenant governor of California that year. A month of days on the front pages of the newspapers hadn't hurt him.

After the trial, the diary was impounded by court order, and with my permission it was incinerated. And late that summer the public finally took its eyes off me when Edward VIII renounced his kingdom for Mrs. Wallis Simpson.

The rest of that summer I spent a lot of time recuperating at home and at the beach with friends. They were fewer now, but they were those who hadn't panicked at the idea of being associated with me in an unsavory episode. It takes a crisis to find out who one's friends are.

And Edith Cortright departed like a friendly, companionable ghost. I had to dismiss her now for I had another picture to do on my contract for Columbia. Just a job, a thing called *Lady from Nowhere,* and completely forgettable. But I felt I was lucky to have a job at all. It had been a possibility that the public might have been shocked and outraged to such an extent that my contract would have been canceled on the morals clause, and my career would have been out the window. But the public remained friends too. One should never underestimate them: They are not fooled.

Lady from Nowhere closed out my contract with Columbia and now I was free-lancing—which was even more precarious. And that trial had been expensive.

But along came a script for the remake of *The Prisoner of Zenda,* with Ronald Colman, Douglas Fairbanks, Jr., Madeleine Carroll and Raymond Massey. I played Antoinette de Mauban, the wife of "Black Michael," Raymond Massey, and the scorned mistress of Rupert of Hentzau, Doug, Jr.

She wasn't much of a "who" character, but she was beautiful, dark and mysterious and beautifully gowned. I worked with my friend Auriol Lee on the script. She had a nice house at the beach; she had directed many of John Van Druten's plays here and in England, and was a good person to help me to try to make a "who" out of Antoinette. She suggested I play her with a French accent but it came out sounding German—I never was a good mimic!—and Auriol said, "Let's just forget it, ducky!"

I hadn't worked with Colman, but I knew him very well. He was

PRISONER OF ZENDA (1937)   *Above:* With Ronald Colman
Below: With Raymond Massey

On the set of PRISONER OF ZENDA   *Above:* With Douglas Fairbanks, Jr.
Below: With Douglas Fairbanks, Jr., C. Aubrey Smith and visitors

one of the group of the English set that I saw frequently: Bart Marshall, Nigel (Willie) Bruce, Leslie Howard, their wives, and David Niven (whose first acting job had been in *Dodsworth*), Dame May Whitty (not yet on the honors list), C. Aubrey Smith and others.

As an actor Ronnie was always excellent. Easy, skillful, never very deeply involved—always a touch of humor. There were some exciting fencing scenes in the picture and both Ronnie and Doug, Jr., were pretty good. The scenes were routined—choreographed, you might say—by an old friend, Ralph Faulkner, who had given up acting long ago to become an Olympic champion in foils and now had a fencing school and also doubled for difficult scenes such as we had in *Zenda*. He had played the lead in one of the little two-reel pictures I had made way back in 1921.

Raymond Massey was a fairly new personality to films—he had not yet played Lincoln—and it would be a long time before he would be Dr. Gillespie in the Kildare series.

I believe this was the third version of *Zenda*, the first in sound. There was still one to come with Deborah Kerr and Stewart Granger in 1952. And it was always successful, proving, I suppose, that people like the "tell me a story" form of entertainment. *Zenda* was always a most unlikely story, but it could have happened, and the sad-sweet ending with its renunciation of love in the face of duty left the audience sad-happy because it had the moral values of another time and there was something gallant and fine and nostalgic about it all. Madeleine Carroll was our princess, fair-haired, gentle and warm, and her farewell scene with Ronnie gave you the feeling that it might just be possible after all the hullabaloo was over, they'd meet on the edge of town and get the hell out of the country.

10

MOVIES WERE PEAKING in quality those closing years of the thirties—and the box office was dropping off. People were staying home listening to other people telling them a story on radio. They were listening to *One Man's Family*, *Allen's Alley*, *Lux Radio Theater*, *Suspense*, *Fibber McGee and Molly*, and found them more interesting than the double features and Giant Giveaway Free Dishes nights at the movies. Radio took it away from us, quite seriously.

A Gallup Poll of the time describes the average moviegoer as 27 years of age, earning $28 a week, strongly averse to pictures about any problems concerning war or its consequences, and with Mickey Rooney as his favorite actor. So a fine picture like *Wuthering Heights*, with Laurence Olivier and Merle Oberon, just didn't have a chance. *Algiers*, with Charles Boyer and Hedy Lamarr, made it on a catch phrase, "Come with me to the Casbah!" and it took *Gone with the Wind* to bring them back into the theaters.

All of which made me wish I were in a less iffy business. Like the century, I too was in my thirties, and I'd had a long career, but I was at my peak of energy and interest. An occasional moment such as that in *Dodsworth* was not enough to fill my needs. I was rooted in Hollywood, emotionally and financially. I longed for what I felt sure the theater could give me—the contact with live audiences and the wider freedom of the stage—but I was too chicken to take a chance on cutting out and maybe having to pinch pennies in New York in the theater, which was even iffier.

Bramwell Fletcher, a charming young English actor, and his lovely wife, Helen Chandler, both of the theater (they had been in a hit, *Outward Bound,* in New York) were in Hollywood to make money but, hungry for their own medium, were forming a group to produce the Noel Coward cycle of one-act plays, *Tonight at Eight-Thirty.* Helen and I would divide the Gertrude Lawrence roles, with Helen doing the comedies, the dancing and singing roles and I the more serious playlets, like *Still Life* and *The Astonished Heart.*

Of course we couldn't hope to achieve the tour de force of Coward and Lawrence who had zipped through the cycle with breath-taking versatility and dazzle. But that was their thing. We could take the same plays, and because they were basically good, play them in our own way, and still make them a good evening's entertainment.

We played the Biltmore Theater in Los Angeles to good box office and good press. And I had something to chew on! Something to learn—and a lot to unlearn. I had to learn to open up—rather to learn it all over again—to widen out my boundaries ("Where you cutting, Andy?" "Shoulders, Mary—couple of feet each side."). I had no mike over my head to catch a low tone or a whisper. But I had learned to be a "thinking actor," and to my great delight it worked—even way out there beyond the proscenium. I had help, lots of it, from the more experienced Bram and Helen, and from Estelle Winwood who did a couple of stunning Cockney roles in the cycle.

In *Still Life,* which came to the movies as the lovely *Brief Encounter* years later, Bram and I played the unhappy lovers who met in a railroad station restaurant for a half hour stolen from their respective and respectable homes. We sat quietly at a table downstage right, while on the other side, a comedy of almost farce level was being played out at intervals. The attention of the audience was supposed to shift back and forth between the two areas.

All through rehearsals I bitched and complained about these scenes. "But what, just tell me *what* is going to make the audience come back to us when they've been laughing and having a good time?" Estelle Winwood with those wondrous blue popeyes and a flaming red wig would assure me. "Darling, br-ring them back to you by your *stillness*. Remember the name of the play, *Still Life*—play that. You'll see, we quit all our nonsense, and when we do, believe me, if you're *still*, they will come to you." Yeah, I thought. I was sure we'd have to wave a flag.

Of course we have to give the author something. Noel Coward had written the piece skillfully, so that the audience was more interested in *our* story, and the nonsense between the two waitresses and the "Stop Me and Buy One" man with his tray of Banbury tarts were simply a diversion and a relief from the emotional intensity of the star-crossed lovers. And Estelle was right. When they were on, Bram and I sipped tea, lighted cigarettes, talked quietly. Then when our cue got close we stopped moving, completely, and you could see the entire audience swivel over—all those heads!

Theater is theater wherever it is. This was just a taste of theater for me. A second company playing the Los Angeles Biltmore is hardly Broadway. But basically it is the same. People are people and audience-actor relationship was as fascinating a challenge, as elusive a thing to capture, as theater anywhere.

The theater-in-the-round has never appealed to me, either as a spectator or as an actor. I played a few in later years during a tour of Shaw's *Don Juan in Hell*. I didn't like people so close, it affected my concentration, and I lost the sense of the audience as a whole, as an entity. It was fragmented, broken up into this person blowing his nose, that woman over there whispering to her neighbor, those two children swinging their feet. And when I attended shows that were either projected or in the round, I didn't like seeing the makeup, the sweat on the brow of a nervous actor. Nor did I like sharing the play with another part of the audience; actors turning their backs on me made me feel left out, so the hell with them. I lost interest.

Yes, I know about Shakespeare's original theater and the Greek theater and later when box seats were on the stage. But I think it was an improvement to separate stage and audience. It placed a veil of illusion between us. I don't think it would be very interesting or help the emotional impact if the audience could see a prop man back stage firing Hedda Gabler's suicide shot.

Anyway. While I was playing the Coward shows I went into a picture for Sam Goldwyn called *The Hurricane*. Dorothy Lamour's first picture with sarong, Jon Hall, and some *good* actors, Thomas Mitchell, Raymond Massey, C. Aubrey Smith, Jerome Cowan, John Carradine. And directed by the greatest, John Ford. The real star was the "special effects" man, James Basevi, and the hurricane. It was all to be shot on the back lot of the Goldwyn Studios and in tanks inside the studio. It had to be to control the elements.

We took the *Tonight at Eight-Thirty* company up to the Lobero Theater in Santa Barbara after I started on *Hurricane*. I worked all week at the studio, left Friday night where we did five shows during the weekend: Friday night, matinee and night on Saturday, matinee and night on Sunday. Then I drove back at the crack of dawn Monday to be ready for work at the studio. I think I did this for three or four weeks. My maid drove the car and I sat in back and removed the movie makeup and dried my hair—soaked from the studio rain—put it back up in pincurls and got to the theater just in time to put on stage makeup, get dressed and have a sandwich. And it was all fun. Really fun.

There wasn't much to the story of *Hurricane* or much required in the way of acting—although there were some good scenes. After we had disposed of the story, so to speak, the hurricane started and that kept us occupied for weeks. We walked against winds, carefully calculated to blow at near hurricane level. Huge propellers kept us fighting for every step, with sand and water whipping our faces, sometimes leaving little pinpricks of blood on our cheeks from the stinging sand.

I think "laconic" is a good word for John Ford and for his technique of direction. No big deal about communication with John. Terse, pithy, to the point. Very Irish, a dark personality, a sensitivity which he did everything to conceal, but once he said to me while I was doing a scene with Ray Massey, "Make it *scan*, Mary." And I said to myself, "Aha! I know you now!"

I saw him do a wonderful piece of direction with a very small Polynesian child playing one of the native boys who were helping in Jon Hall's escape. The boy was being severely, harshly questioned by Ray Massey as to his activities. And Ray could look *very* severe and frightening as he shouted, "Where were you, boy?"

The close-up of the child was to be all big eyes and a lie in just one word, "Fishing." A lie, and a frightened one. And John stood close to the boy and repeated over and over two musical notes, about a fourth apart—like C to F—"Fish-*ing*." "Fish-*ing*." And the boy would say it, and then John, and sometimes the camera would be going and sometimes not, according to his hand signals behind his back. And finally it was all big black eyes and the whopper of a lie, "Fish-*ing*."

However, the picture, as I said, was mostly a technical problem. The little town on the Island of Manakura (remember the song, "Moon of Manakura"?) was built on the back lot around an artificial harbor big enough to float a large schooner tied up at the dock. There was a church and the residence of the governor, a store, and various native shacks and buildings which later would go all to pieces in the water and the wind.

There were several weeks of shooting it intact. The arrival and departure of the schooner, a big luau, lots of people involved and that meant we could only get a few setups a day.

For diversion John instituted afternoon tea for the cast. We'd sit on the veranda of the "government house" and have our tea and cakes and biscuits and jam. I'm sure it was dear Aubrey Smith's idea. He never really left England. For us, tea was a welcome change from the endless cups of bad coffee in cardboard containers.

But then the rains came, the big hoses, the wind machines, the overhead sprinklers and everybody in the crew in boots and raincoats and everything everywhere in a continual dripping, wet, muddy mess.

And there was a tree. Oh, that tree! It was a big one, and it "grew" in front of the church. A huge, twisted trunk, and big branches a foot or more in diameter, into which Jon Hall helped Dotty and me take refuge, tying us to the branches with rope. The tree was to last during most of the storm, then, uprooted, to drift out to sea and we would be safe. That's the way the story went. And there were shots of us during the storm to show the audience that we were still there, scared and clinging to our branches. Of course, each time they came to us, the water had risen. Close-ups had to be done inside the studio with a replica of the tree built into a tank, and it was made of wood and wire and papier-mâché and canvas. There they would turn the wind machines and hoses on us, and there they suspended the tree so that it would turn as though its roots were being loosened. For some shots there was water in the tank, activated by wave machines, and sometimes the tank was drained so that the camera parallel could get closer.

None of this made John very happy. It was tricky and dangerous, and as he sat perched on top of the parallel (I don't recall that they had the huge moving camera booms in those days) he would alternately chew on the stem of a very black pipe or the corner of his handkerchief.

Just before we were ready to go on a shot one day when the tank was dry, there were some unpleasant sounds of creaking and crunching where the branch joined the tree trunk and all of a sudden it gave way (not in the script!) with a sickening scary plunge. It held at the trunk, but I was suspended (Dotty was way above me, yelling!) head downward over the concrete floor of the tank twenty feet below. *If* the branch had come loose completely and *if* I hadn't been tied securely, it would have been serious. The crew rushed to me with ladders and supports and got me untied and down very quickly.

It had happened so fast I didn't really have time to be very scared—only for those few seconds looking at the concrete floor! I looked around for John, for, well for a comforting word, maybe. But he was still atop the parallel. He hadn't moved. There he sat, tearing at his handkerchief with his teeth. It was in shreds.

All he said was, "Go home, Mary. Go home, no more for today!"

With *Hurricane* finished there was some talk of taking the *Tonight at Eight-Thirty* company on another tour, but financially it didn't make sense, so now it was time to listen to the voice of my agent. And take a script over at Metro.

"But I don't *like* it!" I said—as usual!

"It's a big opportunity, Mary—gets you 'in' over at Metro."

"So? Metro's a factory."

"Oh, you're wrong, Mary, they're doing the biggest things in films today."

THE HURRICANE (1937)   *Above:* With Thomas Mitchell
and C. Aubrey Smith   *Below:* With C. Aubrey Smith

"Well, give me one of the big things then, not this piece of junk!"

"They want you Monday in wardrobe. Irene's going to do your clothes."

Monday it was. And Irene was wonderful. She made stunning clothes. The kind I liked: tailored, simple. The expensive-looking simple.

I was standing on the raised, circular platform getting a "lining fitting." From this they would make a dressmaker's dummy. These dummies were kept on file at all the studios where an actress had worked and might work again. Measurements were checked at the beginning of fittings, and time and strength were saved. They looked very odd, those headless forms, standing in one part of the huge workrooms, with the names of the famous ones stamped on their chests. There was Judy Garland, and Greer Garson and Ethel Barrymore and Alexis Smith in the spooky ensemble.

Irene and I had never worked together before, since I had never worked at Metro. She walked around the platform studying my figure, nodding, frowning. She said, "You have beautiful legs, Mary, nice and long and slim. Nice shoulders, arms." She sighed, gustily, and made a frame with her hands which took in the area from my shoulders down to just below my hips. "Now if we could just draw a *veil* over what's between." I knew. Hips a little too wide, a waistline that could be an inch smaller, flat-chested. You don't expect flattery in the intimacy of the fitting room. Irene dressed me for many years but in modern clothes only; there was another designer always for period clothes: That's another kind of talent. It was a tie between Irene and Edith Head (Paramount) as to who did better for me. It wasn't easy!

But lovely Irene clothes didn't help much in a comedy in which I had to compete with such seasoned laugh-getters as Frank Morgan, Reginald Owen, Edna May Oliver, Herman Bing, Siegfried Rumann. Edna May Oliver with that rubber face, and Frank Morgan's high-pitched splutter. Well, I just sat around looking lovely in Irene's lovely clothes.

Then another pair for Columbia, a two-picture deal. One was called *No Time To Marry*, and the other *There's Always a Woman*. The first one had this for a plot: Two reporters, Richard Arlen and I, keep trying to get married but every time we almost get to the altar a big assignment holds us up. Does that vaguely recall a thing called *The Front Page?* Well, vaguely.

The other was described in the ads as a detective battle-of-the-sexes comedy played against a murder mystery. And Joan Blondell and Melvyn Douglas and I were all very bright and funny.

There was a stupid book out recently by a writer who thought he could analyze all the great stars of the past by the kinds of roles they had played during their career. Total bunk. Because actors simply did not choose all the roles they played and it is *choice* that is revelatory. They had limitations; Humphrey Bogart could never be Red Skelton, and I could never be Ginger Rogers. Other than that I don't think there is anything profoundly revealing. I know I was never quite as sweet or clever or darling as most of the parts I played, nor was I ever quite such a bitch as in later roles. You might come to the conclusion after seeing many of my pictures that I was "cool, self-possessed, a woman in excellent control of her life." Well . . .

By now I must have made my point. That a long—and yes, successful—movie career is not quite the life of glamour, champagne and applause, adulation and ease that most people think it is. And to those who think "all that money," I would remind them there were "all those expenses" too. An agent got 10 percent off the top. Then you had to have a business manager, because the very nature of the work precluded one from having much of a business head. I don't think this is true today. Most actors have learned to take care of their money a little better, because of some of the brother-can-you-spare-a-dime stories of actors who had brief, brilliant careers and then nothing. It finally got through our heads that success was not continual and permanent. That you become a has-been, an old-timer and a veteran very quickly. The success life-span is normally very short.

And in those Golden Years it was necessary to possess some status symbols. You didn't run around in a jalopy and old clothes. (In itself a reverse status symbol.) You had to have a house that was impressive, and for that house you had to pay mortgages and have servants and maintenance expenses.

You had to appear at nightclubs, to be seen, and if you were going to be seen, you had to dress the part.

Also, when you've got all that money you want to spend it: It's nice to make big gestures and pay for somebody's hospital bill or finance somebody in a big deal. And *that* can get to be a bad habit. For people have many sad stories. And so you loan money that is never paid back. You help out somebody, usually a somebody who will never learn to help himself, except to your money. Success can make you feel very guilty. You hear, over and over, "Look at all you've got. All I need is a few lousy bucks that you'd never miss. You've had all the breaks." You're a sucker. You give. And you have to keep on working, because you *do* miss those "few bucks"—a few thousand here, a few thousand there.

Those who work, get work. And the hours are just as long, the lights are just as hot, and the required energy is just as great in the routine, dull pictures as in the good ones. In the good ones there are those moments like islands of beauty. The moments that make memories—in the mind of an actor as well as his audience.

I saw almost all of the movies that were made in this era. Mostly in projection rooms, not as entertainment, but to keep up with other work that was being done. I viewed them critically but I didn't become a very good critic! My viewing was often faintly tinged with jealousy: "Now there's a part I would like to have played!" Irene Dunne came in for most of my envy—she *always* seemed to get better parts! I went to previews and like everyone I was happy at a hit and troubled if it was bad. For whatever was good for the business was good for the rest of us.

Back to Culver City and MGM. I always found it a cold place perhaps because it was so big. I believe it had the biggest area of any studio—except for the back lot of Universal. They had more stages—27 to be exact, over 400,000 square feet of sound stages alone.

The back lot had many permanent streets, with big trees and homes that could have their faces changed for whatever period the picture required. The feature player and star dressing rooms were constantly being renewed and redecorated until in the later years they were suites as fine as any hotel.

The studio where I had been happiest was Warner Brothers. You knew everybody, people seemed to keep their jobs there for a very long time; there wasn't the constant turnover for efficiency's sake. People in the front office were available, you could go and pass the time of day or make a complaint to the producers.

(My complaints were usually received with a good-natured, "Stick to acting, Mary.") At Metro, I felt the producers to be remote in their heavily carpeted soundproof offices. And most of them had the psychological gimmick of making the caller uncomfortable by having to walk a long way before he reached the billiard-table-size desk.

But MGM had the best stable of contract players. That gives you an idea: "stable." As in horses, not as in permanence. They could really make "all-star" pictures and they made bad ones too. Like this little job I took: *Woman Against Woman*. Producer Edward Chodorov, Director Robert B. Sinclair, Cameraman Ray June were top men. And stars Herbert Marshall and that beautiful gal Virginia Bruce. Margaret Culkin Banning's nice little short story underwent some unfortunate change on its way to the screen, however.

Let's draw a veil over this "seriocomic marital drama," and move on to one that was at least fun, and had for its star a chunky little fourteen-year-old who sang. Who sang even then, and belted out her songs with more emotional quality than any fourteen-year-old should have.

The studio had big plans for this already veteran song-and-dance girl. *The Wizard of Oz* was coming up, for instance, but in the meantime Judy Garland was in this little semimusical domestic comedy called *Listen, Darling*. The story was light, and it was played lightly, thanks to director Ed Marin. I was Judy's mother (the first of a long career of "Mothers for Metro"). I was a widow whose two other children were Freddie Bartholomew and Scotty Beckett—and they saved me from making the wrong marriage and presented me with Walter Pidgeon. Nice going, kiddies! In it Judy sang "Zing! Went the Strings of My Heart" and something that went "they're playing ten pins in the sky" when Scotty Beckett got frightened of a storm. And at the finish we *all* sang "On the Bumpy Road to Love." It sounds pretty icky, and it was. But working with Judy was sheer joy. She was young and vital and got the giggles regularly. You just couldn't get annoyed, because she couldn't help it—it was no act. Something would strike her funny, and her face would get red and "There goes Judy!" would

With Judy Garland in
LISTEN, DARLING (1938)

be the cry. And we just had to wait until she got over it. She was a kid, a real kid. It didn't take long for her to get over that.

During the picture I went riding one Sunday and took a bad fall from my horse and was laid up in the hospital for a couple of weeks. The injury was to my back and when I returned to the picture I had a gimpy walk, which was "shot around"; I did scenes where I didn't *have* to walk. But the gimpy walk was all Judy needed: "I'm sorry, Mom, but you just look so funny!" And there would go Judy.

There was enough time before the year ended for me to do one picture and then I was going to have to quit for a while. I had married again, to Manuel del Campo, one of the young men of Ruth Chatterton's salon of admirers, and I was carrying a baby. The picture was delayed for story reasons, which made me pretty nervous. Claudette Colbert was the star and she had story approval rights. Stars who had those rights liked to exercise them, not necessarily to the story's advantage. In Claudette's case, she saw to it that the story focused on her at all times. Claudette was a star and had many limitations. She was pretty rather than beautiful; she had some difficult angles to her face—not as difficult as she thought—but every close-up had to be shot showing only the left three-quarters angle of her face. The right side of her face was called "the other side of the moon" because nobody ever saw it. She was a good comedian, and she herself was bright and witty.

In *Midnight* she surrounded herself with good people: Don Ameche (well . . .), Francis Lederer, Rex O'Malley, Monty Woolley—and John Barrymore and his new wife, Elaine Barrie.

The delay on the picture worried both me and the wardrobe department. My waistline was getting thick. The clothes were those of a rich woman, so Edith Head saw to it that I was enveloped in furs; or I was seated behind a bridge table or presiding at luncheon. I was also supposed to lead a conga line at a big party. But we fixed it in the story that I had to be called to the telephone.

Seeing Jack again, working with him, was saddening. He was so changed. He was sick and old (only in his fifties) and he had been through some events in connection with Miss Barrie that had made the country laugh at him. He was vague and quiet and sat on the set barely talking to anyone. For most of his scenes he required prompt cards, carried off-camera by the prop man. This in itself at that time was considered a subject for sniggering: "The old boy's lost his marbles." Of course, later, TV developed cue cards and Teleprompters to a fine art. But even with cue cards and only a faint idea of what the picture was all about, he had enough years of experience behind him to be able to act rings around anyone else.

I played his wife in the picture and we had a few scenes together. It was all very strange. He hardly spoke to me off the set —politely, impersonally. Once we were sitting off-camera in the usual canvas chairs waiting to be called. Saying nothing. I reached over and touched his hand, gently, because I was remembering another time, so very long ago. He snatched his hand away as though it had been burned and he glared at me and said, "Don't." Tears came weakly to his eyes and he fisted them away and laughed and said, "My wife—ah—Miss Barrie—is very jealous."

With Francis Lederer in MIDNIGHT (1939)   *Harry Wilkinson.*

I saw him only once again. A few years later when he was doing a weekly radio show in which he permitted Rudy Vallee to make a clown of him. I was doing a *Lux Theater* or something that immediately followed his show. I was on the second floor of the building where the dressing rooms were. A long bleak fluorescent lighted hall: There was no one else around and I saw him walking alone down the hall ahead of me. I wanted to catch up and say hello, but I didn't. He had stopped, like someone who just couldn't walk another step; he leaned against the wall in sheer fatigue, his body sagged. It was no time to intrude, so I retraced my steps. I couldn't help thinking: Where was everybody? Where were the valets, the little train of admiring hangers-on, the designers with drawings to be approved, secretaries with a sheaf of letters to be signed? I hated all the Barrymore jokes—the sick ones, the dirty ones. I hated the people who said, "I was with Jack at a bar one night . . ." ready to recount a wild story. This was a giant of a man, one of the few greats of our time. He was a man with enormous dignity, and he never lost it. He occasionally threw it away—for his own reasons. But that was *his* business. And now, in that long bleak hall, I saw a man who was catching his breath before doing battle, and quite a battle it was, with death.

My scenes in *Midnight* were finally telescoped into a few days work—it was getting to be too much of a problem—and I retired for a few months to enjoy idleness, to lie in the sun, to prepare my little daughter for the new baby. I could read to be content, relieved of the stress and pressure of picture-making.

11

DO YOU REMEMBER THE MIRACLE of the seagulls in the history of the Mormons and Brigham Young and Salt Lake City? I believe there is a monument to the feathered heroes who appeared just at the right moment to save the crops and the lives of the early settlers.

Well, how are you going to put this event on the screen? Crickets appeared in a great cloud and then settled down to munch everything in their path. The Mormons went out into the fields with anything they could lay hands on, brooms, sticks, pokers, scythes, and flailed away at them, but it was a losing battle. They kept coming in waves, and there was nothing left to do but to pray.

Then out of the west came the gulls and in nothing flat they had the situation under control. It was a miracle. None of the Mormons had ever heard of seagulls flying so far inland.

O.K. Simple enough to get stock shots of a flock of seagulls against the sky. Simple enough to capture a few of them and turn them loose in a small area where the property man has dumped the food they like the best. But what about the crickets?

Dear little things. I'd always loved the funny little lonesome sound they make in the night. The "good luck" to find one in the house. The cricket on the hearth. A cozy picture, a cottagey picture. A kettle singing over the red coals, water for the tea. And someone knitting in a rocking chair. The tiny cages in Chinatown in San Francisco in which to keep a cricket for his small contentment-making song.

Well these babies were another variety altogether. Oh yes, we found them. The location man, like the property man, is undefeatable. They are inventive and resourceful. All they say is, "Tell me what you want."

We were discussing this magician-like quality one day at the studio, and the director for a joke decided to put it to the test. "Hey, Limey!" he called to our property man on the set. "Yes, *sir*," he replied, running over to where we were talking.

"Look, Limey. I need to have a pink ceramic elephant, about two feet high, that will blow green incense from his trunk. Not steadily, you understand, but at intervals, in little puffs about two seconds apart."

Limey nodded, understandingly. "It'll take a minute, boss," he said.

And the location man, the man who scours the countryside or the cities and towns for just the right building, background, streets, has the same ingenuity. He has to check weather conditions, attend to hundreds of details for housing and feeding a movie company, get permits from the local police, permits from people to use their property. Once it has been decided not to build it on the back lot.

Of course, you couldn't find anything that resembled the town of Salt Lake City in its pioneer stages, so "research" went to work, and from drawings and historical descriptions it emerged in a clearing somewhere near Big Bear, with a pine woods background. Streets of log cabins, kitchen gardens, a community well.

The logistics of shooting a picture of epic quality such as *Brigham Young: Frontiersman* were impressive. "Frontiersman" in the title was to steer the audience from thinking it had religion as its theme, or polygamy, or persecution. These matters were touched on briefly to set the stage, and then it was an account of the grueling trip of the band of followers of Brigham Young from Nauvoo, Illinois, through the West and over the Rockies until

With Dean Jagger in
BRIGHAM YOUNG:
FRONTIERSMAN (1940)

one day Dean Jagger as Brigham would stand with the wind in his long-haired wig and exclaim the historical words, "This is the place."

I can't remember how many location trips we made. We had to be in the desert—and heat. We had to be up in the mountains in snow and cold. Not only us, the company and the crew, but the train of covered wagons, the horses, cattle, livestock of a whole community—and the people who took care of all that animal life. We wore the costumes of the 1870s, the women in long skirts, long sleeves, high collars, sunbonnets and aprons. Hot as hell in the desert, cold in the mountains, even with long johns and woolen shawls.

This was the picture that finished off the 1930s for me, and began the 1940s. I had graduated from, I hoped, ever again playing just the "love interest": Linda Darnell and Tyrone Power, bless 'em, carried those dull honors. I had the more mature role of Brigham Young's first wife, Mary Ann. Other wives were barely hinted at. Jean Rogers and a couple of other young women were occasionally seen in another wagon.

The plague of the crickets was the final big episode of the picture. Filming the scenes depended on the crickets. It seems that near the town of Elko, Nevada, about every five years a horde of the creatures would migrate into an area (at that time; I'm sure that with modern extermination methods they have been eliminated), and they were controlled by local experts within a strip about five miles' long and a mile wide. It must have been some sort of cycle of growth because once they found their hunting ground they didn't fly away again. In fact they didn't even jump very high, so that the metal stripping had to be only a couple of feet high, and it was slippery so they couldn't crawl over. They'd come to these barriers and die by the million and the stench was appalling.

The crickets didn't arrive right on schedule, and the location man was in constant communication with the Elko Chamber of Commerce. Once they arrived we would have to drop everything else that was scheduled and get up there, for they didn't last very long in that confined area. We spoke of them as of temperamental actors: "Crickets arrive yet?" "Don't they *know* they're holding up the schedule!"

Finally the call came, "Crickets sighted!" and crew and company, including a hundred or so extras were flown up in chartered planes to Elko.

The schedule was for four days of shooting. It was just to be scenes of the battle lines of the people ineffectually driving the crickets off the precious crops of grain.

The first few hours of the first morning were full of practical jokes, with squeals from the girls when somebody would put a cricket down the neck of a dress. But in a very short time, none of it was a joke.

These particular members of the family of crickets came in a size that was vulgar in comparison to our dear little fellow of hearth and home—about the size of my thumb—and they had beady eyes that moved and could *look* at you. The camera and crew had a metal barricade to protect them, but even so, a few got in—on the pants leg of someone who stepped over the barricade.

A cricket lodged in the finder of the lens on a camera, and when one of the operators started to look through and the cricket looked back at him, his string of violent words was an indication that the situation was getting to be more than just annoying. The script girl found one in her container of coffee and was promptly sick over the side of the barrier. The women of the cast, including myself, went on strike until the wardrobe department could do something about our long dresses so the damn bugs (they were just "bugs" now!) wouldn't crawl up our legs. Hurriedly, a sort of harem pants arrangement was stitched to the bottoms of the skirts, with elastic around our ankles.

At noon it was 110 degrees in the field, and we were having to cope with some cases of sunstroke. We were more or less safe outside the barrier that stretched in a long, shining line clear out of sight over the hill. Against this barrier the crickets had piled up a foot deep, trying to crawl over each other; then they poured some kind of insecticide on them and they were struggling and dying and stinking in the heat.

Long shots, medium shots, close-ups—our lines would form and we'd go after them with our weapons, flailing, yelling, sweating, and we weren't acting!

The end of the first day came, and Henry Hathaway, the director, had a problem. He wouldn't be able to keep the company on this job for any four days. They were conferring in little groups in the hotel rooms. The hell with the pay—they were going back to Los Angeles! Hathaway and the script writer went to work, and with some judicious cutting and telescoping of scenes he found he could condense the work and promised everybody we'd be through by noon tomorrow if we all pitched in and didn't hold things up by grousing and complaining.

We started in as soon as the sun was up, and you never saw a movie company work with such deadly earnestness. There were no jokes. There was little conversation at all. There were no coffee breaks. And the hell with the makeup and hairdos. We looked terrible and that was just fine.

Henry put another camera to work on another part of the field for very close shots—of crickets crawling on someone's arm and hand, of crickets devouring a stalk of wheat in a matter of seconds. Of Brigham's face sweating and despairing. Of my face, ditto.

We didn't make it by noon. But we had it all in the can by four o'clock that afternoon, which in itself was an heroic accomplishment, considering the amount of film we shot. And then we all went back to the location at Big Bear where, comfortably, we could have scenes of looking up into the sky and seeing the miraculous arrival of our rescuers in close-up, sans crickets.

With Bette Davis in THE GREAT LIE (1941). The haircut that
set a fashion and the role that won an Oscar

Many of the people I worked with are now only a dimly remembered name, or familiar only because of *The Late, Late Show*.
Some are dead, others disappeared from public view. But there
are several who are, for all time, unforgettable.

Like Bette Davis. A rare combination: a star *and* an actress. To
her the terms were interchangeable; if you were one, you were
the other.

She is an actress of amazing versatility, in spite of being highly
mannered, easily imitated by the nightclub mimics. (Walk with a
hip-swinging stride, gesture with a cigarette, pounce down heavily
on a few words—and you've got it. Or have you?) Her personal
domination of a character only served to strengthen it. She even
lent emphasis to other characters in a film, for the way she
behaved toward or reacted to other characters often said more
than the actor who was doing the part.

She has made some great films, but, like all of us, she had her
potboilers and contract fillers. One of them was *The Great Lie*

(1940). There was a part in the picture—almost a bit, but interesting. At the time of casting, this character was merely the obstacle to an idyllic love affair between Bette, the charming owner of a Virginia farm, and George Brent, a charming geologist who traveled around a lot. The Other Woman was discussed, rarely seen—merely a threat in the background. She was a concert pianist, famous, aggressive, a real bitch. I was delighted to test for it. The test was mostly to see if the actress playing the part could make her look like an authentic concert pianist. She had to be seen doing some of the Tschaikovsky Concerto # 1 in B-flat minor, with the orchestra. I was no pianist, but I had studied piano for many years, and during the test I sounded off with the opening big chords.

Bette herself telephoned the decision to me: I was it. She had wanted me, but the fact that I didn't play with "spaghetti arms" had clinched it. And I was very happy, for it was a complete departure for me; even though the part was small, it could be effective. It didn't stay small for very long, thanks to Bette's story acumen. I get a little annoyed (or at least I *did!*) when reviewers or commentaries say I stole the picture from Bette or that I out-acted Miss Davis. It *became* the better part, and not because of generosity on Bette's part, but because she was trying to save a lousy story.

I had met Bette only a few times, I had never worked with her, and her manner around the set the first few days did little to recommend her as a person who would be easy to work with.

She was sullen and standoffish. She sat in the canvas chairs, smoked furiously and swung her foot in the angry rhythm of a cat's tail. And I wasn't happy at all. Before the picture began she had been very nice, very helpful, especially with the rather distinctive hairdo we dreamed up. My hair was, in the fashion of the time, in a long bob to my shoulders. We wanted to get a severity to the look and I twisted my hair up into a French roll tight to my head. It looked good, but still a bit too soft. I said, "Why can't we have Perc [Westmore] cut it to this shape?" She grinned and said, "Oh, *Mary!* would you? would you *dare?* It's going to look very extreme." I would and did—and that skull-shaped sculptured hairdo became the next trend in hair fashion after the picture was released. The clothes were stunning, designed by Orry-Kelly. Eddie Goulding, the director, had given me a synthesis of the woman, "A piano, brandy, and men. In that order." That was her life. Totally selfish and ruthless about anything else.

We were shooting a sequence in a restaurant where Bette and I first meet—after quite a bit of the picture has gone by—remember we rarely shot in sequence. I was very uncomfortable; I didn't see how I was going to top this gal as a bitch. And it had to be done. The atmosphere on the set was very sticky.

One morning Bette said to me in a very peremptory manner, "Hey, Astor! let's go talk a minute!" We went to her portable and she closed the door and I had the old "What have I done now!" feeling. She flopped on the couch and said, "This picture is going to stink! It's just too too incredible for words." Well! She went on, "I can't get anywhere up front unless I have something to offer that will make it better. You've got to help." How? "You and I, really just us, because I've talked to writers and to Eddie, and everybody's satisfied but me, so it's up to us to rewrite this piece of junk to make it more interesting. All I do now is mewl to George about 'that woman you married when you were drunk,' and to 'please come back to me' and all that crap. And that's just soap opera." What wasn't soap opera, she went on to explain hopefully, was simply a different point of view: a constant conflict between Sandra and the, so far, sappy southern gal who has lost her childhood sweetheart. That would be the story. A declaration of war between the two women and a negotiable but tenuous peace.

In a few sentences the story still sounds pretty "soapy" but it became unimportant. The confrontations and the conflicts between us would be very interesting. Without using character names too much, to avoid being confusing, this was the gist of the "plot." Bette would find out that I am pregnant, and that I am furious at having my career spoiled by having a baby in my life, along with a rather dull husband. So Bette's proposition is that if I will divorce George without telling him about the baby, she, Bette, can marry him. He is due to go on a geological expedition to South America. While he is gone, she and I will go away someplace and I will have the baby secretly, and she will take it as her own, giving her George's baby and a firm hold on George. Later, when George comes back and is a very proud father, Bette suffers from the lie, I renege and there's hell to pay for a while. Pretty "soapy."

But the interesting part, the fun part, was in the relationship between the two women—the savage bargaining—their strange life together in a small town in Nevada while awaiting the child. These are the scenes that Bette and I rewrote, and they were real "female" scenes. A couple of cats who had to shield their claws for expediency, with the continual threat that one or the other would blow the whole setup.

Bette's concern for this bored, restless, pregnant woman was the solicitude for a prize mare about to drop a foal. Keeping her comfortable and healthy. Bette awakes in the night and hears a noise in the kitchen: The house is remote, primitive, no help. She goes out and surprises me with a flashlight at the refrigerator: "Oh, Sandra, *pickles!*"

They take walks in the desert, they play double solitaire, and they hate each other—and Sandra doesn't take the trouble to conceal it. Finally the baby is born, and while Sandra is being attended in the bedroom of the house, Bette stalks outside in the chilly dawn, in riding boots. The riding boots were Bette's idea. There were some objections: "But they'll laugh—the audience will get the similarity of a husband pacing the floor of a hospital." Bette said, "Let 'em. A laugh at this point is fine!" They laughed.

Earlier and again later in the picture, we see Sandra in the concert hall. I am hardly pianist enough to tackle the Concerto, but they wanted to have the reality of the scene, to *see* Sandra playing instead of just shoulder movements in close-ups. I believe this is the first time that synchronization was used. I "played" on a dummy piano, the music had been simplified so that I could do the arpeggios and the octave runs without having to hit every single note, but I had to be right on the nose in the long jumps back and forth between upper and lower registers. Max Rabino-vitch played a real piano off-camera. And later there were very close shots of Norma Boleslavsky's hands actually playing. It was a very slick job of editing—of both film and sound. I of course had had to memorize and practice the last four pages of the Concerto.

It was very weird when we shot the scene. Here I was in front of a full symphony orchestra following the conductor, hearing Max's piano, and feeling almost as though it were I who was play-ing. It was very exhilarating. José Iturbi paid me a great compli-ment afterward. He said he knew, naturally, that I couldn't play that well, I couldn't have had the time in my life to learn, and yet, "How could you *not* be playing? I have played the Concerto many times, and you were right in there!"

The music gave another facet to Sandra: She had to be a student and a great artist. It gave her dignity, another dimension besides her ruthlessness, her selfish bitchiness. So when I received my Oscar I didn't thank all the "little people" (that phony bit of gratitude in bad taste!). I thanked two great people, Miss Davis and Tschaikovsky. I'm sure Mr. Tschaikovsky would have been terribly pleased.

I think the reason Bette and I could hate each other so effectively on the screen was that we liked each other so much off the screen. There was no impediment of conflicting personalities. Liking each other there was no self-consciousness when the barbed sentences and the acid contempt flowed between us. We could work *together*. We laughed so much at the maliciousness we invented during the scenes. Eddie Goulding would clap a palm to his head and say, "My God! only a couple of women could think of that!" And other times, "Well, ladies—if you're *ready*—would you kindly inform me as to what you are going to do?"

There was a scene where we were playing the everlasting double solitaire after dinner (a not too subtle bit of symbolism), and Sandra needs a drink, badly. Bette says, "O.K., the doctor said you could have some brandy—just an ounce." And I make a noise of disgust. Bette said, "It needs more protest than that. Sandra wouldn't be satisfied with less than a pint." I agreed, "She probably never heard of an ounce of anything in the liquor line." "That's *it!* Why don't you say, 'Whoever heard of an ounce of brandy!' and growl it like you do, Mary." Then we'd laugh at our own inventiveness—at least we were having a good time, even if the audience wouldn't!

We worked very hard, and enjoyed it thoroughly. There wasn't very much we could do about the fact that the story was nothing but a shoddy little melodrama. Bette's southern gal, jilted and tearful, unswerving in her devotion to her ex-fiancé, had one redeeming quality. She was human enough to hold a child over the man's head as a club, which is a neat trick and pretty unpleasant but it's been done. Sandra? Well, I've never known a pianist like her—or a woman like her for that matter. Both of us did a lot of "acting," "effect-getting," "look-at-us-being." I know that I never "put the pot on to boil" before a scene of Sandra. I never

[155]

knew what she was thinking, I just knew what she was doing. I'm
sure that Sandra would never have thought twice about having
an abortion since the child was so completely unwanted, but that
was waved away with a weak excuse when the point came up for
discussion. We would have to assume that she was much too
famous, liable to blackmail affecting her career, etc. The point,
of course, was that then we'd have had no story.

Anyhow, I made it.

The Academy Award in those days was not tainted with the
enormous publicity gimmick that it is today. There was no campaigning. The Academy members were not overwhelmed with
propaganda, records of music, special showings of films, trade
and newspaper ads. It was simply that the members of a profession were allowed to have *their* say, *their* professional opinion, as
to who had done the best job in his or her field during the year.
There were also fewer categories. The awards were given at a big
dinner at one of the hotels—no television then—somebody made a
little speech and then the winner of the year before presented the
statue to the new winner, who acknowledged it by a short—repeat
—short speech of thanks. The press took some pictures afterward,
there was a lot of congratulating and that was that. Frankly, I
think it was much more exciting, much more real. All the stage
production, the entrances and exits, the cued music, has diluted
the whole idea and now it looks simply like an orgy of backslap-
ping. Everybody gets an award for something: "Best screenplay,
based on another medium"; "Best original score, not a musical";
"Best story and screenplay based on material not previously published or produced"; "Best short subject, live action"; "Best short
subject, foreign language." Every category imaginable, and all
those strange characters galumphing up to the podium and mess-
ing up the production! In "my day" there were no absentees, no
one received the Award for the winner. Of course there were no
companies shooting in Europe at that time—at least none of ours
—but no actor with a nomination would have even thought of
staying home that big night if he were in Hollywood, or even on
location. He'd *get* there, because it *was* a great honor.

The Great Lie was filmed in December of 1940 and released
in April of 1941, so it wasn't eligible for Academy attention until
1942. A great deal had happened to me—oh yes, and incidentally
to the world—during that period. I had my own weekly radio

show, called *Hollywood Showcase,* which I emceed, introducing young unknown professionals. Its format was more intimate than the show it copied; it really gave young actors, singers, musicians a chance to be heard, and many got jobs as a result. James Daley was one of the alumni, as were Bea Benaderet and Dane Clark. They had been doing jobs in radio for a long time, with few knowing their names.

I also was appearing regularly on the hour-long radio dramas for Lux and Screen Actors' Guild, *Suspense, The Mercury Theater,* etc.

I made *The Maltese Falcon* early in 1941, and a follow-up with Bogart called *Across the Pacific* which was a story of how the Japanese were thwarted from bombing Pearl Harbor. Only the Japanese double-crossed us, and we had to change our locale to the Panama Canal. Someone said, seriously: "Gee, suppose they bomb the Canal. We'll just have to shelve the picture!"

I too was pretty annoyed with the war because I had just learned to fly, and shortly after my solo flight, the government grounded all private planes. To top it all, because of the war, my Oscar was not the familiar tall shiny metal figurine, but a small plaque with cheap plating, and Oscar was in low relief at one side. (Hey, Academy! I would dearly love to have a real Oscar!) Also, because of the war the Academy dinner was not the dressy affair it had been; everyone wore business suits and daytime dresses. We gals still had our furs, of course!

But our insulation was not perfect; it cracked here and there and the troubles of the times got through to us, at long last, rudely, annoyingly, not very deeply. My *Hollywood Showcase,* which had been running for over a year, was canceled. We had been very successful; the sponsors, the Richard Hudnut cosmetic people, were pleased and happy. Disappointed, I asked my producer, Russ Johnson, "Why?" "Because nobody is interested in getting young men good jobs as actors." And for the first time I heard the phrase, "There's a war on, you know!"

My husband went off to be a flyer in England, and never came back. Oh, nothing like that; I just got "Dear Janed."

I began to think, more often than ever, "What's so damned important about being an actress?" I saw my little world, insulated, self-absorbed, limited. And all the twenty years of hard work seemed sour and futile. It was a partial acceptance of reality, but it still was a bit like a child saying, "You mean there isn't any Santa Claus?" I wasn't aware of, nor ready to accept, the fact that the mere doing, the achieving, was the point. Not *what* I had achieved. For what I had achieved would in due time be forgotten. The *doing* was important, it was part of my being—of what and who I am.

12

BEFORE THE LIGHTS WENT OUT, there was *The Maltese Falcon.* There is very little I can say about that one, because everything has been said. But anyway, "Shall we talk about the Black Bird?"

So often, I have been asked "What was it like?" to work in a picture that was so ahead of its time, such a departure in methods, point of view, etc. Of course you don't know you're making history while you're in there making it. We were, all of us, excited about a good story—one that had everyone confused! However, the "where was who when what happened" could be traced down. There wasn't a loophole in it. It helped a great deal that we shot the picture in sequence, except for some exterior night shots on the street set. But even so, John Huston often had to call time out to clear up matters. All of us had read the Dashiell Hammett book and studied the script, but it got so that when the "now just a minute" look came on to somebody's face, it became a joke to say, "When did Brigid shoot Thursby? On Friday!"

I had a lovely pot to boil for Brigid. It was quite a bitches' cauldron. First of all, she was a congenital liar ("I am a liar. I've always been a liar!"), and slightly psychopathic. And that kind of liar wears the face of truth, although they send out all sorts of signals that they are lying. There is an unstable quality to them like nitro. One of the tip-offs is they can't help breathing rather rapidly. So, I hyper-ventilated before going into most of the scenes. It gave me a heady feeling, of thinking at cross purposes. For there wasn't a single scene in the picture where what I said was even close to what I was thinking. In order not to cross myself up I had to keep it down to mostly one thought, "He's got to believe this." Brigid had to oversell so that when Sam Spade said, "You're good—you're very good!" the grateful smile had to be there, but the respiration rate would go up automatically, because she was scared stiff.

It was Huston's picture, Huston's script. He'd had the wit to keep Hammett's book intact. His shooting script was a precise map of what went on. Every shot, camera move, entrance, exit was down on paper, leaving nothing to chance, inspiration or invention. Nobody improvised their way through this one! So let me hear the one about the "agony" of "limitation." It was highly limited, almost stylized. We never took our time with a scene. When Johnnie said, "Action!" we were off and running. Even for the most deliberate scenes—Greenstreet's settling back to tell the history of the Black Bird—there was an exciting reason, not just dull exposition. For just when you thought he was being pretty damn long-winded about it all, you got it: He was waiting for the knockout drops to work on Spade.

Poor Sydney! He never did live down the Fat Man. I don't think he ever did a picture later in which that evil, hiccupy laugh wasn't exploited. He was a very fine, very versatile actor, within his physical limitations. The *Falcon* was his first picture and he was as nervous in his first scene—that same long-winded monologue—as though all his years in the theater counted for nothing. He said to me, "Mary dear, hold my hand, tell me I won't make an ass of meself!"

We had a more than adequate schedule for the picture. Because John's script was well prepared, and because he took time in rehearsal, the shooting went very quickly. Often there is much time lost in lack of preparation. There was and is too much of "Let's rehearse with film" in the hopes that something might happen that would be spontaneous and fresh, and wouldn't happen again. Sometimes it's true, sometimes it's good, but usually the director who does his homework not only comes in under the wire, but without any loss of quality. Of course, if you have actors who come unstuck, not because they are "artistic" and need "freedom to try something else" but because they lack any kind of professional firmness, or ability to get with it, to concentrate, then it all takes time. And something spontaneous and fresh may, in the finished picture, stand out in limbo. The *Falcon* was a jigsaw puzzle, and each scene related to what had happened before and what was to happen—precisely. In emotional levels, in tempos, in cadence of speech and movement. In passing, it is interesting perhaps to note that imitations of various scenes in the *Falcon,* and there have been many, just don't work. They don't have the chilling quality, because they are out of context.

John used his time to rehearse. He used his own personal intensity to excite us; we were never "back on our heels." And when he said "Let's make it—" we were ready. As a result there were never many takes to a scene and so we had lots of time to play.

And could that company play! If you recall, a tall burly figure staggers into Spade's office late one night, clutching a heavy package wrapped in torn newspapers. He is dressed in the clothes of a seaman, with his peaked cap pulled down over his eyes. He is the captain of the ship which burned in port late that afternoon. He mutters something about "the Falcon—the Bird—" and falls dead on the floor of the office with some bullet holes in him.

Just a bit—you never saw him before—and that's all he has to do, just stagger in and fall and drop the package. John thought it would be great fun to have his father, Walter Huston, come in one morning and do the part. And so did Walter—his son's first movie, etc. A bit of fun-sentiment.

John took hours to film it, and Walter got very grumpy: "Didn't expect to have to put in a day's *work.*"

"Let's do it again. Sorry, Dad, you missed your mark."

"Take seven. Sorry, Dad. This time, try it without staggering so much."

"Take ten, please. Sorry, Dad. We've got to reload."

The next day, after they'd seen the rushes—they were fine, of course—John told me to call Walter's home and pretend to be his, John's, secretary. I called on the set phone and when Walter answered I told him that Mr. Huston was sorry, but that we'd have to retake the sequence that afternoon—something had happened to the film in the lab—and could he be ready to shoot at one o'clock?

I held the receiver from my ear and everybody could hear Walter yelling, "You tell my son to get another actor or go to hell! He made me take twenty falls, and I'm sore all over, and I'm not about to take twenty more. Or even *one!*"

There were other elaborate practical jokes, one of which was "Shock the Tourists." We didn't want people around watching us. We had an odd childlike territorial imperative about our set. It was hard work, and we didn't want anyone looking over our shoulder, so to speak. Also, we had a sneaky feeling that we were doing something different and exciting, and we didn't want to show it to anyone until it was finished. Hard to explain.

It all started one afternoon when we were lined up on a shot where I sit down and cross my knees elaborately—I think it was in Spade's office. I looked down and said, "Hold it a minute, I've got a goddam run in my stocking." I looked up and a little to the side of the camera was the publicity man with a half-dozen gentlemen of the cloth. They were ushered out politely by the publicity man who looked a little pale. When the big doors closed, everybody whooped and hollered and said, "That's our girl! That's the way to get 'em off the set!" After that John dreamed up an act for each one of us—designated by numbers. A stream of Helen Hokinson type club women would come in cooing like pigeons with the excitement of seeing Bogart, and John would sing out, "Number Five, kiddies. Number Five!" At which Bogie would go into the prepared act with Greenstreet. He'd start yelling at him, calling him a fat old fool, "Who the hell do you think you are? You upstaged me, and I'm telling you I'm not having any—" and John would be pleading with him to hold his temper. Very quickly, the uncomfortable and disillusioned ladies would exit and we could go back to work.

"Number Ten" was a bit more involved. I had to get into my portable with Peter Lorre before a group got over to where we were working. When they had been guided into position by the gracious John Huston, saying politely, "I think you'll see just fine right over here," in sight of the door of my dressing room, he would then call out, "O.K., I think we're ready for Number Ten, now." Peter would open the door and come down the steps fastening his fly, and I would stick my head out the door, waving coy fingers as he said, "See you later, Mary."

Our long-suffering publicity man was not stupid. He finally came to John saying, "May I have your permission, *sir,* to bring over some rather important guests this afternoon? Without benefit of your goddam gags?" And John said, "You can try, my friend, you can try." Soon the *Falcon* company became a closed set and we could get our work done without people gaping at us.

The Lakeside Golf Club was just across the highway from Warner Brothers Studio and had a pleasant poolside dining area. Several of us were members and almost every day the company would gather there for a long hour and a half lunch period. People from other companies would eye us suspiciously because we weren't wolfing down sandwiches in a hurry to get back to work. We could boast smugly, "We're 'way ahead of schedule." I remember one sequence that we rehearsed late one afternoon. It would run about seven minutes. Johnnie had it planned to be shot with two cameras, both on tracks. We worked it out in detail in the afternoon and the next morning shot it in two takes and went over to Lakeside about eleven and played around the pool for the rest of the day. Seven minutes is a good day's work.

The combination of Huston, Bogart and Lorre was very fast company in the wit department; there was a kind of abrasive, high-powered kidding-on-the-level thing that went on, and you joined in at your own risk. Just to get into the act, one day at Lakeside I made the mistake of piping up with some kind of naïve smart crack and the ribbing was turned on to me unmercifully. I did the best I could for a while, but it was more than I could handle. I got sort of backed into a corner: "Then you *admit* you don't like pointillism, that the Fauves were a bunch of jerks?" "I didn't say that, I just said——" My eyes started to smart and I whimpered, "I just can't keep up with this!" Bogie laughed his head off, along with the rest and then got up and came around the table to my place. He wiped my tears away with elaborate care. "You're O.K., baby," he said. "So you're not very smart—but you know it and what the hell's the matter with that!" Although it still was on a kidding level, Bogie really meant what he said. "Be yourself. Be yourself and you're in."

THE MALTESE FALCON
(1941) *Above:*
With Humphrey
Bogart and Peter
Lorre *Mack
Elliott, Warner
Bros. Below:* With
Bogie *Mack
Elliott, Warner
Bros.*

THE MALTESE FALCON (1941) *Above:* With Elisha Cook, Jr.,
Sydney Greenstreet and Bogie *Mack Elliott, Warner Bros.*
Below: With Ward Bond, Bogie, Barton MacLane *John Ellis,
Warner Bros.*

Bogie just didn't have time to be anything but himself. He was a hardworking guy, a good craftsman. He would have hooted if anyone had called him an artist. (I would, but not to his face!) To him, "artist" meant someone unpredictable and fancy pants. He would have made a wisecrack if anybody had called him "Humphrey"—or even "Mr. Bogart."

He wasn't very tall; vocally he had a range from A to B; his eyes were like shiny coal nuggets pressed deep into his skull; and his smile was a mistake that he tried to keep from happening. He was no movie hero. He was no hero at all.

I have heard people say he wasn't *really* a good actor. I don't go along with that. It is true his personality dominated the character he was playing—but the character gained by it. His technical skill was quite brilliant. His precision timing was no accident. He kept other actors on their toes because he *listened* to them, he watched, he *looked* at them. He never had that vague stare of a person who waits for you to finish talking, who hasn't heard a word you have said. And he was never "upstage center" acting all by himself. He was there. With you.

As a person he looked at the world, his place in it, at movies and at life in general and he wore no rose-colored glasses. There was something about it all that made him contemptuous and bitter. He related to people as though they had no clothes on—and no skin, for that matter. If they grabbed at their various little hypocrisies for protective cover, his laugh was a particularly unpleasant chortle.

Bogie would have liked a world that was loyal and loving, truthful and generous. There was something in him that responded instantly to anyone or anything that was "for real." Not too closely. Not too deeply. He might get hooked. He was scared of "getting hooked with a dame." He hated the marriage trap, being used, being possessed, being made to buckle down as a provider. I think the remarkable Lauren Bacall knew who he was, let him be who he was and what he was, and in return, he was at last able to give something no other woman could grab from him—his total commitment.

Bogie had his troubles, his longing for a good world, his need to trust and believe in something. Like the rest of us. But he couldn't dismiss it with a philosophy, or stick his head in the sand. He was "aware" and he blew. Violently and often. And when he got drunk he was bitter and smilingly sarcastic and thoroughly unpleasant.

The Bogart cult that has emerged is very understandable. There he is, right there on the screen, saying what everyone is trying to say today, saying it loud and clear, "I hate hypocrisy. I don't believe in words or labels or much of anything else. I'm not a hero. I'm a human being. I'm not very pretty. Like me or don't like me." We who knew him well liked him. Bogie was for real.

I don't think there are many pictures which have had as many reruns as the *Falcon*. When it was first shown on TV it was just another rerun of an old movie, made to fit a time slot. It was a bad print and had been cut to pieces. Over the years it has gained respect. I don't know how they do such things, but they cleaned up the negative and the print is better, the sound has improved and today I'm sure there isn't a cut missing.

Of *course* I watch it! It's a wonderful, rich memory. Of people who were friends. There they all are, Sydney, Peter, Bogie:

Sydney: "But Miss O'Shaughnessy had, by this time, obtained the Bird." [only he says, "MissO—Shaughnessy."]

Peter: "She shtruck me! She attacked me!"

Bogie: "—and then you went down that dark alley, knowing he'd follow you—"

My dear ghosts.

The *Falcon* was eligible for Academy Awards the same year as *The Great Lie*. It got nothing. And if I'd had my druthers, I would have preferred getting my Oscar for Brigid rather than for Sandra.

Across the Pacific was an idea of the studio to cash in on the success of the *Falcon* with a quick follow-up of almost the same cast together again—at least Bogie, Greenstreet and me. They forgot one thing: a story. It was, as I said, too timely. We began filming about a week or ten days before Pearl Harbor. Since much of the plot concerned a ship sailing for Honolulu and thwarting the plans of the Japs to blow up Pearl, there was considerable rewriting to do, so we had to close the picture down. It was kind of a creepy feeling, to have been talking about "the plans of the Japanese" in the picture, and have them practically blueprint

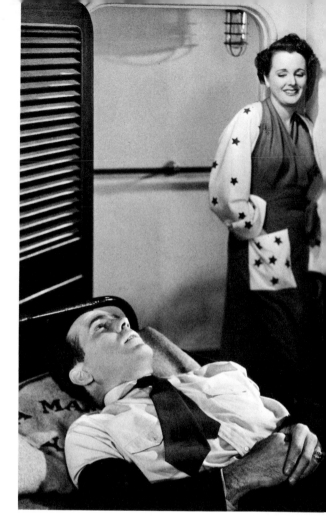

With Humphrey
Bogart in ACROSS
THE PACIFIC
(Released 1942)

our script. There was even some talk about shelving the picture,
but we reopened late in March, and then ran into more difficulty
when the government started shipping out our Nisei cast. A little
indignation and some wire-pulling held them at least until the
picture was finished. A world-shaking tragedy comes into our
lives, and characteristically all anybody was thinking of was, "How
will it affect the picture?"

A very fine Nisei actor played a part in the picture and also
acted as our technical director—translating dialogue into Japanese,
translating direction to those who had little English. We were
shooting night scenes on the back lot one April night, and this
man—call him Tom—was showing me how my name appeared on
the marquees of Japanese theaters. He was explaining and drawing

the detail of the character that indicated my first name when somebody ran up to the set yelling, "Yippee! They're bombing the hell out of Tokyo!" Tom never even lifted his head to listen, but said quietly, "Now this part of the character means . . ." His relatives all lived in Tokyo.

The crew and the company enjoyed being together again, but we missed Peter. He visited us occasionally. One afternoon he donned a white coat and walked through a scene in which Sydney, Bogie and I were being served breakfast on the ship. We didn't know John had made the switch with the actor who was playing the waiter. He was behind us, so we couldn't see him, and Peter served us, making tiny mistakes—holding a platter a bit too far away, just touching Sydney's arm as he lifted a cup of coffee. Finally he leaned down and kissed me on the back of the neck and we all broke up. We could always have fun, even though the subtle sense of success was not a part of this picture.

Most of the action was on board ship, and in the studio they had built a remarkable reproduction of one huge section of the games deck. The slow, gentle roll was effected by supporting the whole structure on hydraulic lifts. It worked constantly, almost unnoticeably, and we had several genuine cases of seasickness. There was no point in stopping it and starting it up again for a scene, for someone might have forgotten to tie down a piece of lighting equipment and have it come skittering into the scene. But the movement, a gentle breeze from the fans and the lighting, all high, like sunlight, and you could close your eyes and believe you smelled the sea.

Then John got a summons from Washington to report immediately to the department of Special Services. So now we'd lost John—and the final scenes of the picture had not been written yet. I'm sure it would have been better if John could have completed it. But as it was it got all hoked up into a chase sequence and who's after who, and a small plane being blown up and "everything turning out all right in the end."

"Turning out all right in the end" just wasn't very good anymore. It was dated. Almost any kind of lightheartedness began to be dated: Silly little jokes around the set and nonsense that seemed hilarious was no longer part of the making of a picture. The world was heavy-hearted.

There has always been an unspoken law among actors: "Don't

bring your troubles to work." Nobody works well if they're upset about something. But an actor who has to play a riproaring tragic emotional scene better feel good. There must be nothing to deplete his energy. If someone from outside brought bad news he would be blocked off: "Don't tell him now—he's got a scene to play." But now we all had troubles. Real ones.

There was nostalgia, there was bittersweetness: There was *Casablanca*, there were *For Whom the Bell Tolls, Watch on the Rhine, Mrs. Miniver*. There was music about "Comin' in on a Wing and a Prayer," "When the Lights Go on Again," "Warsaw Concerto." Even in the lighter vein there was wryness: "Gertie from Bizerte," and "Ac-*cent*-tchu-ate the Positive," and now, more popular than ever, "The Last Time I Saw Paris."

Comedy went a little wild and improbable, all about mad, mad people in Palm Beach or the South of France or something. The forerunners of our jet set. Like the picture I did with Claudette Colbert and Joel McCrea called, of course, *The Palm Beach Story*. The stereotyped ending was kidded, because each of the characters Colbert and McCrea played had a twin and there was some question about who married who.

I wore a blond wig and waved a lorgnette around and Rudy Vallee played my brother, and I could never please Preston Sturges, the director. It was just not my thing. I couldn't talk in a high, fluty voice and run my words together as he thought high-society women did, or at least *mad* high-society women who've had six husbands and six million dollars. Joel McCrea had a line to me, "Don't you ever talk about anything but Topic A?" and I had to say, "*Is* there anything else?" *That* got a real naughty yok in the theaters!

The position of the free-lance player, now that the movie purses had tightened up, was not a very good one. The studios were more inclined to use their own players instead of bargaining with the free-lancer, even though he might be more suited to a role than someone on their own lot.

I was offered a long-term contract with MGM with its secure income of a forty-week year. That twelve week layoff period per year sounds attractive, as though you could count on doing some traveling, doing a play, or even getting acquainted with your own children. But it didn't work out that way. As soon as you finished a picture you went on layoff, even if it was only five days. It was

Joel McCrea, Mary Astor in blond wig, Rudy Vallee and
Claudette Colbert in THE PALM BEACH STORY (1942)
Paramount Pictures, Inc.

never a period of time you could count on. Even if you called the
studio and said you'd like to go to New York for a couple of
weeks, there was always some hesitation before they would clear
you. You really became a piece of property. I didn't like the idea
for other reasons. Under contract, for some weird reason, you
get typed, stuck into the same part over and over again. In my
case it was mother roles. It isn't that I didn't like being a mother:
I had two wonderful kids of my own.

But Metro's Mothers never did anything but mothering. They
never had a thought in their heads except their children: They
sacrificed everything; they were domineering or else the "Eat up
all your spinach" type. Clucking like hens. Eventually every actor
on the Metro lot called me Mom. I was in my late thirties and it
played hell with my image of myself. And my femme fatale image
of the Diary days went right down the Culver City drain.

I signed the contract—for seven years—and felt very trapped,
while all around me said, "Oh, you're lucky!" And the *Reporter*
had the news that I had signed a "termer" and there was a great
deal of handshaking and "Glad to have you with us" and I was
assigned a lovely dressing room and given a lifetime studio pass.

That was like on Friday, and on Friday afternoon Metro casting phoned and said, "Be in Wardrobe eight o'clock on Monday."

"Well—ah," I well-ahed, "mind my asking? What's the picture? I haven't seen a script yet."

"Oh, you'll get one. The final hasn't been mimeoed yet. You play Susan Peters' mother."

Well, that's a big thrill. What do I do as Susan Peters' mother? Do I change her diapers or console her because the boy next door hasn't invited her to the dance? Or maybe I worry because I'm a widow and want to get married again and I'm afraid it will ruin her life. There were a *few* variations, but not many.

And what's happened to the power and the glory of an Oscar? And how long, how long will it be before another *Falcon* comes along? Or a play on Broadway? Forget it. Shut up and be happy; you've got that check coming in every week. There's a war on.

During the making of the picture with Susan Peters, my father died. He and my mother had been living in Lancaster, California, very quietly and he had been ill for some time. They had been in town to visit me and I had taken them to an afternoon showing of *The Great Lie* at our neighborhood theater. Since before my father had decided I was to be a movie star, he had ambitions for me to be a great pianist, somehow in his faltering mind when he saw me playing the piano in the picture he was almost tearfully proud that I had achieved so much. He kept commenting about my tempi and fingering and the way I made the melody *sing*. Disturbed, I tried to explain that it was a dubbing job, that I really wasn't playing, but he merely shushed me. I couldn't have disillusioned him if I'd wanted to. I had finally "pleased Daddy."

Once in a while Metro would get a big showy whopper together which was merely advertising for the company itself, utilizing every star and feature player on their contract list. It was held together by some kind of slim strand of a story which was lost very soon in the production numbers. Such a one was *Thousands Cheer*. NOT *As Thousands Cheer* which was the name of a very fine musical comedy. It had nothing to do with that; of course, if the name sounded a bit familiar you could make your own assumptions.

I played the mother of Kathryn Grayson, a very lovely girl with a fine coloratura soprano. She was quite fascinating in her total concentration on music. Often we stood together in front of the camera waiting for the lighting to be set, saying nothing. Kitty would have a vague, lost look on her face and I'd whisper, "Sing, Kitty Cat!" and out it would pour—the song she'd been singing in her mind—no beginning, no hesitation, just another breath, the middle of an aria, perhaps. It was like squeezing a Mama doll.

I had a lot of time off during the picture. All those production numbers with three bands, Mickey Rooney and Judy Garland doing a big number, and Eleanor Powell and chorus doing a big dance number, and Kathryn Grayson singing in a big number for camp shows—and all in Technicolor.

That was a first for me, being in Technicolor, and it was very flattering: Color is kind to skin, and for the first time I was a redhead on the screen. I had a lot of fan mail afterward saying, "*Why* did you dye your hair? I always loved you as a brunette." Well, I hadn't dyed my hair, and I never was a brunette. My hair was auburn and it grew right out of my scalp that way. But red, or reddish, tones photographed black, remember?

So, besides having a great deal of time during the picture, it seemed I would go on layoff right after it, with nothing scheduled for me. Maybe now was my chance to do a play.

While I was still freelancing, just before *Brigham Young,* I had played with Elliott Nugent in the first tryouts of *The Male Animal.* We played in obscure little theaters, high school auditoriums, banquet halls, up and down the Coast, while Nugent and James Thurber rewrote the show. We'd rehearse in the daytime to incorporate the new material for that evening's show. A new second-act curtain, new dialogue. It was rough, but fun. Then when Elliott asked me to go with them to New York, I had to refuse, because I had signed for *Brigham Young.* I believe the play ran for three years in its original production and then took off from there on the road, and finally summer theaters everywhere.

Now Henry Hull asked me to be with him in a show in New York—a "nice little comedy," *Many Happy Returns* by Clare Kummer. I talked to the people at Metro. There was a good deal of hemming and hawing. Maybe they could give me my twelve-week layoff in one chunk. I said I didn't think it would be right not to sign a run-of-the-play contract. Well, they couldn't let me do that. They'd give me a six-months' suspension, then if the play was a hit we'd "talk about it." I needn't have worried.

MEET ME IN ST. LOUIS (1944). Hovering around Margaret O'Brien and her doctor, Donald Curtis, are Harry Davenport, Judy Garland, Mary Astor, Lucille Bremer, and Marjorie Main

We rehearsed three weeks in New York. Opened in New Haven to frightening notices. We blamed it on a lot of things that weren't really at fault and opened in Philadelphia to more thumbs down. Mr. Hull left the show. Back to New York with a new director, changes in the cast, rewrites and more rehearsals. We opened in Boston, Christmas Day, 1944. More bad notices. And we were thoroughly trounced when we opened in New York. I saved—and savored—a few satisfying crumbs: "She has a flair for comedy hitherto kept a secret by the movies," ". . . a magnetic quality for an audience," and "Come back again, Mary, and let's see you in something good." We played six performances and closed.

I returned home very shortly and reported to Metro. They were quite happy at my failure and said, "Wonderful! We'll have something great for you real soon." A few months went by and they said they had something wonderful for me. I was to play the mother in *Meet Me in St. Louis*. Judy Garland's mother, Margaret O'Brien's mother, Lucille Bremer's mother—and some wonderful production numbers. Really wonderful.

As it happened, it did turn out to be pretty wonderful. In Technicolor. It was all so slick and beautiful. And Judy sang "Clang, clang, clang went the trolley!" and "The Boy Next Door."

I had days and days of fittings for the 1904 clothes, and they made me some beautiful Gibson-girl wigs. There is one dress by Irene Sharaff that was kept as a museum piece until they auctioned off all the memorabilia of Metro.

The dress was for the big event, the fair at St. Louis. It was pale gray silk voile, on which were appliquéd bunches of grapes in pale lavender. Each grape was a flat wooden button, covered with the material. It was very high-necked, boned up to the chin, cinched tight around a real boned corset and dripping with heavy crocheted lace. Underneath there were at least two starched petticoats, a camisole and bust ruffles. With this I carried a parasol, also embroidered and appliquéd with bunches of grapes. I had a beautiful Gibson-girl wig, and topped it with a cartwheel hat trimmed with more grapes. I wore long gloves and carried a reticule and when I got on some scales out of curiosity I found I had indeed put on twenty-five pounds.

There was a lovely romance going on. Judy was in love with Vincente Minnelli, our director. Liza's father, of course.

Judy was no longer a rotund little giggler, but her growing up was not maturing. The fun was still there and she seemed to have great energy. But it was intense, driven, tremulous. Anxious. She was working way over the capacities of any human being. She was recording at night and playing in the picture in the day, and people got annoyed when she was late on the set, and when she got jittery and weepy with fatigue. Including myself. I often felt that her behavior during this period was due to bigshotitis and very unprofessional. Making a movie was a communal effort: Everyone depended on everyone else, and for one person to keep 150 other workers sitting around on a sound stage while she fiddled with her lipstick in her dressing room was just plain bad manners.

I walked into Judy's portable dressing room one tense morning, and she greeted me with her usual cheery, "Hi, Mom!" I sat down on the couch while she went on primping, and said, "Judy, what the hell's happened to you? You were a trouper—once." She stared at me. I went on, "You have kept the entire company out there waiting for two hours. Waiting for you to favor us with your presence. You know we're stuck—there's nothing we can do without you at the moment."

She giggled and said, "Yeah, that's what everybody's been telling me."

That bugged me and I said, "Well, then, either get the hell on the set or *I'm* going home."

She grabbed me by the hand, and her face had crumpled up, "I don't *sleep*, Mom!"

And I said, "Well, go to bed earlier then—like we all have to do. You're not so damn special, baby!" and stalked out in my own unthinking high dudgeon. It was some years later before I really knew what she'd been going through.

She was a hot little flame, and I'm surprised she didn't burn out long ago. She had a great love for her work, but she didn't know how to say "No" to pressure. It was "Go, Judy, go!" all her short life.

There was great perfection of detail on this film—scenically. Its background was my part of the country, the Middle West, and a familiar part of my early childhood: In those days a few years brought no great changes to one's surroundings. The exteriors of the Smith family's home, and the street, were typical. Huge trees formed a leafy arch, the ice wagon, the milk wagon, clop-clopping of horses' hooves, a boy on a bike throwing the paper on the front porch. The lawn-swing in the side yard. An iron deer decorating the front lawn. And the beautiful, hired, shiny black buggy drawn by two horses, in which the family goes in style to the fair.

The interior, lower floor of the house was built in its entirety, not in separate sets. The hall and staircase, the parlor, the dining room, a small conservatory and a huge kitchen. And Mrs. Smith was a dedicated housekeeper with Marjorie Main as a mother's helper. The antimacassars were blinding white and starched and perched on every chair in the place. There were family photographs everywhere (we spent a day in the gallery posing for them!); there were red velvet pompon portieres between the parlor and the hall. And there was a big kettle of soup stock simmering on a great black stove in the kitchen. The girls were costumed beautifully, perhaps a little beyond Mr. Smith's means! Mr. Smith was played by Leon Ames who was right out of a tin-type with his mustache, his gold watch draped across his vest, and a constantly indignant look to keep his head-of-the-house position unquestioned. The only anachronisms were the girls' long-swinging hairdos. Girls "put their hair up" as soon as they got out of pigtails, the first instant they were allowed to by reluctant parents. It was a symbol, like the first long pants for boys.

Margaret O'Brien was at her most appealing (I might say "appalling") age. And she could cry at the drop of a cue. Real tears, an endless flow, with apparently no emotional drain whatsoever. She was a quiet, almost too-well-behaved child, when her mother was on the set. When Mother was absent, it was another story and she was a pain in the neck. There was a long sequence at the dinner table, at which there again was perfection of detail. The white damask cloth, the soup tureen, and all the many odds and ends, crystal bowls for jam and pickles and salt cellars and napkin rings. It was the property man's job to watch these things, and at the end of a scene—or of a take of one scene—to put everything back exactly as it was when the scene started.

It was Maggie's favorite form of mischief, when his back was turned, to put things in disorder again, to reverse knives and forks, to put two napkin rings beside a plate. It would drive him nuts. And remember the strong caste system on the sets: She was a star and he was just a lowly property man, so all he could do was to smile and say, "Please, Maggie dear!" when he'd have liked to have shaken her. At least.

It was indeed a lovely picture, but I think I remember most clearly the end of the day when I could remove my high button shoes, and get out of the heavy clothes and finally—bliss!—get out of the damned corset! After months of this it was very pleasant to get back to chic, Irene clothes.

Irene's great talent was in fitting: She would have you move around, or see how it sits; she paid special attention to shoulder and neckline detail, so it wouldn't detract from the face in close-ups, and still have an interesting line that would compose well. Her evening clothes had great movement, material that would flow around the thighs, revealing and releasing; she paid attention to accessories, dragging out a whole box full of jewelry, pawing through for just the right pin or a clasp for a bag, earrings that would shape the ear and not waggle and detract from the face.

My feminine pleasure in clothes was completely satisfied in Irene's fitting room. The great bolts of exquisite materials, specially woven wools from her designs, and the silks and satins (very few synthetics as yet), the clinging jerseys, the knits, all the textures to make your fingers tingle. I guess that's why I've never cared much about shopping or buying a wardrobe. Every few weeks I had a whole new one made by Irene—and never had to have it altered for next season or sent to the cleaners. It spoils you! ("And, gee whiz, you get to wear all those beautiful clothes!" That's true, my dreaming girl. And wouldn't you just *love* to wear one evening dress every day from eight thirty in the morning until seven at night for two weeks? It happens.)

13

THE PICTURE WAS an adaptation from a Ferenc Molnar play, *Delilah*. Sounds good, doesn't it? The leading man was a fine Dutch actor, new to our country, Philip Dorn. Charming. Directed by a very talented young man, Richard Whorf. Also a new young actress, Gloria Grahame, and another young actor, Marshall Thompson. And Irene clothes. And nice, slick sets. Now how can anything be wrong with all this? Nothing. Except what was *getting* wrong with all movies. They had nothing further to say, and they said it beautifully, efficiently, slickly and boringly. Oh, the lists of *best* pictures of that year were impressive, but they were the exception: *Dragon Seed* with Hepburn, *Gaslight* with Bergman, Crosby's *Going My Way*, *Jane Eyre* with Fontaine and Orson Welles, *The Song of Bernadette* with Jennifer Jones, and *The White Cliffs of Dover* with Irene Dunne. And even the best had the quality of slick, sentimental perfection.

Perhaps it was the "how." I read an article that expresses what I mean, although in a somewhat "Come again?" manner: "We no longer care about what a film says; we care quite as much *how* it is said; because the how is as much a part of the what, as the what is of the how!"

Maybe this little item is a tip as to what was disturbing about the movies at that moment: To commemorate the 50th Anniversary of motion pictures, the U.S. Post Office issued on October 31 a three-cent purple postage stamp. Purple? Indicating regality? or meaning full of phony devices and effects?

And I was "slick and skillful." Confident in my appearance, my ability to wear clothes; I knew all the tricks: how to hit a mark without looking, how to work within the nimbus of my key light. Educated peripheral vision that told me always where the camera was. I had no difficulty with dialogue changes, for I was a quick study. I was dependable, on time, unargumentative. I could do the job sick or well. I was proud of being a pro, I was proud of being called "one-take Astor" for rarely did I fluff a line. I did my job as well as I could, but only because I had a sense of responsibility: "I'm being paid." Do it and get it over with. Stay in good health so as to be able to take long hours, the pressures, the noise, the constant talk. I was a veteran. I knew everybody and everybody knew me.

I had settled in at MGM like a second home. But not contentedly. It wasn't an active, do-something discontent. With the amount of work I was doing, I didn't have enough energy left over even to think about it, to sit down and figure out how to break up the pattern. I hear the voice of my dreaming girl: "You were working in the *movies!*" Unfortunately the human animal is so put together that the most exciting work, if it is done all the time, becomes monotonous and deadly to the spirit. All I could say to myself was, "That's just too bad! Collect your check and shut up!"

I remember the feeling of having to wind up to the level of the day's work ahead. It was about a thirty-minute drive from my house to the studio—no freeways then—almost always before it was light in the winter time, and in the summer it was often foggy and overcast. I remember grayness.

You slow up at the big gate, say "Morning, Mac," and get waved on. Few office people have arrived yet, and the workmen's call isn't until eight, so the narrow streets between the stages are fairly empty except for other actors also arriving, also looking sleepy, puffy and sallow, and reluctant.

You open the door to the makeup and hairdressing department and absorb the shock of people talking over the noise of hair dryers: the warm air laden with a conglomeration of odors of spirit gum and acetone, of soap and hair sprays, Max Factor's products, coffee, and people.

Your girl, Betty let's say, who is on a twenty-minute schedule for each person assigned her, is bright and talkative and cheerful. You're not quite ready for that. "Want some coffee, sweetheart?" "Uh-uh." "Get you pinned up first, O.K.?" You get a shampoo so thorough, it's as though your girl was under the impression you'd just come out of a coal mine; but yesterday's hair spray and pancake around the edges and the dust from the set has to be removed. Still mute, you sit in front of a brightly lighted mirror, which doesn't help, and Betty checks with you, saying, "Still in the library set, huh? Just like yesterday? That's what I have on my sheet, honey." "That's right."

She starts with a comb full of setting lotion, and while she swiftly rolls dozens of little bird's-nest pincurls she continues a conversation with the hairdresser at the next chair—or maybe the one five chairs away. In the mirror you catch the eye of others being done and you mouth, "Morning," with a finger salute and close your eyes.

"Now just five minutes under the dryer and then finish up after Eddie gets through with you, darling."

The makeup booths across the hall are a little quieter. Makeup men or women consider themselves artists and are somewhat more sensitive to this early morning gloom. Somewhat. "Like a Danish, sweetheart? I gotta fresh cuppa coffee for you." I still smell the strong, bitter coffee, the various perfumes of an array of foundations and powders and creams, and mostly "Sea Breeze," a lotion that Eddie and other makeup people use on a sponge as a moistener for the pancake. Under his hands, a face begins to emerge that you might be willing to expose to public scrutiny. Actually it's not bad at all! It's getting late and the adrenalin has started stirring and you hurry back into the hairdressing department. "Let's go, Betty!" "Are you dry, angel? How about another five minutes under the dryer?" "Let's comb it out on the set." "No, you're still damp—I'll be careful of your makeup. And you can get body makeup while you're under." The dryer is hot and the girl, the "body makeup" girl who does nothing else, starts sponging the pancake moistened with icy "Sea Breeze" onto your neck and ears and hands and arms. Assistant directors, no, *second* assistant directors are beginning to appear, carrying invisible blacksnakes, *"Let's* go, let's *go!"* "You're in the first shot, you ready?" and people begin scurrying and the place gets a bit empty, except for those who have later calls.

Only a few of the very privileged are attended to in their own dressing rooms. For efficiency's sake. It takes time for operators to gather their material and walk to and from the dressing-room building. And also, there is too great a temptation to take more than the minimum time for preparation in one's own room.

In front of the department are several of the big black studio cars to take people to the stage. You could walk over to, let's say, Stages Four, Eight and Eleven, but if you happen to be on Twenty-seven or Sixteen, it's maybe two or three city blocks away, so you and the makeup man, hairdresser and a wardrobe lady, and a couple of others in the cast, bus to the stage.

There, in your portable, more coffee is waiting for you, and the prop man says, "Want a Danish, Miss Astor? Or just a dough-nut?" I *hate* Danish and doughnuts, and besides I had breakfast before I left the house, but I follow the ritual, "Thanks, Johnny, but I gotta watch my weight."

Now you're all dressed and you emerge and make your way over to the set, picking through the "spaghetti," the endless tangle of electric cable. "Morning, Alec." "Morning, Joe—boy it's cold, isn't it?" "Morning, Louise." "Morning, Ivan." It's 8:45 and the day has begun.

One of the reasons I enjoy writing—one of the very minor rea-sons—is that it is work done alone. The movies spoiled me for any kind of gregariousness. For what is known as getting out with people once in a while. My social life began at the age of fourteen in the movies. Every day on the set for all those years, all day long, I was within a foot or two of another person, in the midst of from fifty to a hundred or more people; in the midst of talk, chatter, a constant exchange of words. How, I ask you, can I *possibly* enjoy a cocktail party? The times of concentration ("putting the pot on to boil") lasted only minutes. A long scene runs only four or five minutes, and even that is rare. The moment the camera stops, all hell breaks loose again. The crew makes corrections for the next take.

I still hear, after all this time, "Why do they take it over and over?" Or from a visitor: "I stood around there all one morning and all they did was this one simple little scene!" One take is almost a miracle. Let's say the actors do everything just right; they're skillful, they've achieved the proper emotional level, said all the words correctly, action has been coordinated perfectly. In the first place, this is rare. Very small changes can make it better. But, consider how many other things are going on that must function perfectly. The complex camera, moving, changing focus, aperture; the film itself occasionally jams. The sound apparatus, from the mike to the boom man to the console on the set to a sound truck on the street: Many things along the line can go wrong. And the lights, which illuminate not only the actor but also the environment around him. One of them slips a notch, and the light on the shadow of leaves on the windowsill slips; a fuse blows; an actor takes two steps instead of three and misses a light set for him and is "in the black." O.K., so two steps are better than three—the light is readjusted—and the next time he takes three steps, and misses the light. Then *he* gets mad, and grumbles about restrictions. But this is the nature of the job. It is exceedingly complex, but there are a hundred people around doing their best to make it right. And they often get in each other's way, and they also are under pressure of the clock. So they start shouting to one another over the heads of others who are shouting about something else.

And over it all the assistant keeps up his ineffectual plea: "Now, let's keep it quiet, PLEASE!"

I don't think I ever got used to it. On the way home, my head would rock with the sound memory: "Al—up high—drop that one down here." "Siggy—get the phone willya?" "Quiet—we're on a bell!" "Put a barn door on the eighty." "I'm tellin' you, it can't be ready until Monday." "Can I help it if he's late?" "I'm getting a kick off that mirror—spray it down." "Let's go, let's *go!*" "What's this number—26 Chicago?" "Let's re-mark 'em." "Give 'em new marks, Bernie." And the bell. The "quiet bell," an enormous thing, loud enough to be heard all over the stage. One ring (one *blast*) for "Quiet," two for "Go ahead and make as much noise as you want," I suppose. And if the stage isn't completely soundproof, there's another bell out on the street attached to a wig-wag red light to stop cars and trucks.

But when the man at the console, the sound man, said in a very quiet voice, "We—are—rolling," it worked better than all the bells and shouts for quiet ever did. Everything became sepulchral. And because you'd been hearing this previous level of sound— often rehearsing in it—you'd find yourself talking too loud when the scene began. Usually a director's voice, with a last-minute ad-monition, or encouragement, or reminder, would give the pitch— like a musical conductor: "Okay, build it slow now. And—action!"

Then there was lunch time. You could have a sandwich in your portable dressing room, but you needed hot food after the long morning. You could have a tray brought to your room in the dressing-room building, but that might take too much time out of the allotted one hour for lunch. So you went to the commissary. The commissary at Metro was like a restaurant in Grand Central Station. Also running at a high-decibel level, with the clatter of dishes and the scrape of chairs, and greetings from table to table —and everybody in a hurry!

At night, it took a while to unwind. No matter how tired I was, it seemed I couldn't relax until that hot shower hit me. Then dinner, and an hour with the script for next day's work and to bed.

From the newspaper columns one would think that movie people partied all the time—they were seen here and there, at parties, at nightclubs, at openings. Of course, there are often weeks —months—between pictures, so you'd read about maybe fifteen or twenty people out on the town, or traveling, or being seen at the theater in New York. But at the same time, several hundred would be having dinner, working on a script and hitting the pillow at about nine o'clock. The dawn of a new day really cracks.

When a picture was over, I wanted nothing but quiet—lots of it—and sleep and reading and loafing around. I always had to fight the reproach, "But you're not working! You *should* get out more!" Getting out and seeing people was never a holiday for me. I had friends and I liked seeing them, talking to them. I still do! Not just being with them in the midst of a lot of other people. I have never learned the social game: your turn, my turn; I owe them, they owe me. And I loathe dates made weeks in advance, "Cock-tails and buffet, January 20." It contains an assumption that you just can't wait for January 20. Or that one's social life is so complicated and full that you must keep a calendar. Perhaps it's just a personal preference for something more spontaneous.

Twenty years ago I was beginning to feel has-been-ish. Various crew members, a carpenter, a cameraman, an actor or a prop man would want to talk about the good old days and I wasn't ready for that. Nostalgic obsession with the past has always seemed like so much ballast. Because when I was just starting in pictures I was bored to tears with some old ham talking about the good old days when he "had 'em in the aisles in Hoboken on the Pan-Time" or "The Vitagraph days." Now, of course, me and my contemporary old-timers, we did have something pleasant to remember, and there were many who wished they could turn back the clock, when it was all a bit more fun. Now there were unions and big money involved, and there was rush, rush, rush. Now there was no more "resting" after a tough scene. Nobody ever said, "Let's kill the lights a minute," so that we could sit around in the cool gloom and talk about what we'd just done, think about it, even maybe come up with something better. "Hey, that's a good idea. Let's make one like that." Now we'd have to have approval from up front for any change. Of course, then we had seven-day weeks and quit when we finished, even if it was eleven at night. Once, because an actor had to open in a play on a certain date in New York, we worked thirty-six hours straight through.

Now, everything seemed to have reached its peak of efficiency. Just like the scripts: Establishing shot, medium shot, close-up.

You practically had to go to the front office if you wanted something as real as having your hair mussed. You'd argue, "I've been out in the wind. When did I get a chance to reset it?" "Well, it won't look good. Just loosen a strand, maybe." Everyone had that "just from a beauty parlor" look. The sets were perfect, all automobiles were shiny. A picture never hung crooked, a door never squeaked, stocking seams were always straight and no actress ever had a shiny nose.

Every detail was watched with jealous eyes by the department responsible for that detail. After every take a swarm of bees would surround me. The wardrobe lady to adjust a belt. The makeup man to brush on more powder. The hairdresser with her swoosh gun. The body makeup girl to dab at an ear with that icy Sea-Breezed sponge. And everybody talking, explaining what and why they were doing whatever it was: "Just want to pull this down a little," "Little shiny, right here," "There's a white spot I didn't catch," "Couple of wild hairs catching the light." And all those hands, touching, picking, patting; the various breaths being blown at one. Well, it was their job. And to them an actor was only busy when the camera was turning. But if something showed up badly in the rushes, like a bit of shine around the nostrils, somebody'd catch it: "What the hell have we got makeup people for?"

Nobody ever seemed to say, "What are we making pictures for?" The answer was so obvious. "To make money." Keep doing the same thing, just perfect it, no rough edges, no bugs, no shiny noses. And when the box office would slip they tried to remedy it with all the wrong things, the wrong tags and labels. "They want new faces." "The star system is dead." (The *pseudo*-star system, the manufactured star, was on the way out, but there will always be stars.) "Westerns are the thing they want." "They want situation comedy." "They want the documentary type: simple, hard-hitting." "Disney's making millions; maybe they want fantasy." "More sex."

But it never was—and it isn't today—any *one* of those particular things. Audiences have always been hungry for entertainment. They don't care too much what kind of a package it's wrapped up in—gangsters or Gothic, cheesecake or sex, tall-in-the-saddle or slice-of-life. Man is that strange creature, a spiritual animal, with his head in the stars and his feet in the muck, and one of his basic needs is escape from himself, temporarily but thoroughly. The man who goes fishing gets something more than the fish he catches. All the entertainment media should supply this need: sports, books, TV, theater, movies.

Things had to change. The world was changing so rapidly that it seemed to be skidding out from beneath one's feet. Mores and morals, customs and clothes and computers and politics and space programs: everything in evolution and revolution, and entertainment should reflect these changes *but* keep its identity as entertainment and never try to be life itself.

I admire the young film-makers for trying new things, new concepts, but I think they are just as much in danger of getting trapped in clichés as at any time in film-making history. Audiences will get just as tired of people wrestling on a bed as they did of Tom Mix kissing his horse. I think all the tremendous enthusiasm for movie-making, for trying, for discarding is great. As long as the more sophisticated don't keep on making movies just for each other. Soon nobody's going to understand their myths and symbolic significance except themselves. And movies cost money, and money comes from people who want to be entertained. So why make movies that interest only a special few who think they are raising the level up to Art? Or who rigidly proclaim "the way it is, baby." That's a pretty arrogant phrase, because it really doesn't speak for everyone. There are many people for whom the way it is, just isn't. So why lock them out? Why cut off the source of revenue with which to make more movies?

I get a bit hung up when I start talking about present-day film material—whether it is original or taken from books or plays. I *am* skittish about criticism and I shy from the probable comment, "What the hell do *you* know? You're old-fashioned." Perhaps. But no one longed for innovation, for change, more than I did, for I was often up to my knees in dreck. What troubles me is the direction that the changes and innovations have taken. For they are just as drecklich and boring in their own way.

The "how" is what's new—and good. The "what" is neither good nor new. And there are those few who think it's great, and I read a great deal of windy-foggery about it: ". . . elegantly sordid . . ." ". . . re-created stunningly and sickeningly." ". . . downbeat has become box office." The *hell* it has!

It seems to me there is a great deal of self-conscious striving for Art. You can't *make* anything *be* Art—and the minute you try, it eludes you. And if you behave like an artist you'll never be one. It's difficult to define Art without getting into an argument. So I'll try! Not really to define it, but to say how it can happen. First of all, you have to be absolutely bugged with the idea of producing something with the material you love the best. Then learn all about the material—a guitar or a kithara or your own voice, a chunk of red clay, a piece of onyx, some oil paints, a length of movie film—whatever it is. Subdue it, make it as much a part of your life as breathing. Then, *then* you produce. And not with the idea you're going to produce a work of Art. It's just *there,* so much of it, you're so full of it, it has to come out. And it never enters your mind: This is artistic. Nor do you give a damn

[187]

whether anyone ever thinks it is; by then you are, or should be, producing something else. The producing is the satisfaction.

As for movies being an Art Form, I'm not sure. It is a form in which Art can happen—like in a lot of things. I don't think it carries Art in the very sprockets of its film. It can happen, and has—but rarely. There is much art in photography, but as soon as it moves it gets tricky. It's faddy or fashionable. It's awfully greedy about money to support it, and that filters down to the product itself. It has too many fingers in the pie. And it travels. Art, like wine, doesn't travel well.

As an example, I don't think I can match the experience I had when I was in Rome the first time. I chose *not* to be part of a sight-seeing tour, even though time was short and I might miss something. I went to St. Peter's by myself, and I turned to the right as I went inside and there was the Pietà. It was a gray, chilly day, nobody was around, the light was pale. But there she was. She and her Son. I don't know how long I stood there. No words, no cheap teary feelings. She was there and I was there.

Then she "traveled" and got set up on an appropriate pedestal and got beautiful lighting and background music. And thousands of people saw a piece of exquisite sculpture with great prestige. But I don't think they saw what I saw, or felt. A work of Art in context. I'm sure they were thrilled, those thousands, and they were entertained—but that is something else.

Even so, being thrilled is fun. Being excited about something is fun. Identifying is fun: It's an ego-stroker. Even weeping is fun. For fun is an emotion. One of them. It's the emotion that makes play good for the health and the tone of one's being. And movies are like seeing the Pietà with background music and blue spotlights. It stirs the emotions and it's fun. It's a Christmas tree ornament with a nugget of pure gold inside.

And whatever we did—we old movie-makers—we gave people a lot of fun. Through depressions and wars and calamities we gave them "the sound of brass, the sense of glory, of a future that would be braver than today."

We gave them chiffon and moonlight and rose petals; tinkling glasses and penthouses; heart-lifting melodies and dancing and soft words; and ordinary Americana like a Fourth of July picnic with fried chicken and kids in a swing. And ambitious young people who wanted to leave the farm and make their way to glory in the big city. And tears—of loss, of pain, of pride.

I know this is gone. I know that such material would have no appeal to audiences of today. But to replace it with stories of drug addiction, homosexuality, pederasty, sadomasochism, seems to denote a poverty of spirit. My stomach is queasy when I watch it —and I feel a deep sadness.

Now if someone will be so kind as to help me down from this platform, we'll go back to a time when World War II was in its last year. FDR had died in April. In San Francisco a charter had been signed in which the signatories pledged "to save succeeding generations from the scourge of war . . . to maintain international peace and security . . . to employ international machinery for the promotion of the economic and social advancement of all people." We were trying.

We were dancing to "Dig You Later—a Hubba Hubba Hubba." Hoagy Carmichael was singing "Doctor, Lawyer, Indian Chief" and "Ole Buttermilk Sky."

And I was on my way to Mexico City for locations in a picture called *Fiesta*. In which picture I played Esther Williams' and Ricardo Montalban's mother. In the picture they were twins. That's what it said in the script. And one of the twins became a sensational matador and the other composed music. The switch was that it was Esther who became the matador.

For reasons that had nothing to do with Mexico, I hated the whole trip, and thought I hated Mexico. I stayed in my room at the Reforma Hotel with Montezuma's revenge and nosebleeds from the altitude.

I had only a few scattered scenes. As *Mamacita* I was a well-protected Mexican mother and never left the hacienda to go to those old bull fights. I welcomed guests at the gate of the *zaguan*, and strolled down a balcony thoughtfully. And I got home in time to get married for the last time on December 25, 1945. This marriage was to last eight years. A very nice guy by the name of Thomas Wheelock whom I'd met at the home of the writer John Lee Mahin.

I was holing up, going to ground once more. A husband, a new home, my kids. I was lost in the enormous shuffle that was MGM. If they were happy to pay me a weekly salary and not use me, why should I kick? I didn't kick, but it was making me ill. I was only thirty-nine years old, and for me to sit around waiting for a call from the casting office was just all wrong. I had a cable from

With Dorothy McGuire in CLAUDIA AND DAVID (1946)

Noel Coward to play the second wife in *Blithe Spirit*, in London. No dice. "There may be something coming up in the near future —we can't risk it." *What* risk? Occasionally I was asked to report for a gallery session, "We need a new set of photos for the files." File under "Who's that?" A day spent making a test with a young man who was a possibility for their stable, a young actor, thrilled and earnest at being given this big opportunity. Never heard of him again.

In the summer of 1946 they loaned me out to 20th-Century Fox for *Claudia and David* with Dorothy McGuire and Robert Young. I enjoyed it—I loved it—I wasn't anybody's mother and I looked lovely in beautiful clothes—and I was *working*. The working habit is a deep one. I have complained bitterly—bitched about how hard the work is—but I can't sit and twiddle my thumbs and watch the world go by, and I firmly believe that the day or the time when I can no longer work at *something*, I will die.

It's funny, the things you remember about a picture. In this one, mostly I remember a sequence concerning oysters.

There was a big formal dinner, perhaps twelve people. Quite a long episode, with a lot of dialogue. I think it was two or three days' work. Table scenes are difficult, technically. People can't be moved around, there are cross cuts, you are *attached* to the table. It's a lighting and camera problem mainly, and takes time.

The first course—and the only course, because the scene ran long enough for that course to be eaten—was oysters. Lovely fresh bluepoints on the half shell served on an iced plate with the usual accompaniments. You can fake eating only up to a point in front of a camera. There comes a time when you must put food into your mouth and swallow it. The first day we were all delighted with the excellence of the oysters that the studio had provided us, and nobody even tried to fake it. In the long shot, the establishing shot, we enjoyed ourselves very much. Now the camera moves in closer for "a tight two." The plates have been replenished with ice and oysters, and the sauce and the horseradish, and the little lemon slices, etc. But we'd all had enough oysters, for the long shot had gone three takes.

The first two shot you spear an oyster, dip it into the sauce and swallow it quickly in time for whatever it is you have to say. While the other person is speaking, you have time to eat another, or to wipe your lips with a napkin. But, careful! it has to match: You ate an oyster at that point in the establishing shot!

The morning hasn't even begun! We should have taken a hint from the stack of huge kegs over in a corner, packed in ice. As long as we ate 'em, the property man could furnish us with another dozen.

No lunch that day. Just, "I think I'll lie down during lunch hour."

After three days of eating nothing but oysters and crackers, the body rebels. And there was nothing wrong with the oysters. They were delicious, fresh, iced—as good as you'd get in the finest restaurant. Dorothy and I had the longest scenes, the most close-ups—and in spite of frequent visits to the ladies' room, we both looked rather pale and wan in the sequence that followed—after a short, recuperative layoff.

Later on in the year Metro decided they could use me in a nice little vehicle for Elizabeth Taylor—as her mother. A very B-type movie, except Metro never stinted on their B-type movies. A kitchen apron for me (I asked, out of curiosity) cost them about seventy-five dollars. Just the ordinary bib-type checked apron with a pocket in it and rickrack around the borders. The pocket was appliquéd, and the rickrack was hand-stitched. At so much a yard, and so many hours of hand work by the union wardrobe seamstresses—you figure it out. Of course, there was a duplicate also, in case I spilled ketchup or something on it. I remember this apron because it caused a small crisis. I *did* spill water on it. And the cry went up, "It's O.K., it's O.K.! We have a dupe." But then I said, heretically, "I *want* the water on it."

In the kitchen I was supposed to have been washing dishes. I entered the living room to answer the doorbell and I was wiping my hands on a towel. Offstage, just before the scene, I told the prop men, "Slosh me in the front a little." I've never washed dishes without getting sloshed, and it looked right. But it was one of those problems.

O.K., I know you're in a hurry to get to Elizabeth. She was in her teens, only a couple of years after *National Velvet,* and just beginning to turn into an exquisite beauty. A figure just beginning to blossom, beautiful skin that needed no makeup and those violet eyes with lashes that needed no mascara. She was a young, well-mannered English girl, with her mother on the set—very unobtrusively, I hasten to add.

I had seen Elizabeth from a distance in the MGM commissary during the making of *National Velvet,* and she had at that time, a serious, "dedicated" look. That was gone, she was no longer quite as shy, and she was beginning to be conscious in a very normal, teen-age way of her own beauty. She was also bright. *Very* bright. Head-of-the-class type of brightness. For a kid, she concentrated very well on the work—and I liked her. But I liked another "daughter" better—Judy Garland. Judy was warm and affectionate and exuberant. Elizabeth was cool, and slightly superior. More than slightly. There was a look in those violet eyes that was somewhat calculating, as though she knew exactly what she wanted and was quite sure of getting it. Maybe all she wanted was that great big hunk of a diamond ring. It seems to symbolize what she got.

George Murphy played my husband, Elizabeth's father. The Senator himself. If ever a man telegraphed what he'd be in later years, George really did. Not much interested in acting, perhaps because he was bored with playing father and friend-of-the-family roles, and it had become merely a job. Off the set he read a daily newspaper, *not* turned to the drama section. He talked about politics at great length, local and national, and our own union politics. He was boring to the rest of us, because of our habit of not facing or caring what was going on in the rest of the world. We were still self-enchanted.

So the appellation, "song-and-dance-man-turned-politician," never fitted him. He was a politician who'd earned his living at one time as a song-and-dance man.

Like Ronald Reagan, with whom I worked many years later in one of his General Electric shows. Ronnie made up for his deficiency in acting by his attractive personality. Aggressively attractive. He used it. He was an organizer, enthusiast, a doer—and he worked tirelessly for us in the Screen Actors Guild. When he was campaigning for governor I heard him speak at a rally in my neighborhood. I was walking back to my car afterward and I overheard a couple of nice-old-lady types talking about him. ". . . but if he gets elected governor, he won't be able to make any more movies, will he? What a shame!" They loved him.

In general I might say that a politician may be a good actor, but a good actor would never make a successful politician. Just in case you might be asked to consider George C. Scott for mayor of New York.

Cynthia was a sweet little picture, but I'm sure even the greatest admirers of Elizabeth Taylor won't remember it—or her. And I'll bet a quid she's never had it shown for Richard.

14

THERE IS A VERY OLD JOKE in the profession about the five stages in the life of an actor. Supply the name of any well-known player, and the producer/director/casting office says,

1. Who's Mary Astor? 2. Get me Mary Astor. 3. Get me a Mary Astor type. 4. Get me a young Mary Astor. 5. Who's Mary Astor?

I was between stages 4 and 5, and I was troubled and angry and unhappy about it. I was not doing that absurdity, trying to hang onto my youth; I had watched too many of those pathetic, futile attempts. At forty I was not an unattractive woman. O.K., I'd play all the mothers they wanted: the selfish, domineering mother; the warm, understanding mother. Mother. M.O.T.H.E.R. Fine. But there wasn't a mother in every script, and was I to sit around until there was?

I marked time. I went to a local art school and dug my hands into clay, I took a course in anatomical drawing. I went out to Birmingham Veteran's Hospital and worked in the Arts and

Skills Department of the Red Cross. I wrote, and put reams of stuff into the wastebasket.

Many people have suffered from the dreadful affliction of contractitis. Writers have told of sitting around in the California sun collecting their pay—and of what it did to them—and there are some truly tragic stories.

Try to tell a non-pro what it's like and you hear, "Boy, I'd sure like to get paid for doing nothing!" And how do you explain that it's demoralizing? Insidiously the thought sneaks into your head: "You're no good. They're on to you. You're finished, washed up."

I had a bit in *Cass Timberlane* with Spencer Tracy. Another bit in something else, picture and cast forgotten.

There was another loan-out to Paramount—a picture called *Desert Fury*. I played Lizabeth Scott's mother. O.K., a mother role, but not the conventional one. This mother was called Fritzi and she was the owner of a gambling club someplace near Reno. She was tough, dominating, determined to keep her daughter from being tainted by the environment of corruption in which Fritzi lived.

Fritzi was good for my nerves. I could use all my accumulated bitterness and bad temper and do a little exploding. There were some good, strong actors around me, good "opponents": Burt Lancaster, John Hodiak, Wendell Corey—and Liz Scott, whom I liked, very much, and who was also a good "opponent." I needed "opponents." I needed a target. I needed to fight with somebody.

My own daughter, Marylyn, made a very astute comment one evening when I got to the house after work. I banged the front door, threw my bag and script onto the couch, looked at the clock which showed 7:30 and said, "Why aren't you doing your homework! And why the hell isn't dinner ready—what's the matter with that girl in the kitchen—what am I paying her for!" A real tirade. My daughter never stirred, just kept turning the pages of her magazine, and said, "You brought Fritzi home with you, didn't you, Mom?"

I had, indeed. And I would shed Fritzi under a hot shower. As hot as possible, so I wouldn't inflict her on the innocent.

The following year—yes, it was like that!—I was assigned the role of Marmee in *Little Women*. Now, I'm of the generation that read and loved *Little Women*, *Jo's Boys* and *Little Men*. I had read and reread them when I was in sixth or seventh grade. I'd

DESERT FURY (1947). At the gambling table with Lizabeth Scott, while John Hodiak and partially hidden Wendell Corey look on

been in love with Laurie and wanted Jo to marry him instead of that old Professor Baer. And in order to be like Jo, I went up to the attic at home and scribbled short stories; things that began, "Dear Boy, boy that I am to meet one day. I wonder where you are this beautiful October afternoon, and I wonder if you know the poem about 'October's Bright Blue Weather.' " But I wasn't quite ready to become a writing prodigy, selling stories to the amazement of my classmates at school.

Now, while I was glad to go to work again, it seemed a bit ho-hum. I knew it would be "pretty." I knew that the MGM settings and costumes, in color, would be superb. And that Mervyn LeRoy would make it a very slick show with due emphasis on "heart" and comedy. Jo's scorched dress, the one pair of gloves between her and Meg, the rebellious docking of Jo's beautiful locks. (*Aside:* Wonder what the Freudians would say about the connection between rebellion and hair!)

And, of course, Marmee with her girls around her, reading the gallant letter from the distant soldier-father.

June Allyson was to be Jo; Elizabeth Taylor in a blonde wig,

Amy; Janet Leigh was Meg; and Margaret O'Brien was Beth who died. And was that ever a death scene!

I was not well, physically or emotionally. I had not accepted gracefully the months of idleness, I was not cut out or trained for the role of housewife. It was substitute role-playing for me. I'd learned to cook by researching dozens of cookbooks; there were none of our "quick foods" of today.

If you didn't like canned peas, you had to go to the market and buy fresh ones. They didn't look much like the peas I used to see on vines on the farm! Then they must be hulled, etc. But other women did it, why couldn't I? I learned to clean a house and to iron a man's shirt and do my kids' washing and ironing and make school lunches. I did it all rather well—but this was supposed to be a temporary engagement; I didn't want to play this part forever.

Actors are spoiled rotten as far as self-help or do-it-yourself is concerned. You peel off a pair of stockings and you never see them again. There's always somebody to zip you up. You want some coffee? It's at your elbow. Here's a chair, sit down a minute and rest. We'll get a car to take you over there. Can't do your Christmas shopping? Give the girl some money and she'll do it for you. You say "Cigarette, please" and there's one in your hand —your brand and lighted. You feel faint—there's a glass of brandy under your nose. Now all this is not because of your pearly teeth or your charm or anything else. These people are prepared to take care of the "product": keep it happy, keep it well, cater to its every desire. It works harder. You reward a puppy with a goodie, don't you? Well, that's got more honest feeling in it than seeing that Miss X has a magnum of champagne in her dressing room. But the person who is the product gets some very odd ideas, begins to expect it as his due. Now take this person out of the hothouse milieu and he does a bit of floundering around for a while.

Furthermore, my financial situation was extremely bad. My father had protected me from having to "bother" about money. And since then, there had been a whole series of people anxious to relieve me of the worry about money. And my marriages were all financial disasters, so at this point, there just wasn't any. Even though I was still earning. At the end of every year, for reasons I was told not to worry about, I seemed to *owe* money, instead of having accumulated any.

My approach to the part of Marmee was not an enthusiastic one. Everybody else had fun. The girls all giggled and chattered and made a game of every scene. Taylor was engaged, and in love, and talking on the telephone most of the time (which is fine normally, but not when that production clock is ticking away the company's money). June Allyson chewed gum constantly and irritatingly, and Maggie O'Brien looked at me as though she were planning something very unpleasant.

In the scene where Jo got her hair cut, Peter Lawford was supposed to arrive at the house and say, "What have you done! You look like a porcupine!" Except that for some reason the pronunciation of porcupine eluded him. It came out "porkypine." It took an entire afternoon, and everyone, even Mervyn LeRoy, was doubled up with laughter. The scene would begin, with Peter insisting, "I've got it! I've got it now!" and then, nearly at the end of the scene, he would burst in the door and say, "What have you done! You look like a porkypine!" And everybody went to pieces.

My sense of humor, my sense of fun, had deserted me long ago. And it just wasn't all *that* funny. It was getting on toward six o'clock, the clothes (heavy with hoop skirts and corsets) felt like a ton, and I'd been standing in the same spot in the lights while all the joke was going on. The floor felt soft, as though I were sinking into it. My head felt odd. The scene began again and I had the first line. With a real sense of panic, I realized I hadn't the faintest notion of what I was supposed to say. Mervyn said, "Cut! Where's your line, Mary?" And all I could say, rather weakly, was, "I don't know, Merv." And that broke everybody up. They thought I meant that I too was so overcome by the overpowering joke, that I couldn't go on.

It gave me a moment. I couldn't say, "I'm ill." I didn't want the kind of attention that would have brought on. Finally we shot it, with Mr. Lawford successfully saying "porcupine." Or did he say "porkypine?" I don't remember.

The schedule was a long one. And there were many sequences in which I didn't appear. Fred Zinnemann was doing a picture called *Act of Violence* at the time and there was a small but interesting part he wanted me for.

So for two weeks or so I was with the Zinnemann company

With Van Heflin in ACT OF VIOLENCE (1948)

playing a sleazy, aging whore, with Van Heflin and Robert Ryan. It was such a contrast that it was stimulating—and reviving. I had something to do.

I worked out the way this poor alley cat should look, and insisted firmly (with Zinney's help) that the one dress in the picture would *not* be made at the MGM wardrobe, but be found on a rack at the cheapest department store. We made the hem uneven, put a few cigarette burns and some stains on the front. I wore bracelets that rattled and jangled and stiletto-heeled slippers. I had the heels sanded off at the edges to make walking uncomfortable. I wore a fall, a long unbecoming hairpiece that came to my shoulder. And I put on very dark nail polish and chipped it. I used no foundation makeup, just too much lipstick and too much mascara—both "bled," that is, smeared, just a little. Zinney said, "You look just right!" And camera helped with "bad" lighting.

One afternoon when I had some time between shots I walked over to the lovely *Little Women* set just for the hell of it. Mervyn, who for some reason didn't know I was moonlighting in another production, took a startled look at me, came over to me, shocked, and said, "What the hell have you got that kind of an outfit on for? What's the matter with you anyway—you look like a two-bit tart!" I was very pleased.

Playing some of the scenes with Van Heflin, working with an artist like Zinnemann—after years of literally *nothing*—was a tonic. The way we worked, talking about it, thinking about it, using, discarding, trying something else. It was good. It was the way it ought to be—always.

After this drab, black-and-white wonderful little picture, I went back to the picture-postcard sumptuousness of *Little Women*.

To make a mixaphor, I had a good berth in the MGM stables. I was told that my contract would be renewed for another seven years and I could consider myself part of the family: in my berth, in their stables. Also they were creating an annuity for their contract players, which should work out in my case at fifty-five. It was before the era of fringe benefits and pensions and all the goodies that people fight for in these days. At least I had never heard of them but then I didn't know anything about money! I had the simple idea that you work, you get paid, and that it was a personal matter as to whether you blew it or saved up for when you couldn't work.

The whole idea completely sunk me. "Age fifty-five" was still more than a decade away, and it smelled of servitude, of lost hope, of morbid planning for old age, of a benevolence that seemed patronizing.

I went all stubborn and rebellious. I felt trapped in an "until death do us part" situation, and I knew I would never have the opportunity to do work that I enjoyed and had the skills for. I wanted out, I wanted my contract canceled. I wanted to get well, without the pressure and obligation of getting well. The studio was most cooperative: They offered me a year of "sick leave" without pay. But I knew I would never get well feeling that the casting office would be calling regularly, pressuring, saying, "How you doing, Mary? Be ready to work soon?"

There were other pressures and opinions—agents, husband, friends—that I was a fool to throw away such an opportunity.

The arguments went something like this: "Why shouldn't you want to take it and ease off? They sure as hell don't work you very hard. You've had all the goodies, the fame and the headlines and the recognition that anybody could ever want. . . . You've said you're tired of movies: So make a picture or two a year—you've got enough energy left for that—and then in twelve or fifteen years you can really quit and sit on your annuity."

Oh, it made sense—and my arguments didn't.

There was a generation about to be born that would understand perfectly what was bugging me. I wanted to be free to do my thing, but at the time I was wrong. I was a fool and people shook their heads and said, "She's just not well." "Women often get funny ideas at this time of life." That *was* part of it. A very insignificant part.

I canceled my contract and went to ground like an animal putting on fat during hibernation.

It took me two years before I began to stick my nose out again. "How'd you like to go on the road with the Shirley Booth play, *Time of the Cuckoo?*" I would. And it was *my* decision. I didn't have to call up the studio and ask permission. I needed money. Badly. But I wanted to go and maybe learn something. And work.

In the thirty some years since I first saw the light of a Klieg lamp, in all the films where I sat around looking beautiful and being the answer to my father's dream of fame and fortune, somewhere along the line something had filtered through that had nothing to do with beauty or fame and fortune. It had nothing to do with the skills I had learned, of speech and movement and presence. There had been moments—and baby, you can have manufactured combinations of chemicals, inhaled, swallowed or injected, there is no comparison to the kick. You aren't "way out," you are totally "here and now." With a sense of perfection, a sense of joy. It doesn't last long—but it's unforgettable.

There's a hitch to it, however. It isn't now. It isn't instant and it can't be induced. Nor can you wait around for it to happen. You have to work. You have to be full of curiosity about everything—and extremely docile. (In the sense of teachable, not meek!)

I'd got hooked on this. I don't think it's namable, it's too elusive. It can't be called "artistic satisfaction" because it isn't satisfying: It's a goad. And I don't know how much it has to do with Art.

I got to New York. And the next four years, from 1952 to 1956, I never saw the inside of a movie studio and I never stopped working. Theater, television, road shows, stock.

Whatever the troubles, and there were plenty, whatever the discomfort and fatigue and worry, these are the years of my career that finally had meaning for me. There were successes and bitter failures; neither was important.

The tour of *Time of the Cuckoo,* for instance, was a disaster. It was a wry comedy, which Shirley Booth had made into a mild success on Broadway. Her company had adored her, and there were few cast changes when I came into it. And I was an interloper. I learned a great deal in that show, mainly never to follow an actress of such stature who has made a personal hit. I watched a few performances and the part looked like a piece of cake. It wasn't; it was a virtuoso at work. And when it came my turn I played it straight and all the weaknesses of the play came glaringly to light, in spite of all the help I received from the other actors in the company. "Shirley did this." "Shirley did that." It destroyed considerable confidence, because, naturally, I couldn't do it "like Shirley." About the time the closing notice went up in San Francisco, one of the members of the company, a "lowly understudy" who had been watching my misery, came to my aid, and pointed out what should have been obvious, that I was studying Shirley instead of the character, Leona. And it all fell into place—it was the old trick of "putting the pot on to boil." The last few audiences got their money's worth and had a good time. And so did I.

After that came winter stock, and summer stock up and down the Eastern Seaboard and then, *finally,* I had the great honor and joy of an opening night on Broadway in a play with Eva Le Gallienne. In a long scene in the second act with her, I got a taste of "my drug." It happened. The heightened reality that mesmerizes an audience into unmoving attention. Something flows, or is, or exists between actor and audience, that is full of wonder and love and listening. And it is all very still and very alive. And it has nothing to do with applause or adulation or success—for the play was a flop. It wasn't a very good play on the whole, really. But that's not the point. I had been enriched.

On tour with TIME OF THE CUCKOO (1952)   *Louise Pote.*

15

A ND BEFORE AND DURING and after appearing in plays, there was television, a whole new experience—another one! I was never bored during this time. Of course, I'm talking about what they call the "early days" of television—live, and *alive*. It was experimental, crazy and wonderful.

I was in them all: *Studio One, Philco, Producers Showcase, Playhouse 90, U.S. Steel Hour*. I met the "new breed" of directors, writers, actors. I wasn't confined to playing mothers; I played everything, and had a ball.

The working form was close to theater inasmuch as we took time for rehearsals. A week to three weeks. At first sitting around long tables in some banquet hall or loft just reading the parts aloud, getting used to the sound of each other's voices, getting familiar with the play, getting acquainted with each other, the play, the director. Then someone would lay out the sets in chalk marks on the floor, and we'd get on our feet and really go to work. (It reminded me of when I was a child and kids would outline "leaf houses"—dead leaves raked into squares, with spaces left for doors and windows—and we'd pantomime going in and out of the house, turning an imaginary key, saying, "Click-clack, you're locked out, you can't come in!" Now we played the same game: The technical director over in the corner said, "Ring!" and you walked through an opening in the chalk lines, put a fist to your cheek and said, "Hello!" You were answering a phone. One time an actor who had been answering the phone with the gesture of the fist to the cheek, all during rehearsal, completely ignored the telephone on the desk during air time: He just put a fist to his cheek and said, "Hello!"

It was fun, it was concentrated, unmarred by the noise and confusion of a studio. No light crews, camera crews, no hurry, hurry, let's get the shot before lunch. We had that too, of course, but it was over very quickly. "Camera Day," when the technical crews would join us in the TV studio, and the show would be turned over to them, and all we had to do was to walk through it, establishing where we'd be and when. Then there'd be a stop-and-start rehearsal and a final dress rehearsal, and the tension would begin to build, and you'd think, "It'll never get on the air." But the time finally came, together with butterflies in the stomach and sweaty palms and everybody trying to make jokes: "Have fun! It's Magic Time!" And then the first red light on the first camera came on, and you were on your own, and in a minute the hour was over, and you felt as though you'd never touched the floor.

Every show was as exciting as an opening night in the theater. You didn't have to give a damn whether you had a hit or not. You didn't sit up most of the night waiting for the reviews. And you didn't have to do the whole thing over again, tomorrow and tomorrow and tomorrow. I'd never been in a hit in the theater, so I can't tell what it's like to do a show for a year or more. I've heard various opinions: that it's a job just to re-create that enthusiasm, that strength and energy necessary to do a perform-ance eight times a week. As much as he loved the theater, John Barrymore told me that he never went through that stage door before a performance without the deepest sense of reluctance and fatigue, wondering where the strength was going to come from. Others like the charge of walking across the stage, the excitement, the audience contact, and still others have said that the demand itself is a stimulus: "Gotta please the customers."

Live TV never had slickness or polish. It was immediate—always could have been a little better. This line wouldn't have been fluffed, that door wouldn't have stuck, spoiling an entrance or an exit. A scene that dragged could have been tightened up in the writing. But what it had was the spontaneity, the right-nowness of theater. It added a lot to the excitement when you realized that maybe a few million people would be watching. Although I shied away from that image—it was too unbelievable! I couldn't play to a million people; I couldn't even conceive the idea. That single red light on the side of a camera was the symbol of your audience, and it followed you around and you could almost forget it—except in that constant discipline of the peripheral vision. For if it wasn't there you were in limbo.

Eventually, of course, live TV was just too risky; there was no margin for error. If anything serious went wrong, you'd have to "go to black."

I remember once, during air time, seeing one of the cameras starting to smoke ominously. It had developed a short-circuit and was hauled out quickly; but that meant rerouting all of the other cameras which had to take over, and cables untangling while trying to be quiet, and everybody in the booth looking panicky. It was a lousy show, we all lost our concentration, and there were fluffs and missed cues all over the place. Another time, something got fouled up, and in the midst of a quiet scene our loudspeaker on the stage blasted with the screams of a child, "Mommie, Mommie, Mommie—I had only two cavities!" Toothpaste had entered Eden.

Once I had a costume change to make behind a flat—a thing like the old "goboes"—and about forty-five seconds to do it in. The dress was made for quick changing, zippered from hem to neck. And the zipper stuck. Right beneath my bra. The wardrobe lady was in tears, and nothing we could do would unstick it. My cue was coming up and the stage manager was relaying the trouble via his headset to the control booth. I told him, "Warn Camera—I'll play it in the mirror." There was a vase of flowers just off-scene where I had to enter, and I picked it up and carried it in front of me, getting a startled look from the actor who was already on-scene—I *think* it was George Grizzard. I placed the vase on a table in front of a mirror and arranged flowers, looking at him in the mirror, and we got away with it. When I came off, somebody had a pair of scissors so I could make the next change. But that kind of thing can give you ulcers.

The man who really got ulcers was the director in the booth. I always said he was kept behind glass so we actors couldn't hear what he called us. As in one instance where a pair of very experienced men destroyed a scene simply because they wouldn't shut up.

It is customary during rehearsal before a part is thoroughly memorized to ask for help of the technical director by saying, "Line, please." He has the script and supplies the forgotten word or words.

In the middle of a scene an actor snapped his fingers and turned to the nearby T.D., saying, "Line, please." The T.D. opened his eyes in horror and whispered the line. His expression must have irritated the actor, for he said, "Don't worry, I'll know it by air time." At which the man playing opposite him fell completely apart and said, "You sonofabitch, we're *on* the air!"

Those were good times, exciting times. I worked with the finest actors of that period, the new directors: Delbert Mann, John Frankenheimer, Franklin Shaffner, Arthur Penn, and Vincent Donehue, who would soon become giants. It's hard to believe that it's gone, that it lasted only a few years. Tomorrow comes suddenly.

When I came back home to California, I found that movies were totally unaware of my very real success, and my wealth of experience. And that I had developed a whole new popularity. Movies, in their usual insular manner, were desperately trying to avoid TV, as though it were something that would go away.

Oh, yes, there was a mother role for me—a week's work in a picture called *A Kiss Before Dying*. During which a young starlet looked at me, her beautiful eyes popping, "*Mary Astor!* I thought you were dead!"

I'd been away for four years, and I was interested in seeing what changes must have occurred by now. Surely, a different pace, crisper styles in acting. Technical advances, yes. But it was the same old hurry up and wait. Scenes played long and cumbrously with every thought blueprinted and telegraphed like a lousy fighter's punch. And audiences way ahead of them.

I found old friends in the crew, and people I'd see around the studio from various departments greeted me warmly, "Mary!

Where the hell have you been? Heard you'd been ill—O.K. now?"
(That was four years ago!) "Fine, marvelous, thanks." "Didn't I
see you on TV not long ago?" And believe this: It wasn't said
enthusiastically but rather in a conspiratorial manner, as though
they meant, "What were you doing on *TV!*" And I had to say,
"Quite a bit—grocery money you know!" "Oh sure, sure." Poor
Mary!

There is a kind of attitude, a manner of speaking, a look in the
eye, the kind of smile you get, the embrace from a director or
producer that carries the most depressing hypocrisy: "Hey! You
know you're still looking pretty sexy!" "Wow, you still got it, you
know!" "You haven't got a worry in the world—you can be right
up there again." Translated, it means "The old girl looks pretty
good." But the old girl, now nearing fifty, is *not* a young girl, is
not sexy and has no intention of competing with anybody. Competition has never been my thing, and I wasn't sure I wanted to
be right up there again. And anyway just where is right up there?
Who's kidding who? I wanted to put my craft, what I had learned,
my experience to work. The myth of *Sunset Boulevard,* with the
old glamorous actress looking at all her old movies in the sumptuous, decaying mansion, is just that. It may have been taken from a
factual story of some kind of nut—but believe me, that isn't where
all old actresses go! It would have been sheer desperate vanity to
go through all the trouble to be right up there again. Beauty
devices, face lifts and face peels, and body conditioning and contact lenses. And what would you get?

There was a road company being formed for *Don Juan in
Hell,* a section of Shaw's *Man and Superman.* Agnes Moorehead,
Charles Laughton and Charles Boyer had been enormously successful in a very interesting theatrical innovation. It was presented
without scenery by four players who carried large, impressive,
leather-bound manuscripts onto the stage, opened them on lecterns, and sat or stood and *apparently* read the play to the audience. It wasn't read, it was memorized and played, the "readers"
gradually becoming the characters in the play.

The company assembled in a small, attractive playhouse-cum-
workshop above Santa Monica Boulevard for rehearsals. Kurt
Kasznar, Ricardo Montalban, Reginald Denny, and I, and Agnes
Moorehead as our director.

Here there was none of the depressing "You're lookin' fine,

sweetie!" None of that "dear old girl" crap. Here we concentrated on Shaw and his words and his thinking. Agnes, besides
being an excellent actress, is a fine director and was most generous
with her own experience in the show. (This was not a case of
following a personal success by another actress. For Agnes gave
me all sorts of little goodies which she had found had worked
when she originated the show. I wasn't working blind.)

Don Loper made me a magnificent fuchsia evening gown: long,
flowing, timeless in style—almost Grecian. It seemed to move of
its own accord, for there were yards and yards of the material
swirling around my feet.

We opened in San Francisco to great notices and good box office
and played three weeks. We seemed to be off and running. Then
we went on to one-night stands—twenty-eight of them in a row,
Sundays included—throughout the Northwest and Western
Canada. And then we continued east with one-nighters and split
weeks. We traveled by commercial plane, since the scenery could
be "traveled" in one big box: the stools, lecterns, books and our
clothes. Plane travel was not what it is today, and some of our
city to city to small town to university connections were pretty
scary.

The play was wonderful to do and in university towns we had
great audiences.

But somebody had the quick buck in mind and didn't provide
for the fact that actors need sleep occasionally. Playing every night
and hopping by some intercity, single-engine carrier in all kinds
of weather, waiting around chilly airports where even a coffee
shop hasn't opened as yet, not eating properly—it all took its toll
on our small company. I have toured in station wagons and buses
and played one-night stands with a Pullman car waiting on a side
track with at least food and a decent berth. But never anything
like this.

Somebody—I can't even remember his name; he was producer
and backer and nonprofessional—must have come up with a nice
tax deduction, for he spent nothing on advertising. He didn't
think an advance man was necessary; "Please bulieve me." (I've
heard these "Please bulieve me" guys before! It means, "We ain't
got it!") "I've got a great advance man," he would say. "He's in
Boise right now, you got reservations at the best hotel and the
advertising is all out and we've got a great advance already." He

didn't travel with us, naturally. He stayed in Hollywood and "never got our telegrams." For there were towns where no reservations had been made and they were sorry they couldn't accommodate us because there was a convention in town, and we might get something down the street. Then we'd play to an empty auditorium of maybe a hundred people who just stopped by to see what was going on.

One night, someplace in Canada, we played on a platform on a skating rink where the local hockey team was wont to compete with other local hockey teams. The audience came properly attired in furs and overshoes and blankets, and I had purple skin to go with my fuchsia gown. There was no such thing as a dressing room, naturally. There were a couple of locker rooms, unheated, and I sat on a stool and put my makeup on, using my compact mirror from my handbag, with my makeup laid out on a kind of shelf. I happened to look up, trying to find some better source of light than the dangling single light globe, and above my head was a row of pegs with men's jock straps hanging on them. It just broke me up with laughter. I was hungry and tired and discouraged, but this just wasn't to be believed. It seemed to me that I carried giggles under my ribs all during the performance that evening, and once they threatened to get out of hand.

There was a pretty good house—people who'd come to watch the show. Not particularly a Shaw audience. Down to the right of our platform a black cat walked with unhappy paws on the ice and leaped up onto the platform right at Kurt Kasznar's feet. We were about to get the usual "cat walks across the stage" laugh when Kurt, with great presence of mind, leaned down and scooped the cat up into his arms. Kurt was playing the role of the Devil and was about to go into his great speech, "Have you walked upon the earth lately—?" which would only have added to the laughter, except that he beat the audience to it. He addressed the cat instead of us, stroking it, making it knead his shoulder and purr —using it as a prop—a black cat and the Devil? Totally acceptable. And there wasn't even a titter. Our panic-stricken stage manager was hovering close by the platform by now, and when Kurt finished the speech he simply tossed the cat into the arms of the man below. Later when we all spoke our thanks and our admiration for his inventiveness, Kurt said, "What would I have done if it had been a white Angora?"

I should like to recommend George Bernard Shaw to the student actor. If he wants to find out what it's like to get immediate results from an audience. All he and a company have to do is to say the words *as he wrote them* with a reasonable amount of intelligence, loud enough to be heard clearly by an audience not made up of morons (am I asking too much?) and his funny line will get a laugh—just like that. His dramatic moment will obtain the most satisfactory stillness. Shaw has done all your work for you. Way back there, two or three pages of dialogue preceding your moment, he's set up the bowling pins and you knock 'em over, and it works.

An interviewer once asked Mr. Shaw, "What do you consider to be the mission of the dramatist of the future?" "To write plays," Shaw answered. I wish he were around today. We'd all have a lot of fun.

As far as movies were concerned, I had had them. And they, apparently, had had me. There were "cameos" around in which to pick up a good week's fee. *Cameo:* a lovely, euphemistic word for bit part with screen credit.

Also, by now there was lots of TV. Still "live." Some of it beginning to be taped. Some of it beginning to invade California. Once more I commuted to New York and back to Hollywood. But by plane now.

Once, when I had the time, I returned to California from an engagement in New York by train—for sentimental reasons. It's not good to take sentimental journeys. You see the differences instead of the samenesses. I was aware of the shabbiness of the train. The food wasn't as excellent as I remembered it. The porters and waiters weren't quite as starched and smiling, and they didn't open a heavy door between cars and say pleasantly, "Having a good trip, Miss Astor?" and "It's gonna be right cold going through the mountains tonight. Bring you a hot water bottle for your berth?" Outside, the country still stretched, broad and wide and incredibly beautiful, but the little towns we'd pass through at night—with that diminishing sweet-and-sour note, "*dang-dang-dang*" of the warning at a crossing, would glare with neons instead of gently twinkling their "Here I am!" greeting that I remembered.

Funny. You can even miss cinders. Diesel engines now. No soft surf rattling over pebbles sound of cinders blowing over the roof of the car. Windows sealed tight. Air-conditioned. No acrid smell of smoke from the engine up a mile ahead. And no soft odors from the desert or whiff of pine in the mountains. And that over-powering fragrance of citrus fruit blossoms that would envelop the train on the final morning, and white-pated Mount Baldy gleaming in the distant blue sky—and sunshine—and you knew you were in California at last. When even the word "California" made you smile with anticipation and pleasure. Sunshine and flowers and broad beaches and the blue Pacific.

No. It's not a good idea to go back. Memories are fine and healthy. A person without a memory is either a child or an amnesiac. A country without a memory is neither a child nor an amnesiac, but neither is it a country.

But to try to live it over is pure escapism—the wrong kind, for it gets distilled into a romantic mixture that isn't all true or real.

For I remember, very clearly, those other trips so long ago when I was full of confused fears of the new work I had been thrust into. Fears of Daddy because he was asking so much of me. To be a movie star. To be one of those creatures with so much élan, so smiling and vivid and proud when I would have preferred skittering into a hidey hole and pulling it in after me.

Well . . . Now I would have liked to have been a little younger, to have had more energy and vitality, for there was still work to do. But the "get the hell out" bug had really bitten me. I knew I no longer had the stamina for another tour. I wanted to stop moving around and living out of suitcases. The movies I was offered weren't bad, but I was bored down to my shoes with them: Cornel Wilde's mother in *The Devil's Hairpin,* June Ally-son's mother-in-law in *Stranger in My Arms,* somebody else's mother in *Return to Peyton Place.* That's right! *Return* to . . . You see, they hadn't changed. Movies were still making a good picture, and then trying to imitate their own success, with "Return to—" or "Son of —" Now they turn it into a TV series, and they make a lot of money and end up with an inferior product.

And getting up at four or five A.M. Well, it's a lovely time of day if you get up because you want to, not because you have to— "there's a bright star still shining in the sky and a pinkish bluish

As Brett Halsey's mother in RETURN TO PEYTON PLACE (1961) *20th-Century Fox Film Corporation.*

tinge to the horizon—" *and* then there's a thirty- or forty-mile drive to the studio and the same old makeup departments and the hair dryers buzzing and "How about a Danish, honey?" and then on to the sound stage and you brace yourself for the noise: "Hit the eighty, Harry!" "Gotta kill this set before noon so let's romp on it!" "Hey, greens man—spray the hedge willya . . . ?" "Where you gonna be, Mary? Little more to the right, maybe? . . ."

I had a new love. A new absorbing interest. Requiring a great deal of time and attention. I'd seen my name on a hard-cover book and I had found it a bigger thrill than seeing it in marquee lights. I had been a reader since I was a child—and I was at the feet of writers and their mysterious skill.

Back at MGM I used to head for the writers' table in the commissary just to listen to their talk. They were mostly contract writers, churning out the MGM product. Some were distinguished or would become distinguished: George Oppenheimer, Anita

Loos, Robert Benchley, Dorothy Parker and Alan Campbell, F. Scott Fitzgerald, Louis Bromfield, Donald Ogden Stewart.

Auriol Lee, my English director friend, brought John Van Druten, Noel Coward and Somerset Maugham to my house. In New York I'd been at parties attended by George Jean Nathan, George Kaufman, Marc Connelly and Moss Hart. Playwright, newspaperman, novelist: Part of what made them attractive to me was that they all sat at a typewriter, put one word down after another, and the product was something that was of the mind, while my product was simply me. Me being someone else. Now I too had produced words.

My Story had been published and because of curiosity had sold very well. It came out right at the time of the genre of *I'll Cry Tomorrow* and *Too Much Too Soon*, and it was hot stuff. It started as a great stack of material that I had written as a sort of assignment to help me during a short period of psychotherapy. I didn't have the time or the money for the luxury of the daily couch sessions but I had needed help and my very wise therapist said, "Write it down." It was not meant for public eyes, but someone convinced me it should be a book.

Now the ghost-writers were after me like the *paparazzi* in Rome. "Movie actors can't write; just let me have the material and I'll do it for you." "You'll make a fortune." "You'll *help* people!" Personally I thought that the confession-type document was one of the more boring types of entertainment, but I was listening. Finally it got mauled and changed and cut down to book size and all that seemed to remain was booze and sex. It didn't make a fortune and maybe it helped half a dozen people. Fine. But it *did* open that unexpected door.

I met a most excellent editor, Lee Barker. During the final drafts of *My Story,* he would say, "I need about four pages here—" "There are a couple of spots that don't seem clear. Can you do me about five hundred words that expand the situation and let me have it by Friday?" And to myself I would say, "My God! He's treating me like a *writer!*" Then he suggested I take a crack at fiction, and I've been hooked ever since.

But it was a whole new discipline. You work alone, and it takes time, time, time, to write a book. It does for me. When I've got a book in work I feel as though I have a lump of something in my stomach and wish I could take something for it. I don't want to be bothered until I get rid of it. Finally, words, paragraphs, pages begin to happen and there is relief. Some. Not much!

I think it is about the only "if only" in my life. If only I could have put all that time and work and study into writing I might have learned to write well—I mean *really* well—and could have been a Solzhenitzen or a Conrad, or Rumer Godden or Daphne du Maurier—or Simenon. (*Not—please!* like a girl named Sue.) But I didn't, and regret is a waste of time. Mine is a Johnny-come-lately ambition and so now I have to take some of my own advice and remember that it isn't the product, or the name, or the fame that is important. It's the producing—without one eye cocked on the result.

I was beginning to resent the time spent even on a week of work in a filmed TV show. I guest-starred in almost all the anthologies and series. Of course that was familiar ground: like the old B-movie days, with no time at all to do anything right. "Set it up and shoot it." There was no dearth of work: A Hitchcock one week, a *Defenders*, a *Rawhide*, a *Dr. Kildare*.

My first novel came out—hard-cover, paperback, English edition, Good Housekeeping condensation. Whee! I went to work on my second. And my third . . .

But there comes a day when you have to make up your mind what you must do. I couldn't carry two jobs. I had to retire one. So I decided on a cutoff time. I made a *Ben Casey* in which I died. That's good enough. I'm dead—nice little private joke between me and me. No more TV.

My agent called: "There's this cameo in a movie with Bette Davis. It's a hell of a part; it *could* put you right up there again."

I read the script. The opening shot described a severed head rolling down the stairs, and each page contained more blood and gore and hysterics and cracked mirrors and everybody being awful to everybody else. I skipped to my few pages—a little old lady sitting on her veranda waiting to die. There was a small kicker to it inasmuch as it was she who was the murderess in her youth and had started all the trouble. And then in the story, she died. Good! Now, I'd really be dead! And it was with Bette, which seemed sentimentally fitting.

It was called *Hush, Hush, Sweet Charlotte*, and the locale was the deep South, and we went on location to Baton Rouge and it

As the murderous little
old lady in HUSH, HUSH,
SWEET CHARLOTTE (1964)
Courtesy of 20th-Century
Fox Film Corporation.
© 1964 by Associates and
Aldrich Co., Inc., and
20th-Century Fox Film
Corporation.

was hellish hot. We worked at one of the magnificent decaying old pillared mansions with an avenue of moss-hung trees leading down to the levee. It was an hour's drive from the hotel and we had to get up at the crack of dawn—naturally!

The first day of shooting I was, as always, full of anxiety tremors. Every actor worth his salt has them, and you *never* get over it. I had lots of dialogue in a southern accent, and I had never worked with the director, Bob Aldrich. Bette was not in the scene and so naturally had the day off. But she had the sensitivity and courtesy to take the long drive out to the location and be a friendly, familiar face on the sidelines. "Hi, Astor!" said she, "You look great!" And I knew that *she* didn't mean the usual Hollywood flattery. She took a quick look at my costume, listened to my accent, watched a rehearsal, and said to Aldrich, "Turn her loose, Robert, you might learn something!"

Back home I went through the process of retiring without any nonsense. I simply turned in my union cards and moved out of town, far enough away so I wouldn't be tempted by the telephone, for something that "would take only a few days—that would pay a lot."

After 45 years—over 100 feature-length films, two-reelers, radio, TV, theater—it was with an extraordinary sigh of relief that I could let it go. I was not of the artist caliber that feels so burningly important. I had no tag on me marked "Special"—the kind of person who feels since he has so much to give to people he is divinely obligated to go on giving, whether they want him to or not!

So now I would never be one of those famous faces seen in a crowd of extras; I'd never be one of those aging beauties, with hardworking smiles and drops in their eyes to make them sparkle, parked in casting offices, waiting desperately for the comeback that would put them right up there again.

And I had no intention of letting retirement sickness get me. I had some adjustments to make, of course. I had to learn to stop role-playing—like living in a senior citizens' community, where all you hear is rheumatism, backaches, fallen arches and who died yesterday. I didn't want to be like the lady who admired the view from my efficient senior citizens' apartment window, "My, isn't this nice! You can sit here and watch the cars go by!" I didn't want to sit around on my behind and "tsk-tsk" and say, "What's the world coming to?"

I knew that the century had almost gone on without me, but I didn't want to be *that* square. Nor did I want to become neurotically stuck in the past. It's interesting to have been there in my particular past. Many people ask me about it, want me to talk about it. It's not my favorite topic of conversation. I'd rather refer those who are interested to a book—this one. Or to that previous one written about fifteen years ago that concerned the more personal part of my life. Then we can talk about something else.

I wanted to meet new people—people not connected with the antic arts—and I did. But because I was in the *moo*-vies communication was difficult. In almost any group, conversation would grind to a halt, especially among those who remembered me. And it wasn't so much of "You were always my favorite!" but they seemed to need to impress me that they, of course, had met movie people before; or they knew someone who knew me: "She was in the commissary at RKO for a while—did you ever meet her?" "Errol Flynn once winked at me in a bar—what was he like?"

I got some odd reactions. One very nice man, slightly drunk, came up to me at a party and said, "I don't give a damn if you were the Queen of Sheba!" and walked away. And then there was the person who was afraid if he remembered me too well, it would reveal his age. "Why, I remember you when I was just a child!" And the southern lady who obviously would never see seventy again who sneered behind delicate fingers, "That ole Ma'y Asta!"

Young people were more fun. They were informed and curious. I had a house at the beach at one time, and one afternoon my little black puppy tumbled out of his depth in a wave that rolled high up onto the sand. A couple of kids scooped him out and helped me calm his fears and dry him off.

The talk went beyond my thanks because they said, "Aren't you . . . ? and I said I was, and it resulted in a couple of good talk sessions with some of their friends. We built a fire against one of the big rocks and had hot dogs and Cokes, and I asked them about their music and they asked me a lot of questions about the movies. The right questions. They weren't in awe, they wanted to know.

I think they were the springboard for this book, or at least they helped me write it, because I keep hearing those questions.

But I'm not a teacher, and I'm no good on the lecture platform, and I wanted to write.

I went to Mexico.

There was a little town far from the big cities and tourism, full of age and great beauty. It had clean, sweet air, no TV and only two telephones. Cobbled streets and views of the mountains framed by arches covered with flowering vines.

In such a place the moon, even though it's been stepped on, still gives a lovely light. You can take a walk at night and that dark figure approaching you won't attack you, but will pass by with a soft *"Bueno' noches!"* You can walk to the top of a hill and look down into the town and see lamplight and the flicker of candlelight. And dark, mysterious ruins.

Perhaps in this serenity—for there is no drone of the bulldozer and no jet planes howling down the skies—perhaps I could rest and escape the twentieth century for a while. I could park my typewriter and put down one word after another and see what happened.

Since my retirement, I have been constantly asked, "But don't you *miss* it?" To the "it" *they* mean—no. To the "it" *I* mean—yes.

No, to the work. I've had it. In fact, as I said in the beginning, during the first two months of hanging around the Famous Players-Lasky studio in Astoria in 1920, I distinctly remember feeling, "Is that all?" I'm not quite sure what I expected, any more than I'm sure today what people mean when they say that it must be glamorous work. A woman can feel glamorous, when she is beautifully dressed and walks into a restaurant and people turn and look at her. But when the restaurant is a movie set and the people who turn to look are extras getting paid to do just that, and the woman is an actress who has to make that same entrance a dozen times—it ceases to be glamorous. Glamour is in the eye of the movie fan.

I don't underrate the satisfactions by any means. But it's like pressing food through a sieve: You obtain a delicious purée, but the bulk remains in the sieve. The extraneous things, the things that add up to fatigue and boredom. A painter paints, a musician plays, a writer writes—but a movie actor waits.

Yes, I *do* miss my "family." That great big family I accumulated over the years. The people. Hundreds of people with whom I spoke the same language—that strange shorthand speech of the sets. The jokes and the gags and the gossip and the getting along together; or the arguments and disagreements, the blowups and the cooling-downs. We shared the ephemeral quality, the sense of impermanence of the medium we worked in. Often when a scene was being worked over in rehearsal, experimenting, nit-picking about words and moves, somebody would break up the overseriousness with the question, "Who's waiting for this opera anyway?" and we'd laugh and realize it was all something that shouldn't be taken too seriously—and yet, if it wasn't taken seriously it wasn't any good.

I miss these people who were part of my life—co-workers, co-actors. Friends. And I watch the new ones, the new breed, and when they do something great and fine, I'm proud. And when they do things that are blatantly bad, I am ashamed. But I can't disinherit them, for no matter how much they may feel that it is a whole new thing, it isn't really. It is a continuation. For what they have today was built upon the great and fine and the blatantly bad jobs that we did—we old movie-makers.

[219]

MARY ASTOR'S FEATURE FILMS

Compiled by DeWitt Bodeen

1. JOHN SMITH. Lewis J. Selznick Films. Released in June, 1922. Directed and story written by Victor Heerman. Cast: Eugene O'Brien, Vivian Ogden, William J. Ferguson, Tammany Young, Ester Banks, Frankie Mann, George Fawcett, J. Barney Sherry.
2. THE MAN WHO PLAYED GOD. United Artists. Released October 8, 1922. Director: F. Harmon Weight. Scenario: Forrest Halsey, adapted from a play by Jules Eckert Goodman, founded on Governeur Morris' story of the same name. Cameraman: Harry A. Fishbeck. Cast: George Arliss, Ann Forrest, Ivan Simpson, Edward Earle, Effie Shannon, Miriam Battista, Mickey Bennett, Pierre Gendron, Margaret Seddon, J. B. Walsh.
3. SECOND FIDDLE. A Tuttle Waller-Film Guild production, released through the W. W. Hodkinson Corporation, January 14, 1923. Directed and written by Frank Tuttle. Supervisor and cameraman: Fred Waller, Jr. Cast: Glenn Hunter, Townsend Martin, Leslie Stowe, Mary Foy, Helena Adamowska.
4. SUCCESS. Metro. Released February 25, 1923. Director: Ralph Ince. Cast: Brandon Tynan, Naomi Childers, Dore Davidson, Lionel Adams, Stanley Ridges, Helen Mack.
5. THE BRIGHT SHAWL. First National-Inspiration. Released April 22, 1923. Director: John S. Robertson. Scenario: Edmund

Goulding, adapted from Joseph Hergesheimer's novel. Cast: Richard Barthelmess, Dorothy Gish, Edward G. Robinson, Jetta Goudal, William Powell, Andre de Beranger, Margaret Seddon, Luis Alberni, Anders Randolph.

6. THE RAPIDS. Produced by Sault Ste. Marie Films and released through the W. W. Hodkinson Corporation, June 24, 1923. Director: David M. Hartford. Cameramen: Walter L. Griffin and Oliver Sigardson. Cast: Harry T. Morey, Walter Miller, Harlan Knight, Charles Slattery, Charles Wellesley, John W. Dillon.

7. PURITAN PASSIONS. W. W. Hodkinson Corporation. Released September 9, 1923. Director: Frank Tuttle. Scenario: Ashmore Creelman and Frank Tuttle, adapted from the play *The Scarecrow* by Percy Mackaye. Cameraman: Fred Waller, Jr. Cast: Glenn Hunter, Osgood Perkins, Maude Hill, Frank Tweed, Dwight Wiman, Thomas Chalmers.

8. THE MARRIAGE MAKER. Paramount. Released September 30, 1923. Director: William C. de Mille. Scenario: Clara Beranger, adapted from Edward Knoblock's play *The Faun*. Cameraman: L. Guy Wilky. Cast: Charles De Roche, Agnes Ayres, Jack Holt, Robert Agnew, Ethel Wales, Bertram Johns.

9. WOMAN PROOF. Paramount. Released October 28, 1923. Director: Alfred E. Green. Scenario adapted from a George Ade comedy. Cast: Thomas Meighan, Lila Lee, John Sainpolis, Louise Dresser, Robert Agnew, Edgar Norton, Charles A. Sellon, George O'Brien, Vera Reynolds.

10. THE FIGHTING COWARD. Paramount. Released March 14, 1924. Diretocr: James Cruze. Scenario: Walter Woods, adapted from Booth Tarkington's play *Magnolia*. Camerman: Karl Brown. Cast: Cullen Landis, Ernest Torrence, Noah Beery, Phyllis Haver, G. Raymond Nye, Richard Neal, Helen Dunbar.

11. BEAU BRUMMEL. Warner Brothers. Released March 30, 1924. Director: Harry Beaumont. Scenario: Dorothy Farnum, adapted from Clyde Fitch's play which had starred Richard Mansfield. Cast: John Barrymore, Willard Louis, Irene Rich, Alec B. Francis, Carmel Myers, William Humphreys, Richard Tucker, Andre de Beranger, Claire de Lorez, Michael Dark, Templar Saxe, Clarissa Selwynne.

12. FIGHTING AMERICAN. Universal. Released May 26, 1924. Director: Tom Forman. Scenario: Harvey Gates. Adapted by Raymond L. Schrock from a story by William Elwell Oliver, winner of Universal Studio's Intercollegiate Scenario Contest. Cameraman: Harry Percy. Cast: Pat O'Malley, Raymond Hatton, Warner Oland.

13. UNGUARDED WOMEN. Paramount. Released June 22, 1924.

Director: Alan Crosland. Scenario: James Creelman, adapted from a *Satevepost* story, "Face," by Lucy Stone Terrill. Cast: Bebe Daniels, Richard Dix, Walter McGrail, Frank Losee, Helen Lindroth, Harry Mestayer.

14. THE PRICE OF A PARTY. Howard Estabrook Productions. Released November 23, 1924. Director: Charles Giblyn. Cameraman: John F. Smith. Cast: Hope Hampton, Harrison Ford, Arthur Edmund Carewe, Dagmar Godowsky.

15. INEZ FROM HOLLYWOOD. First National. Released December 14, 1924. Director: Alfred E. Green. Scenario: J. G. Hawks, adapted from Adela Rogers St. Johns' story "The Worst Woman in Hollywood." Cast: Anna Q. Nilsson, Lewis Stone, Lawrence Wheat, Rose Dione, Snitz Edwards, E. H. Calvert.

16. OH, DOCTOR. Universal. Released February 23, 1925. Director: Harry Pollard. Scenario: Harvey Thew, adapted from a Harry Leon Wilson story. Cast: Reginald Denny, Otis Harlan, William V. Mong, Tom Ricketts, Lucille Ward, Mike Donlin, Blanche Payson.

17. ENTICEMENT. First National. Released in March, 1925. A Thomas H. Ince Production. Director: George Archainbaud. Scenario: Bradley King, adapted from a novel by Clive Arden. Cast: Clive Brook, Ian Keith, Louise Dresser, Edgar Norton, Vera Lewis, Lillian Langdon, Larrimore Johnston, Maxine Elliott Hicks, Fenwick Oliver, Florence Wix, Roland Bottomley, Aileen Manning.

18. PLAYING WITH SOULS. First National. Released April 30, 1925. A Thomas H. Ince Production. Director: Ralph Ince. Supervisor: John Griffith Wray. Scenario: C. Gardner Sullivan, adapted from a story by the Countess de Chambrun. Cast: Jacqueline Logan, Clive Brook, William Collier, Jr., Belle Bennett, Jessie Arnold, Josef Swickard, Charles H. Mailes.

19. DON Q, SON OF ZORRO. United Artists. Released July 21, 1925. Director: Donald Crisp. Scenario: Jack Cunningham, adapted from *Don Q's Love Story*, a novel by K. and Esketh Prichard, a sequel to *The Mark of Zorro*. Cameraman: Henry Sharpe. Cast: Douglas Fairbanks, Jack McDonald, Donald Crisp, Warner Oland, Jean Hersholt, Lottie Pickford Forrest, Albert MacQuarrie, Charles Stevens.

20. THE PACE THAT THRILLS. First National. Released October 18, 1925. Director: Webster Campbell. Cast: Ben Lyon, Charles Beyer, Tully Marshall, Warner Richmond, Evelyn Walsh Hall, Thomas Holding, Fritzi Brunette, Paul Ellis.

21. THE SCARLET SAINT. First National. Released November 15, 1925. Director: George Archainbaud. Cast: Lloyd Hughes,

Frank Morgan, Jed Prouty, Jack Raymond, George Neville, Frances Grant, J. W. Jenkins.

22. THE WISE GUY. First National. Released May 30, 1926. Director: Frank Lloyd. Scenario: Jules Furthman. Cast: James Kirkwood, Betty Compson, George F. Marion, Mary Carr, George F. Cooper.

23. DON JUAN. Warner Brothers. Released August 6, 1926. Director: Alan Crosland. Scenario: Bess Meredyth. Cameraman: Byron Haskins. Cast: John Barrymore, Willard Louis, Estelle Taylor, Helene Costello, Myrna Loy, Jane Winton, John Roche, June Marlowe, Yvonne Day, Phillipe de Lacy, John George, Helene D'Algy, Warner Oland, Montagu Love, Josef Swickard, Lionel Brahm, Phyllis Haver, Nigel de Brulier, Hedda Hopper.

24. FOREVER AFTER. First National. Released October 17, 1926. Director: F. Harmon Weight. Scenario adapted from a play by Owen Davis, Sr. Cast: Lloyd Hughes, Hallam Cooley, David Torrence, Eulalie Jensen, Alec B. Francis, Edward Everett Horton, Lila Leslie.

25. HIGH STEPPERS. First National. Released in December, 1926. Director: Edwin Carewe. Scenario: Louis Leeson. Adapted by Finis Fox from Philip Gibbs's novel *Heirs Apparent*. Cast: Lloyd Hughes, Dolores Del Rio, Emily Fitzroy.

26. THE ROUGH RIDERS. Paramount. Released March 20, 1927. Director: Victor Fleming. Original Story and Research: Hermann Hagedorn. Scenario: John Fish Goodrich. Cast: Frank Hopper (as Teddy Roosevelt), Charles Farrell, Charles Emmett Mack, Noah Beery, George Bancroft, Fred Kohler, Colonel Fred Lindsay.

27. THE SEA TIGER. First National. Released April 24, 1927. Director: John F. Dillon. Scenario: Carey Wilson, adapted from Mary Heaton Vorse's story "A Runaway Enchantress." Cameraman: Charles Van Enger. Cast: Milton Sills, Alice White, Larry Kent, Kate Price, Arthur Stone, Emily Fitzroy.

28. SUNSET DERBY. First National. Released June 18, 1927. Director: Albert Regell. Scenario adapted from the story by William Dudley Pelley. Cast: William Collier, Jr., Ralph Lewis, David Kirby, Lionel Belmore, Burt Ross, Henry Barrows, Bobby Doyle, Michael Visaroff.

29. ROSE OF THE GOLDEN WEST. First National. Released October 2, 1927. Director: George Fitzmaurice. Scenario: Bess Meredyth, adapted from a story by Minerva Caroline Smith and Eugenia Woodward. Cast: Gilbert Roland, Gustav von Seyffertitz, Montagu Love, Flora Finch, Andre Cheron, Romaine Fielding, William Conklin.

30. TWO ARABIAN KNIGHTS. A Caddo Production released by United Artists. Released October 30, 1927. Producers: Howard Hughes and John W. Considine, Jr. Director: Lewis Milestone (who won an Academy Award for comedy direction in the first year of the awards, 1927–28). Scenario: James T. O'Donohue and Wallace Smith, adapted from a Donald McGibney story. Cast: Louis Wolheim, William Boyd, Michael Vavitch, Ian Keith, DeWitt Jennings, Michael Visaroff, Boris Karloff.

31. NO PLACE TO GO. First National. Released December 25, 1927. Producer: Henry Hobart. Director: Mervyn LeRoy. Scenario: Adelaide Heilbron, adapted from Richard Connell's Satevepost story "Isle of Romance." Cast: Lloyd Hughes, Hallam Cooley, Virginia Lee Corbin, Myrtle Stedman, Jed Prouty, Russ Powell.

32. SAILORS' WIVES. First National. Released January 22, 1928. Producer: Henry Hobart. Director: Joseph E. Henabery. Scenario: Bess Meredyth, adapted from Warner Fabian's best-selling novel. Cameraman: Syd Hickox. Cast: Lloyd Hughes, Earle Foxe, Burr McIntosh, Ruth Dwyer, Olive Tell, Gayne Whitman.

33. DRESSED TO KILL. Fox. Released March 18, 1928. Director: Irving Cummings. Scenario: Howard Estabrook, adapted from a William M. Conselman story. Cameraman: Conrad Wells. Cast: Edmund Lowe, Ben Bard, R. O. Pennell, Robert Perry, Joe Brown, Tom Dugan, John Kelly, Robert Emmet O'Connor.

34. HEART TO HEART. First National. Released August 19, 1928. Producer-Director: William Beaudine. Scenario: Adelaide Heilbron, adapted from a Juliet Wilbor Tompkins story, "Once There Was a Princess." Cameraman: Sol Polito. Cast: Lloyd Hughes, Louise Fazenda, Lucien Littlefield, Thelma Todd, Raymond McKee, Aileen Manning, Virginia Grey.

35. THREE-RING MARRIAGE. First National. Released August 26, 1928. Producer: Henry Hobart. Director: Marshall Neilan. Scenario: Harvey Thew, adapted from Dixie Wilson's story "Help Yourself to Hay." Cameraman: David Kesson. Cast: Lloyd Hughes, Lawford Davidson, Yola d'Avril, Alice White, Harry Earles, George H. Reed, Anna MacGruder, Del Henderson, Rudy Cameron, Skeets Gallagher.

36. DRY MARTINI. Fox. Released November 11, 1982. Director: Harry A. D'Arrast. Scenario: Douglas Z. Doty, adapted from a story by John Thomas. Cameraman: Conrad Wells. Cast: Matt Moore, Jocelyn Lee, Sally Eilers, Albert Gran, Albert Conti, Tom Ricketts, Hugh Trevor, John T. Dillon, Marcelle Corday.

37. ROMANCE OF THE UNDERWORLD. Fox. Released January 13, 1929. Director: Irving Cummings. Scenario: Douglas Z.

Doty, adapted from a story by Doty and Sidney Lanfield. Cameraman: Conrad Wells. Cast: Ben Bard, Robert Elliott, John Boles, Oscar Apfel, Helen Lynch.

38. NEW YEAR'S EVE. Fox. Released April 14, 1929. Director: Henry Lehrman. Scenario: Dwight Cummins, adapted from a story by Richard Connell. Cameraman: Conrad Wells. Cast: Charles Morton, Earle Foxe, Arthur Stone, Helen Ware, Freddie Frederick, Florence Lake, Sumner Getchell, Jane La Verne, Virginia Vance, Stuart Erwin.

39. WOMAN FROM HELL. Fox. Released July 28, 1929. Producer-Director: A. F. Erickson. Scenario: Ray Doyle. Adapted by Charles Kenyon from the play *From Hell Came a Lady* by Lois Leeson, Jaime del Rio, George Scarborough. Cameraman: Conrad Wells. Cast: Robert Armstrong, Dean Jagger, Roy D'Arcy, May Boley, James Bradbury, Sr.

40. LADIES LOVE BRUTES. Paramount. Released May 18, 1930. Director: Rowland V. Lee. Scenario: Waldemar Young and Herman J. Mankiewicz, adapted from Zoë Akins' play *Pardon My Glove*. Cameraman: Harry Fishbeck. Cast: George Bancroft, Fredric March, Margaret Quimby, Stanley Fields, Ben Hendricks Jr., Lawford Davidson, Ferike Boros, David Durand, Freddie Burke Frederick, Paul Fix, Claude Allister, Crauford Kent, E. H. Calvert.

41. THE RUNAWAY BRIDE. RKO-Radio. Released May 18, 1930. Director: Donald Crisp. Scenario: Jane Murfin, adapted from the play *Cooking Her Goose* by Lolita Ann Westman and H. H. Van Loan. Cameraman: Leo Tover. Cast: Lloyd Hughes, David Arnell, Natalie Moorehead, Maurice Black, Paul Hurst, Edgar Norton.

42. HOLIDAY. RKO-Pathe. Released June 15, 1930. Director: Edward H. Griffith. Scenario: Horace Jackson, adapted from Philip Barry's play. Cameraman: Norbert Brodine. Cast: Ann Harding, Edward Everett Horton, Robert Ames, Hedda Hopper, Monroe Owsley, Will Holden, Elizabeth Forrester, Mabel Forrest, Creighton Hale, Hallam Cooley, Mary Forbes.

43. THE LASH. First National. Released January 4, 1931. Producer-Director: Frank Lloyd. Screenplay: Bradley King, based on the novel *Adios* by Lanier Bartlett and Virginia Stevens Bartlett. Cameraman: Ernst Haller. Cast: Richard Barthelmess, Fred Kohler, Marian Nixon, James Rennie, Robert Edeson, Arthur Stone, Barbara Bedford, Mathilde Comont, Erville Alderson.

44. THE ROYAL BED. RKO-Radio. Released February 1, 1931. Director: Lowell Sherman. Screenplay: J. Walter Ruben, adapted from Robert E. Sherwood's play *The Queen's Husband*. Camera-

man: Leo Tover. Cast: Lowell Sherman, Nance O'Neil, Anthony Bushell, Robert Warwick, Alan Roscoe, Hugh Trevor, Gilbert Emery, J. Carrol Naish, Frederick Burt, Desmond Roberts.

45. BEHIND OFFICE DOORS. RKO-Pathe. Released March 22, 1931. Director: Melville Brown. Screenplay: Carey Wilson, adapted from Alan Brener Schultz's story "Private Secretary." Cameraman: Roy Hunt. Cast: Robert Ames, Ricardo Cortez, Kitty Kelly, Edna Murphy, Catherine Dale Owen, Charles Sellon, William Morris.

46. SIN SHIP. RKO-Radio. Released April 5, 1931. Director: Louis Wolheim. Screenplay: F. Hugh Herbert, adapted from a story by Keene Thompson and Agnes Brand Leahy. Cameraman: Nick Musuraca. Cast: Louis Wolheim, Ian Keith, Hugh Herbert, Russell Powell, Alan Roscoe, Bert Stanley.

47. OTHER MEN'S WOMEN. Warner Brothers. Released April 26, 1931. Director: William Wellman. Screenplay: Maude Fulton and William K. Wells, adapted from "Steel Highway," a story by Maude Fulton. Cameraman: Chick McGill. Cast: Grant Withers, Regis Toomey, James Cagney, Joan Blondell, Fred Kohler, J. Farrell MacDonald, Lillian Worth, Walter Long.

48. WHITE SHOULDERS. RKO-Radio. Released May 17, 1931. Director: Melville Brown. Screenplay: J. Walter Ruben, adapted from a Rex Beach story. Cameraman: Jack Mackenzie. Cast: Jack Holt, Ricardo Cortez, Sidney Toler, Kitty Kelly, Nicholas Soussanin.

49. SMART WOMAN. RKO-Radio. Released October 11, 1931. Director: Gregory La Cava. Screenplay: Salisbury Field, adapted from Myron C. Fagan's play *Nancy's Private Affair*. Cameraman: Nick Musuraca. Cast: Robert Ames, Edward Everett Horton, Noel Francis, Ruth Weston, John Halliday.

50. MEN OF CHANCE. RKO-Radio. Released January 3, 1932. Director: George Archainbaud. Screenplay: Wallace Smith and Louis Stevens, adapted from a story by Louis Weitzenkorn. Cameraman: Nick Musuraca. Cast: Ricardo Cortez, John Halliday, Kitty Kelly, Ralph Ince, George Davis, Tom Francis, James Donlin, Andre Cheron, Albert Petit, Jean De Briac.

51. THE LOST SQUADRON. RKO-Radio. Released March 6, 1932. Director: George Archainbaud. Screenplay: Wallace Smith and Herman J. Mankiewicz, based on a story by Dick Grace. Cameramen: Leo Tover and Edward Cronjager. Cast: Richard Dix, Erich von Stroheim, Joel McCrea, Dorothy Jordan, Hugh Herbert, Robert Armstrong, Arnold Grey, Dick Grace.

52. A SUCCESSFUL CALAMITY. Warner Brothers. Released

August 24, 1932. Director: John G. Adolfi. Screenplay: Austin Parker, Maude Howell, and Julian Josephson, adapted from the play by Clare Kummer. Cameraman: James Van Trees. Cast: George Arliss, Evalyn Knapp, Grant Mitchell, William Janney, Hardie Albright, David Torrence, Richard Tucker.

53. THOSE WE LOVE. World Wide. Released September 13, 1932. Director: Robert Florey. Screenplay: F. Hugh Herbert, adapted from the play by S. K. Lauren and George Abbott. Cameraman: Arthur Edeson. Cast: Kenneth MacKenna, Lilyan Tashman, Hale Hamilton, Tommy Conlon, Earle Foxe, Forrester Harvey, Virginia Sale, Pat O'Malley, Harvey Clark, Cecil Cunningham, Edwin Maxwell.

54. RED DUST. MGM. Released November 5, 1932. Producer: Hunt Stromberg. Director: Victor Fleming. Screenplay: John Lee Mahin, adapted from Wilson Collison's play. Cameraman: Harold Rosson. Cast: Clark Gable, Jean Harlow, Gene Raymond, Donald Crisp, Tully Marshall, Forrester Harvey, Willie Fung.

55. THE LITTLE GIANT. First National. Released April 14, 1933. Director: Roy Del Ruth. Original Screenplay: Robert Lord and Wilson Mizner. Cameraman: Sid Hickox. Cast: Edward G. Robinson, Helen Vinson, Kenneth Thomson, Russell Hopton, Shirley Gray, Donald Dillaway, Louise Mackintosh, James H. Doyle.

56. JENNIE GERHARDT. Paramount. Released June 9, 1933. Producer: B. P. Schulberg. Director: Marion Gering. Screenplay: Josephine Lovett and Joseph Moncure March. Adapted by S. K. Lauren and Frank Partos from the novel by Theodore Dreiser. Cameraman: Leon Shamroy. Cast: Sylvia Sidney, Donald Cook, Edward Arnold, H. B. Warner, Louise Carter, Cora Sue Collins, Theodore Von Eltz, Morgan Wallace, Frank Reicher, Rose Coghlan, Jane Darwell, Lillian Harmer.

57. THE WORLD CHANGES. First National. Released October 28, 1933. Director: Mervyn LeRoy. Screenplay: Edward Chodorov, based on Sheridan Gibney's story "America Kneels." Cameraman: Tony Gaudio. Cast: Paul Muni, Aline MacMahon, Donald Cook, Alan Dinehart, Guy Kibbee, Margaret Lindsay, Henry O'Neill, Jean Muir, Anna Q. Nilsson, Theodore Newton, Patricia Ellis, Willard Robertson, Douglas Dumbrille, Jackie Searles, Marjorie Gateson, Mickey Rooney, George Meeker, Gordon Westcott, Arthur Hohl, William Janney, Philip Faversham, Sidney Toler, Oscar Apfel, Alan Mowbray.

58. THE KENNEL MURDER CASE. Warner Brothers. Released October 28, 1933. Director: Michael Curtiz. Screenplay: Robert E.

Lee and Peter Milne, adapted from the novel by S. S. Van Dine. Cameraman: William Reese. Cast: William Powell, Eugene Pallette, Ralph Morgan, Helen Vinson, Jack LaRue, Paul Cavanagh, Robert Barrat, Arthur Hohl, Henry O'Neill, Robert McWade, Frank Conroy, Étienne Girardot, Spencer Charteris.

59. CONVENTION CITY. First National. Released December 14, 1933. Director: Archie Mayo. Screenplay: Robert Lord, adapted from a story by Peter Milne. Cameraman: William Reese. Cast: Joan Blondell, Adolphe Menjou, Dick Powell, Guy Kibbee, Frank McHugh, Patricia Ellis, Ruth Donnelly, Hugh Herbert, Grant Mitchell, Hobart Cavanaugh, Gordon Westcott, Douglas Dumbrille, Samuel Hinds, Johnny Arthur.

60. EASY TO LOVE. Warner Brothers. Released January 13, 1934. Director: William Keighley. Screenplay: Carl Erickson and Manuel Seff. Adapted by David Boehm and Carl Erickson from the play by Thompson Buchanan. Cameraman: Ernest Haller. Cast: Genevieve Tobin, Adolphe Menjou, Guy Kibbee, Edward Everett Horton, Patricia Ellis, Hugh Herbert, Hobart Cavanaugh.

61. UPPER WORLD. Warner Brothers. Released May 25, 1934. Director: Roy Del Ruth. Screenplay: Ben Markson, adapted from a Ben Hecht story. Cameraman: Tony Gaudio. Cast: Warren William, Ginger Rogers, Andy Devine, Dickie Moore, Ferdinand Gottschalk, Robert Barrat, J. Carroll Naish, Theodore Newton, Robert Greig, Sidney Toler, Willard Robertson, John Qualen, Henry O'Neill.

62. RETURN OF THE TERROR. First National-Warner Brothers. Released July 11, 1934. Director: Howard Bretherton. Screenplay: Eugene Solow and Peter Milne, adapted from an Edgar Wallace story. Cameraman: Arthur Todd. Cast: Lyle Talbot, John Halliday, Frank McHugh, Irving Pichel, J. Carrol Naish, Frank Reicher, Robert Barrat, George E. Stone, Robert Emmet O'Connor, Étienne Girardot, Frank Conroy, Cecil Cunningham, Charley Grapewin.

63. MAN WITH TWO FACES. First National. Released July 12, 1934. Director: Archie Mayo. Screenplay: Tom Reed and Niven Busch, adapted from the play *The Dark Tower* by George S. Kaufman and Alexander Woollcott. Cameraman: Tony Gaudio. Cast: Edward G. Robinson, Ricardo Cortez, Mae Clarke, Louis Calhern, Arthur Byron, Margaret Dale, Henry O'Neill, Virginia Sale, John Eldredge, David Landau, Emily Fitzroy, Arthur Aylesworth, Dorothy Tree.

64. THE CASE OF THE HOWLING DOG. Warner Brothers. Released October 17, 1934. Director: Alan Crosland. Screenplay: Ben Markson, adapted from the novel by Erle Stanley Gardner.

Cameraman: William Reese. Cast: Warren William, Helen Twelvetrees, Allen Jenkins, Grant Mitchell, Dorothy Tree, Helen Lowell, Gordon Westcott, Harry Tyler, Arthur Aylesworth, Russell Hicks, Frank Reicher, Addison Richards, Harry Seymour.

65. I AM A THIEF. Warner Brothers. Released January 2, 1935. Director: Robert Florey. Original Screenplay: Ralph Block and Doris Malloy. Cameraman: Sid Hickox. Cast: Ricardo Cortez, Dudley Digges, Robert Barrat, Irving Pichel, Florence Fair.

66. STRAIGHT FROM THE HEART. Universal. Released March 22, 1935. Director: Scott R. Beal. Producer: B. F. Zeldman. Original Screenplay: Doris Anderson. Cameraman: Charles Stumar. Cast: Roger Pryor, Baby Jane Quigley, Carol Coombs, Andy Devine, Henry Armetta, Grant Mitchell, Virginia Hammond, Robert McWade, Doris Lloyd, Hilda Vaughn, Louise Carter, Willard Robertson, Douglas Fowley, Clara Blandick, Rollo Lloyd, Frank Reicher, Jack Mulhall, Marion Lord.

67. DINKY. Warner Brothers. Released June 28, 1935. Director: Ross Lederman. Screenplay: Harry Sauber. Cameraman: Arthur Edeson. Cast: Jackie Cooper, Roger Pryor, Henry Armetta, Betty Jean Haney, Henry O'Neill, Edith Fellows, Sidney Miller, Richard Quine, Frank Gernardi, Florence Fair, Addison Richards, James Burke.

68. PAGE MISS GLORY. Warner Brothers-Cosmopolitan Productions. Released July 8, 1935. Director: Mervyn LeRoy. Screenplay: Delmar Daves and Robert Lord, adapted from a play by Joseph Schrank and Philip Dunning. Cameraman: George Folsey. Cast: Marion Davies, Dick Powell, Pat O'Brien, Frank McHugh, Lyle Talbot, Patsy Kelly, Allen Jenkins, Barton MacLane, Berton Churchill, Hobart Cavanaugh, Joseph Cawthorn, Al Shean, Helen Lowell, Lionel Stander, Mary Treen, Harry Beresford, Gavin Gordon.

69. RED HOT TIRES. Warner Brothers. Released October 25, 1935. Director: Ross Lederman. Original Screenplay: Tristram Tupper. Cameraman: Warren Lynch. Cast: Lyle Talbot, Roscoe Karns, Frankie Darro, Gavin Gordon.

70. MAN OF IRON. Warner Brothers. Released December 11, 1935. Director: William McGann. Screenplay: William Wister Haines. Adapted from a Dawn Powell story, "Country Boy." Cameraman: L. W. O'Connell. Cast: Barton MacLane, John Eldredge, Dorothy Peterson, Joseph Crehan, Craig Reynolds, Joseph King, John Qualen, Joseph Sawyer, Florence Fair, Edward Keene.

71. THE MURDER OF DR. HARRIGAN. First National. Released January 21, 1936. Director: Frank McDonald. Screen-

play: Peter Milne and Sy Bartlett. Based on a novel by Mignon G. Eberhardt. Cameraman: Arthur Todd. Cast: Ricardo Cortez, Kay Linaker, John Eldredge, Joseph Crehan, Frank Reicher, Phillip Reed, Gordon Elliott, Don Barclay, Johnny Arthur, Joan Blair.

72. AND SO THEY WERE MARRIED. Columbia. Released May 14, 1936. Director: Elliott Nugent. Screenplay: Doris Anderson, Joseph Anthony, and A. Laurie Brazie, adapted from a story by Sarah Addington, "Bless Their Hearts." Cameraman: Henry Freulich. Cast: Melvyn Douglas, Edith Fellows, Jack Moran, Donald Meek, Dorothy Stickney, Romaine Callender, Douglas Scott.

73. TRAPPED BY TELEVISION. Columbia. Released June 16, 1936. Director: Del Lord. Screenplay: Lee Loeb and Harold Buchman, adapted from a story by Sherman Lowe and Al Martin. Cameraman: Allen G. Seigler. Cast: Lyle Talbot, Nat Pendleton, Joyce Compton, Thurston Hall, Henry Mollison.

74. DODSWORTH. United Artists. Released September 9, 1936. Producer: Samuel Goldwyn. Director: William Wyler. Screenplay: Sidney Howard, adapted from his dramatization of Sinclair Lewis' novel. Cameraman: Rudolph Maté. Cast: Walter Huston, Ruth Chatterton, Paul Lukas, David Niven, Gregory Gaye, Maria Ouspenskaya, Odette Myrtil, Kathryn Marlowe, John Payne, Spring Byington, Harlan Briggs, Charles Halton, Beatrice Maude.

75. LADY FROM NOWHERE. Columbia. Released December 23, 1936. Director: Gordon Wiles. Screenplay: Fred Niblo, Jr., Arthur Strawn, and Joseph Krumgold, adapted from a story by Ben G. Kohn. Cameraman: Harry Freulich. Cast: Charles Quigley, Thurston Hall, Victor Kilian, Spencer Charteris, Norman Willis, Gene Morgan, Rita La Roy.

76. THE PRISONER OF ZENDA. Selznick-United Artists. Released September 2, 1937. Director: John Cromwell. Screenplay: John L. Balderston. Adapted by Wells Root from Anthony Hope's novel and Edward Rose's dramatization of the same. Cameraman: James Wong Howe. Cast: Ronald Colman, Madeleine Carroll, Douglas Fairbanks, Jr., C. Aubrey Smith, Raymond Massey, David Niven, Lawrence Grant, Ian Maclaren, Byron Foulger, Howard Lang, Philip Sherman, Alexander D'Arcy, Ben Webster.

77. THE HURRICANE. United Artists. Released November 10, 1937. Producer: Samuel Goldwyn. Director: John Ford. Screenplay: Dudley Nichols and Oliver H. P. Garrett, adapted from the novel by James Norman Hall and Charles Nordhoff. Cameraman: Bert Glennon. Special Effects: James Basevi. Cast: Dorothy Lamour, Jon Hall, C. Aubrey Smith, Thomas Mitchell, Raymond Massey,

John Carradine, Jerome Cowan, Al Kikume, Kuulei De Clercq, Layne Tom, Jr., Mamo Clark, Movita Castenada, Spencer Charteris, Ines Courtney.

78. PARADISE FOR THREE. MGM. Released January 30, 1938. Producer: Sam Zimbalist. Director: Edward Buzzell. Screenplay: George Oppenheimer and Harry Ruskin, adapted from Erich Kaestner's novel *Three Men in the Snow*. Cameraman: Charles Lawton. Cast: Robert Young, Florence Rice, Frank Morgan, Reginald Owen, Edna May Oliver, Herman Bing, Siegfried Rumann, Henry Hull, Walter Kingsford.

79. NO TIME TO MARRY. Columbia. Released February 5, 1938. Producer: William Perlberg. Director: Harry Lachman. Screenplay: Paul Jarrico, adapted from "The Night Before Christmas," a short story by Paul Gallico. Cameraman: Allen G. Siegler. Cast: Richard Arlen, Lionel Stander, Virginia Dale, Marjorie Gateson, Thurston Hall, Arthur Loft, Jay Adler, Matt McHugh, Paul Hurst, George Humbert, Louis Jean Heydt.

80. THERE'S ALWAYS A WOMAN. Columbia. Released March 19, 1938. Producer: William Perlberg. Director: Alexander Hall. Screenplay: Gladys Lehman, adapted from a story by Wilson Collison. Cameraman: Henry Freulich. Cast: Joan Blondell, Melvyn Douglas, Frances Drake, Jerome Cowan, Robert Paige, Thurston Hall, Pierre Watkin, Walter Kingsford, Lester Matthews.

81. WOMAN AGAINST WOMAN. MGM. Released June 18, 1938. Producer: Edward Chodorov. Director: Robert B. Sinclair. Screenplay: Edward Chodorov, adapted from a short story, "Enemy Territory," by Margaret Culkin Banning. Cameraman: Ray June. Cast: Herbert Marshall, Virginia Bruce, Janet Beecher, Marjorie Rambeau, Juanita Quigley, Zeffie Tilbury, Sarah Padden, Morgan Wallace.

82. LISTEN, DARLING. MGM. Released October 18, 1938. Producer: Jack Cummings. Director: Edwin L. Marin. Screenplay: Elaine Ryan and Anne Morrison Chapin, adapted from a Katherine Brush short story. Cameraman: Charles Lawton, Jr. Cast: Judy Garland, Freddie Bartholomew, Walter Pidgeon, Alan Hale, Scotty Beckett, Barnett Parker, Gene Lockhart, Charley Grapewin.

83. MIDNIGHT. Paramount. Released March 15, 1939. Producer: Arthur Hornblow, Jr. Director: Mitchell Leisen. Screenplay: Charles Brackett and Billy Wilder, adapted from a story by Edwin Justus Mayer and Franz Schulz. Cameraman: Charles Lang, Jr. Cast: Claudette Colbert, Don Ameche, John Barrymore, Francis Lederer, Elaine Barrie, Hedda Hopper, Rex O'Malley, Monty Woolley, Armand Kaliz.

84. TURNABOUT. United Artists. Released May 7, 1940. Director: Hal Roach. Screenplay: Mickell Novak, Berne Giler, John McClain. Based on a novel by Thorne Smith. Cameraman: Norbert Brodine. Cast: John Hubbard, Carole Landis, Adolphe Menjou, Verree Teasdale, William Gargan, Joyce Compton, Donald Meek, Ines Courtney, Polly Ann Young, Norman Budd, Ray Turner, Burton Churchill, Franklin Pangborn, Marjorie Main.

85. BRIGHAM YOUNG: FRONTIERSMAN. 20th Century-Fox. Released August 27, 1940. Executive Producer: Darryl F. Zanuck. Associate Producer: Kenneth MacGowan. Director: Henry Hathaway. Screenplay: Lamar Trotti, adapted from an original screen story by Louis Bromfield. Cameraman: Arthur Miller. Special effects: Fred Sersen. Cast: Tyrone Power, Linda Darnell, Dean Jagger, Brian Donlevy, Jane Darwell, John Carradine, Vincent Price, Jean Rogers, Ann Todd, Willard Robertson, Moroni Olsen, Marc Lawrence, Stanley Andrews, Frank Thomas, Fuzzie Knight, Dickie Jones, Selmer Jackson, Frederick Burton, Russell Simpson, Arthur Aylesworth, Chief Big Tree, Davidson Clark, Claire Du Brey, Tully Marshall.

86. THE GREAT LIE. Warner Brothers. Released April 4, 1941. Director: Edmund Goulding. Screenplay: Lenore Coffee, adapted from a Polan Banks novel, *Far Horizons*. Cameraman: Tony Gaudio. Music Score: Max Steiner. Cast: Bette Davis, George Brent, Lucile Watson, Hattie McDaniel, Grant Mitchell, Jerome Cowan, Sam McDaniel, Thurston Hall, Charles Trowbridge, Russell Hicks, Virginia Brissac, Olin Howland, J. Farrell MacDonald, Doris Lloyd, Georgia Caine, Charlotte Wynters.

87. THE MALTESE FALCON. Warner Brothers. Released September 30, 1941. Director: John Huston. Screenplay: John Huston, adapted from the novel by Dashiell Hammett. Cameraman: Arthur Edeson. Cast: Humphrey Bogart, Gladys George, Peter Lorre, Barton MacLane, Lee Patrick, Sydney Greenstreet, Ward Bond, Jerome Cowan, Elisha Cook, Jr., James Burke, Murray Alper, John Hamilton, Emory Parnell.

88. ACROSS THE PACIFIC. Warner Brothers. Released August 18, 1942. Producers: Jerry Wald and Jack Saper. Director: John Huston. Screenplay: Richard Macaulay, adapted from a *Satevepost* serial by Robert Carson, *Aloha Means Goodbye*. Cameraman: Arthur Edeson. Cast: Humphrey Bogart, Sydney Greenstreet, Charles Halton, Sen Young, Roland Got, Lee Tung-Foo, Frank Wilcox, Lester Matthews, Paul Stanton, John Hamilton, Tom Stevenson, Monte Blue, Kam Tong, Chester Gan, Richard Loo, Keye Luke, Spencer Chan, Rudy Robles, Bill Hopper, Frank Mayo.

89. THE PALM BEACH STORY. Paramount. Released November 2, 1942. Producer: Buddy G. De Sylva. Director and Original Screenplay: Preston Sturges. Cameraman: Victor Milner. Cast: Claudette Colbert, Joel McCrea, Rudy Vallee, William Demarest, Franklin Pangborn, Robert Dudley, Sig Arno, Jack Norton, Esther Howard, Jimmy Conlin, Monte Blue, Dewey Robinson, Ester Michelson, Robert Warwick, Roscoe Ates, Arthur Hoyt, Chester Conklin.

90. YOUNG IDEAS. MGM. Released August 2, 1943. Director: Jules Dassin. Producer: Robert Sisk. Original Screenplay: Ian McLellan Hunter and Bill Noble. Cameraman: Charles Lawton. Cast: Susan Peters, Herbert Marshall, Elliott Reid, Richard Carlson, Allyn Joslyn, Dorothy Morris, Frances Rafferty, George Dolenz, Emory Parnell, Rod Rogers, Roberta Smith, Grady Sutton, Robert Emmet O'Connor, Ava Gardner.

91. THOUSANDS CHEER. MGM. Released September 15, 1943. Producer: Joseph Pasternak. Director: George Sidney. Screenplay: Paul Jarrico and Richard Collins, based on their story "Private Miss Jones." Cameraman: George Folsey. Cast: Kathryn Grayson, Gene Kelly, John Boles, Jose Iturbi, Ben Blue, Connie Gilchrist, Dick Simmons, Frances Rafferty, Marta Linden, Frank Morgan, Mary Elliott, and a list of guest stars that included almost all of the MGM contract players: Mickey Rooney, Judy Garland, Red Skelton, Eleanor Powell, Lionel Barrymore, Virginia O'Brien, Ann Sothern, Lucille Ball, Lena Horne, Marsha Hunt, Marilyn Maxwell, Donna Reed, Margaret O'Brien, June Allyson, Gloria DeHaven, John Conte, Sara Haden, Don Loper, Maxine Barrat, with Kay Kyser, Bob Crosby, Benny Carter and their orchestras.

92. MEET ME IN ST. LOUIS. MGM. Released November 1, 1944. Producer: Arthur Freed. Director: Vincente Minnelli. Screenplay: Irving Brecher and Fred Finklehoffe, based on the book by Sally Benson. Cameraman: George Folsey. Music: Hugh Martin and Ralph Blane. Cast: Judy Garland, Margaret O'Brien, Lucille Bremer, June Lockhart, Tom Drake, Marjorie Main, Harry Davenport, Leon Ames, Henry A. Daniels, Jr., Joan Carroll, Hugh Marlowe, Robert Sully, Chill Wills, Robert Emmet O'Connor.

93. BLONDE FEVER. MGM. Released December 5, 1944. Producer: William H. Wright. Director: Richard Whorf. Screenplay: Patricia Coleman, adapted from the Ferenc Molnar play *Delilah*. Cameraman: Lester White. Cast: Philip Dorn, Gloria Grahame, Felix Bressart, Marshall Thompson, Curt Bois, Elisabeth Risdon, Arthur Walsh, Paul Scott.

94. CLAUDIA AND DAVID. 20th-Century Fox. Released July

25, 1946. Producer: William Perlberg. Director: Walter Lang. Screenplay: Rose Franken and William Brown Meloney. Cameraman: Joseph La Shelle. Cast: Dorothy McGuire, Robert Young, John Sutton, Gail Patrick, Rose Hobart, Harry Davenport, Florence Bates, Jerome Cowan, Else Janssen, Frank Tweddell, Anthony Syder, Pierre Watkin, Henry Mowbray, Clara Blandick, Betty Compson, Eva Novak, Eric Wilton, Frank Darien.

95. CYNTHIA. MGM. Released May 20, 1947. Producer: Edwin H. Knopf. Director: Robert Z. Leonard. Screenplay: Harold Buchman and Charles Kaufman, adapted from Viña Delmar's play *The Rich Full Life*. Cameraman: Charles Schoenbaum. Cast: Elizabeth Taylor, George Murphy, S. Z. Sakall, Gene Lockhart, Spring Byington, James Lydon, Scotty Beckett, Anna Q. Nilsson, Charles Bradstreet, Morris Ankrum, Kathleen Howard, Harlan Briggs, Will Wright, Minerva Urecal.

96. FIESTA. MGM. Released June 12, 1947. Producer: Jack Cummings. Director: Richard Thorpe. Screenplay: George Bruce and Lester Cole. Cameramen: Sidney Wagner, Charles Rosher, William Cline. Music: Johnny Green. Cast: Esther Williams, Ricardo Montalban, Akim Tamiroff, John Carroll, Cyd Charisse, Fortunio Bonanova, Hugo Haas, Frank Puglia, Los Bocheros (Basque Singers), Alan Napier, Soledad Jimenez, Robert Emmet O'Connor.

97. DESERT FURY. Paramount. Released August 1, 1947. Producer: Hal B. Wallis. Director: Lewis Allen. Screenplay: Robert Rossen, adapted by A. I. Bezzerides and Ramona Stewart from the novel *Desert Town* by Ramona Stewart. Cameramen: Charles Lang and Edward Cronjager. Cast: Burt Lancaster, John Hodiak, Lizabeth Scott, Wendell Corey, Kristine Miller, William Harrigan, James Flavin, Jane Novak.

98. CASS TIMBERLANE. MGM. Released November 7, 1947. Producer: Arthur Hornblow, Jr. Director: George Sidney. Screenplay: Donald Ogden Stewart. Adapted by Stewart and Sonya Levien from Sinclair Lewis' novel. Cameraman: Robert Planck. Cast: Spencer Tracy, Lana Turner, Zachary Scott, Tom Drake, Albert Dekker, Selena Royle, Josephine Hutchinson, Margaret Lindsay, Rose Hobart, John Litel, Mona Barrie, John Alexander, Frank Wilcox, Cameron Mitchell, Howard Freeman, Betty Blythe.

99. ACT OF VIOLENCE. MGM. Released December 21, 1948. Producer: William H. Wright. Director: Fred Zinnemann. Screenplay: Robert L. Richards, adapted from a Collier Young story. Cameraman: Robert Surtees. Cast: Van Heflin, Robert Ryan, Janet Leigh, Phyllis Thaxter, Barry Kroeger, Nicholas Joy, Harry Antrim, Connie Gilchrist, Will Wright, Dick Simmons.

100. LITTLE WOMEN. MGM. Released February 25, 1949. Pro-

ducer-Director: Mervyn LeRoy. Screenplay: Andrew Solt, Sarah Y. Mason, Victor Heerman, and Sally Benson, based on Louisa May Alcott's novel. Cameramen: Robert Planck and Charles Schoenbaum. Cast: June Allyson, Margaret O'Brien, Elizabeth Taylor, Janet Leigh, Peter Lawford, Rossano Brazzi, Lucile Watson, Sir C. Aubrey Smith, Elizabeth Patterson, Leon Ames, Harry Davenport, Richard Stapley, Connie Gilchrist, Ellen Corby.

101. ANY NUMBER CAN PLAY. MGM. Released June 2, 1949. Producer: Arthur Freed. Director: Mervyn LeRoy. Screenplay: Richard Brooks, based on the novel by Edward Harris Heth. Cameraman: Harold Rosson. Cast: Clark Gable, Alexis Smith, Wendell Corey, Audrey Totter, Frank Morgan, Lewis Stone, Barry Sullivan, Edgar Buchanan, Marjorie Rambeau, Leon Ames, Caleb Peterson, Mickey Knox, William Conrad, Richard Rober, Darryl Hickman, Charles Arnt, David Opatoshu, Art Baker, John "Skins" Miller, Dorothy Comingore, Philo McCullough.

102. A KISS BEFORE DYING. United Artists. Released June 12, 1956. Producer: Robert L. Jacks. Director: Gerd Oswald. Screenplay: Lawrence Roman, based on a novel by Ira Levin. Cameraman: Lucien Ballard. Cast: Robert Wagner, Jeffrey Hunter, Virginia Leith, Joanne Woodward, George Macready, Robert Quarry, Howard Petrie, Bill Walker, Molly McCart, Marlene Felton.

103. THE POWER AND THE PRIZE. MGM. Released September 12, 1956. Producer: Nicholas Nayfack. Director: Henry Koster. Screenplay: Robert Ardrey, based on the novel by Howard Swiggett. Cameraman: George Folsey. Cast: Robert Taylor, Elisabeth Mueller, Burl Ives, Charles Coburn, Sir Cedric Hardwicke, Nicola Michaels, Cameron Prud'homme, Richard Erdman, Ben Wright, Jack Raines, Thomas Browne Henry, Richard Deacon.

104. THE DEVIL'S HAIRPIN. Paramount. A Theodora Prod. Released October 4, 1957. Producer-Director: Cornel Wilde. Screenplay: James Edmiston and Cornel Wilde. Cameraman: Daniel L. Fapp. Cast: Cornel Wilde, Jean Wallace, Arthur Franz, Paul Fix, Larry Pennell, Gerald Milton, Ross Bagdasarian, Morgan Jones, Jack Kosslyn.

105. THIS HAPPY FEELING. Universal-International. Released March 19, 1958. Producer: Ross Hunter. Director and Screenplay: Blake Edwards based on the play For Love Or Money, by F. Hugh Herbert. Cameraman: Arthur E. Arling. Cast: Debbie Reynolds, Curt Jurgens, John Saxon, Alexis Smith, Estelle Winwood, Troy Donahue, Hayden Rorke, Gloria Holden, Alex Gerry, Joe Flynn, Alexander Campbell, Clem Fuller.

106. STRANGER IN MY ARMS. Universal-International. Released

March 11, 1959. Producer: Ross Hunter. Director: Helmut Kautner. Screenplay: Peter Berneis, based on a novel by Robert Wilder, *And Ride a Tiger*. Cameraman: William Daniels. Cast: June Allyson, Jeff Chandler, Sandra Dee, Conrad Nagel, Charles Coburn, Peter Graves, Hayden Rorke, Reita Green, Bartlett Robinson. Howard Wendell.

107. RETURN TO PEYTON PLACE. 20th-Century Fox. Released May 3, 1961. Producer: Jerry Wald. Director: José Ferrer. Screenplay: Ronald Alexander, based on the novel by Grace Metalious. Cameraman: Charles G. Clarke. Cast: Carol Lynley, Jeff Chandler, Eleanor Parker, Robert Sterling, Luciana Paluzzi, Tuesday Weld, Brett Halsey, Gunnar Hellstrom, Kenneth MacDonald, Joan Banks, Emerson Treacy, Bob Crane, Bill Bradley, Tim Durant, Casey Adams, Pitt Herbert, Warren Parker, Arthur Peterson, Jennifer Howard, Wilton Graff, Hari Rhodes, Colette Lyons.

108. YOUNGBLOOD HAWKE. Warner Brothers. Released November 4, 1964. Producer-Director-Screenplay: Delmar Daves. Adapted from the novel by Herman Wouk. Cameraman: Charles Lawton. Cast: James Franciscus, Suzanne Pleshette, Genevieve Page, Eva Gabor, Lee Bowman, Edward Andrews, Don Porter, Mildred Dunnock, Kent Smith, John Dehner, John Emery, Hayden Rorke, Werner Kemperer, Berry Kroeger.

109. HUSH, HUSH, SWEET CHARLOTTE. 20th-Century-Fox. Released December 23, 1964. Producer-Director: Robert Aldrich. Screenplay: Henry Farrell and Lukas Heller. Cameraman: Joseph Biroc. Cast: Bette Davis, Olivia de Havilland, Joseph Cotten, Agnes Moorehead, Cecil Kellaway, Victor Buono, William Campbell, Wesley Addy, Bruce Dern, George Kennedy, Dave Willock, John Megna, Frank Ferguson, Ellen Corby, Helen Kleeb, Marianne Stewart.

INDEX

INDEX

MacKenna, Kenneth, 89
MacLane, Barton, *165*
Mahin, John Lee, 189
Main, Marjorie, *174*, 176
Makeup, 9, 32, 52, 97
Male Animal, The, 173
Maltese Falcon, The, xi, 157, 159–167, *164*, *165*; credits for, 233
Man and Superman, 208
Man of Iron, 110; credits for, 230
Man Who Played God, The, credits for, 221
Man with Two Faces, The, 107; credits for, 229
Mann, Delbert, 207
Many Happy Returns, 173
Marceau, Marcel, 36
March, Florence, 77, 112
March, Fredric, 77, 77, 112
Marin, Ed, 141
Marriage Maker, The, credits for, 222
Marsh, Mae, 5
Marshall, Bart, 130
Marshall, Herbert, 141
Mary Rose, 119
Massey, Raymond, 127, *128*, 130, 134
Maugham, Somerset, 214
Mayer, Louis B., 125
Mayfair Club, 66
Mayo, Archie, 107
McAvoy, May, 9
McCrea, Joel, 170, *171*
McGuire, Dorothy, 190, *190*
McHugh, Frank, 107
Meet Me in St. Louis, *174*, 175–178; credits for, 234
Meighan, Thomas, 18
Menjou, Adolphe, 107
Men of Chance, credits for, 227
Mercury Theater, The, 157
Metro Goldwyn Mayer, 125, 134, 136, 140–141, 170, 172, 173, 174, 179, 191–193, 200, 213
Midnight, 143, *144*, 145; credits for, 232
Milestone, Lewis, 69
Millay, Edna St. Vincent, 41
Minnelli, Vincent, 175
Miracle, The, 29
Mitchell, Thomas, 134, *137*
Mix, Tom, 187
Moby Dick, 43, 46, 48
Molnar, Ferenc, 179
Montalban, Ricardo, 189, 208
Montgomery, Robert, 109
Moore, Colleen, 73
Moorehead, Agnes, 208
Morgan, Frank, 138
Motion Picture Magazine, 2, 5, 42

Movie magazines, 80, 105
Movietone, 75
Mrs. Miniver, 170
Mumblers, 103
Muni, Paul, 106
Murder of Dr. Harrigan, The, 107; credits for, 230–231
Murphy, George, 192–193
Murray, Mae, 9, 62, 63
Murray, Nicholas, 41
Myers, Carmel, 22
My Story, xii, 214

Nagel, Conrad, 55
Naldi, Nita, 18
Name dropping, 81
Nathan, George Jean, 214
National Velvet, 192
Nazimova, 5
Negri, Pola, 18, 62
New Year's Eve, credits for, 226
Niven, David, 120, 130
No Place to Go, 67; credits for, 225
Nostalgia, 89, 170, 185
No Time to Marry, 138; credits for, 232
Nudity in films, 91–93
Nugent, Elliott, 62, 173

Oberon, Merle, 131
O'Brien, Margaret, *174*, 175, 177, 197, 198
O'Brien, Pat, *108*
Oh, Doctor, credits for, 223
Oland, Warner, 36, 48
Oliver, Edna May, 138
Olivier, Laurence, 131
O'Malley, Rex, 143
Oppenheimer, George, 213
Orry-Kelly, 152
Other Men's Women, 89; credits for, 227
Ouspenskaya, Maria, 122
Outward Bound, 132
Owen, Reginald, 138
Owsley, Monroe, 83

Pace That Thrills, The, 42; credits for, 223
Page Miss Glory, 107, *108*; credits for, 230
Palm Beach Story, The, 170, *171*; credits for, 234
Paradise for Three, credits for, 232
Paramount Pictures, 19, 78, 195
Parker, Dorothy, 112, 214
Parsons, Louella, 1, 41
Part-talkies, 75. See *also* Sound films
Penn, Arthur, 207
Pensions, 200

[243]